HONDA
50 - 65 - 70 - 90
SINGLE CYLINDER
O.H.C. MODELS
1959 to 1983

WORKSHOP MANUAL

A Floyd Clymer Publication
This edition published in 2022 by
www.VelocePress.com

All rights reserved. This work may not be reproduced or transmitted in any form without the express written consent of the publisher.

INTRODUCTION

Welcome to the world of digital publishing ~ the book you now hold in your hand was printed using the latest state of the art digital technology. The advent of print-on-demand has forever changed the publishing process, never has information been so accessible and it is our hope that this book serves your informational needs for years to come. If this is your first exposure to digital publishing, we hope that you are pleased with the results. Many more titles of interest to the classic automobile and motorcycle enthusiast, collector and restorer are available via our website at www.VelocePress.com. We hope that you find this title as interesting as we do.

NOTE FROM THE PUBLISHER

The information presented is true and complete to the best of our knowledge. All recommendations are made without any guarantees on the part of the author or the publisher, who also disclaim all liability incurred with the use of this information.

TRADEMARKS

We recognize that some words, model names and designations, for example, mentioned herein are the property of the trademark holder. We use them for identification purposes only. This is not an official publication.

INFORMATION ON THE USE OF THIS PUBLICATION

This manual is an invaluable resource for those interested in performing their own maintenance. However, in today's information age we are constantly subject to changes in common practice, new technology, availability of improved materials and increased awareness of chemical toxicity. As such, it is advised that the user consult with an experienced professional prior to undertaking any procedure described herein. While every care has been taken to ensure correctness of information, it is obviously not possible to guarantee complete freedom from errors or omissions or to accept liability arising from such errors or omissions. Therefore, any individual that uses the information contained within, or elects to perform or participate in do-it-yourself repairs or modifications acknowledges that there is a risk factor involved and that the publisher or its associates cannot be held responsible for personal injury or property damage resulting from the use of the information or the outcome of such procedures.

WARNING!

One final word of advice, this publication is intended to be used as a reference guide, and when in doubt the reader should consult with a qualified technician.

CONTENTS

CHAPTER ONE

GENERAL INFORMATION ... 1

    Service hints   Expendable supplies
    Tools   Safety first

CHAPTER TWO

TUNE-UP AND TROUBLESHOOTING PRINCIPLES ... 5

    Service operations   Carburetor adjustment
    Valve adjustment   Oil and filter change
    Spark plug   Electrical equipment
    Air cleaner   Drive chain
    Battery service   Cam chain tensioner
    Fuel strainer   Troubleshooting

CHAPTER THREE

ENGINE, TRANSMISSION, AND CLUTCH ... 22

    Preparation for engine disassembly   Right crankcase cover
    Engine removal   Clutch
    Left crankcase cover   Primary driven gear
    Posi-torque mechanism (8-speed)   Shifter linkage
    Magneto   Oil pump
    Alternator   Splitting crankcase halves
    Cylinder head   Crankshaft
    Cylinder   Kickstarter
    Piston   Transmission
    Cam chain tensioner   Bearings

CHAPTER FOUR

FUEL SYSTEM ... 62

    Carburetor operation   Keihin carburetor (1978)
    Carburetor overhaul   Miscellaneous carburetor problems
    Carburetors (1963-1977)

CHAPTER FIVE

ELECTRICAL SYSTEM 81

Battery ignition
Magneto ignition operation
Magneto ignition troubleshooting
Charging system (magneto ignition)
Charging system (battery ignition)
Electric starter
Battery
Lights and signals
Horn
Wiring diagrams

CHAPTER SIX

FRAME, SUSPENSION, AND STEERING 112

Handlebars
Wheels
Brake
Steering stem and forks
Rear suspension
Drive chain

APPENDIX

SPECIFICATIONS 126

C50
C50M
S50
Z50A
C65
S65
C65M
CL70
C70
C70M
CT70
SL70
C90
CL90
CL90L
CD90
CT90 (before frame No. 000001A)
CT90 (after frame No. 000001A)
CT90 (K9)
S90
SL90
ST90

QUICK REFERENCE DATA 136

INDEX 139

NOTES

CHAPTER ONE

GENERAL INFORMATION

This book was written to provide complete service and repair information to owners of Honda 50cc through 90cc four-cycle motorcycles.

SERVICE HINTS

All procedures can be performed by anyone reasonably handy with tools. Special tools are required for some procedures; their operation is described and illustrated. Sources of supply for special tools are suggested, together with their approximate cost. It should be borne in mind that many of these devices will pay for themselves after the first or second use.

Service will be far easier if the machine is clean before beginning work. There are special cleaners for washing the engine and related parts. Just brush or spray on the cleaning solution, let it stand, then rinse it away with a garden hose. Clean all oily or greasy parts with cleaning solvent as they are removed. *Never use gasoline as a cleaning agent*, as it presents an extreme fire hazard. Be sure to work in a well ventilated area when using cleaning solvent. Keep a fire extinguisher handy, just in case.

Before undertaking a job, read the entire section in this manual which pertains to it. Study the illustrations and text until you have a good idea of what is involved. If special tools are required, make arrangements to get them before starting. It's frustrating and sometimes expensive to get under way and then find that you are unable to finish up.

TOOLS

Every motorcyclist should carry a small tool kit to help with minor roadside adjustments and repairs. A suggested kit, available through most dealers, is shown in **Figure 1**.

An assortment of ordinary hand tools is also required. As a minimum, have the following available.

a. Metric combination wrenches
b. Metric socket wrenches
c. Assorted screwdrivers
d. Pliers
e. Feeler gauges
f. Spark plug wrench
g. Small hammer
h. Plastic mallet
i. Parts cleaning brush

Advanced troubleshooting and tune-up requires a few special, more advanced tools. The first four can be considered essential.

1. *Flywheel puller* (**Figure 2**). On all but 90cc bikes, it is necessary to remove the flywheel to gain access to the breaker points. This tool makes flywheel removal easy. Its cost is around

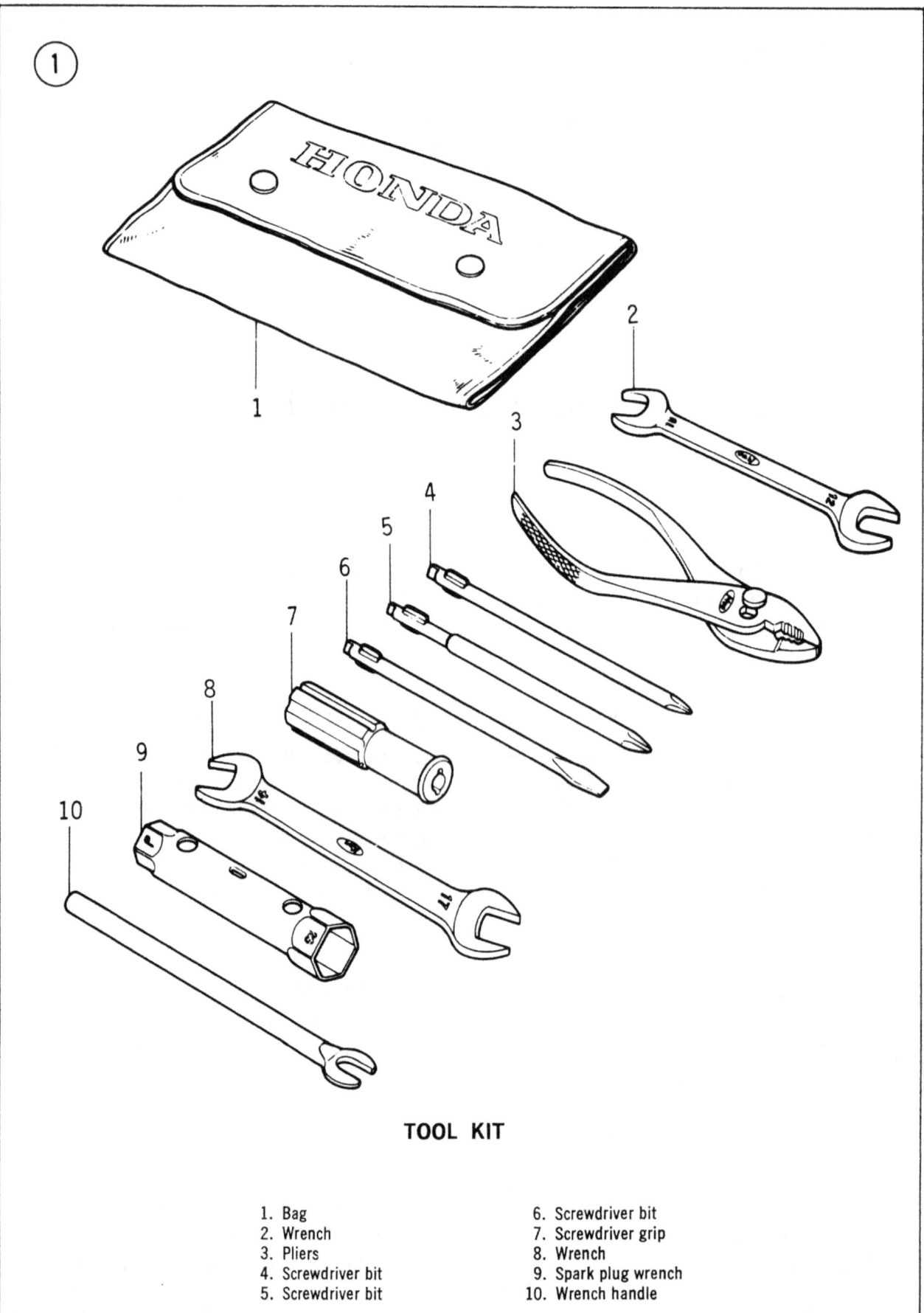

TOOL KIT

1. Bag
2. Wrench
3. Pliers
4. Screwdriver bit
5. Screwdriver bit
6. Screwdriver bit
7. Screwdriver grip
8. Wrench
9. Spark plug wrench
10. Wrench handle

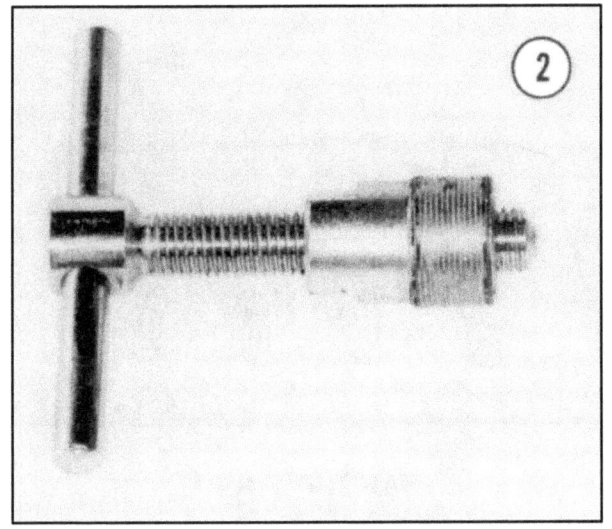

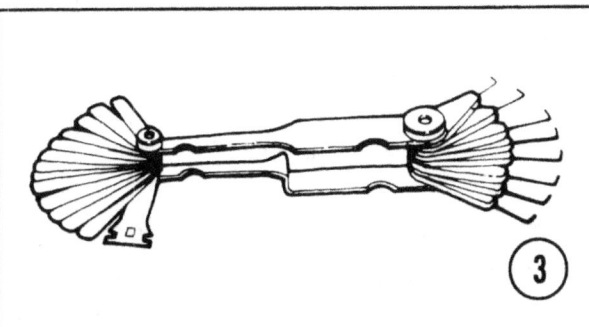

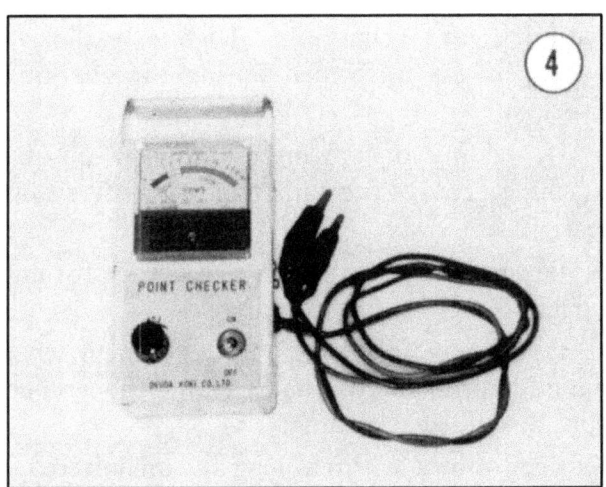

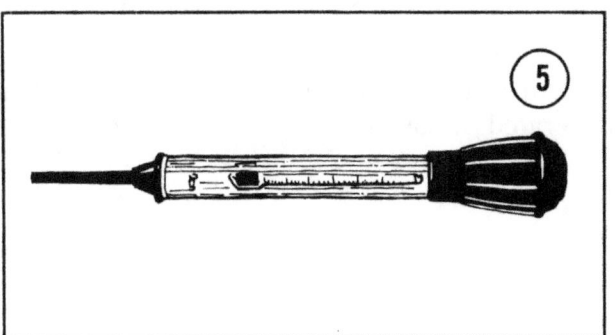

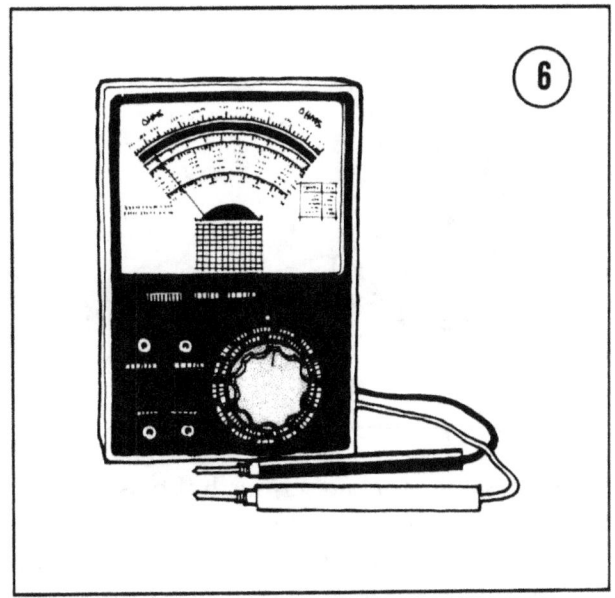

$6, and it is available from most motorcycle shops or by mail order from accessory dealers. Be sure to specify the model of your machine when ordering. There is no satisfactory substitute for this tool, but there have been many unhappy owners who had to buy expensive new crankshafts and flywheels after trying makeshift flywheel removal methods.

2. *Ignition gauge* (**Figure 3**). This tool combines round wire spark plug gap gauges with narrow breaker point feeler gauges. Bikes with magnetos require that point gap be adjusted through a narrow slot in the flywheel. Standard feeler gauges will not fit through this slot, making point gap adjustment difficult or impossible. This tool costs about $3 at auto accessory stores.

3. *Timing tester* (**Figure 4**). This unit signals the instant when breaker points just open. On models with magnetos, this point is sometimes difficult to determine with a test light or ohmmeter, because the points are shunted by a low-resistance coil.

4. *Hydrometer* (**Figure 5**). This instrument measures state of charge of the battery, and tells much about battery condition. Such an instrument is available at any auto parts store and through most larger mail order outlets. Satisfactory ones cost about $3.

5. *Multimeter, or VOM* (**Figure 6**). This instrument is invaluable for electrical system troubleshooting and service. A few of its functions may be duplicated by locally fabricated

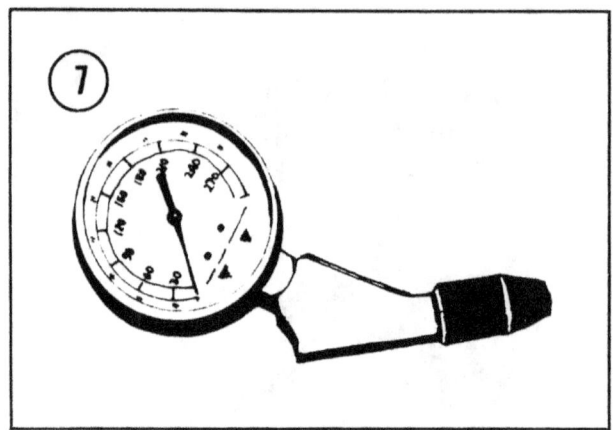

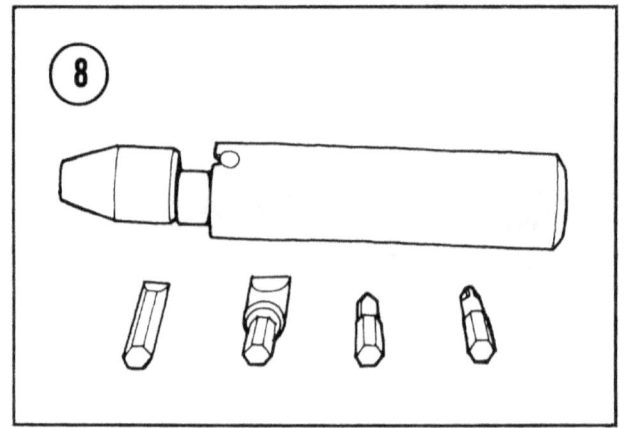

substitutes, but for the serious hobbyist, it is a must. Its uses are described in the applicable sections of this book. Prices start at around $10 at electronics hobbyist stores and mail order outlets.

6. *Compression gauge* (**Figure 7**). An engine with low compression cannot be properly tuned and will not develop full power. A compression gauge measures engine compression. The one shown has a flexible stem, which enables it to reach cylinders where there is little clearance between the cylinder head and frame. Cheap ones start at around $3 available at auto accessory stores or by mail order from large catalog order firms.

7. *Impact driver* (**Figure 8**). This tool might have been designed with the motorcyclist in mind. It makes removal of engine cover screws easy, and eliminates damaged screw slots. Good ones run about $12 at larger hardware stores.

EXPENDABLE SUPPLIES

Certain expendable supplies are also required. These include grease, oil, gasket cement, wiping rags, cleaning solvent, and distilled water. Cleaning solvent is available at many service stations. Distilled water, required for battery service, is available at most supermarkets. It is sold for use in steam irons, and is inexpensive.

SAFETY FIRST

Professional mechanics can work for years without sustaining serious injury. If you observe a few rules of common sense and safety, you can also enjoy many safe hours servicing your own machine. You can also hurt yourself or damage the bike if you ignore these rules.

1. Never use gasoline as a cleaning solvent.

2. Never smoke or use a torch near flammable liquids, such as cleaning solvent in open containers.

3. Never smoke or use a torch in an area where batteries are charging. Highly explosive hydrogen gas is formed during the charging process.

4. If welding or brazing is required on the machine, remove fuel tank to a safe distance, at least 50 feet away.

5. Be sure to use the proper size wrench for nut turning.

6. If a nut is tight, think for a moment what would happen to your hand should the wrench slip. Be guided accordingly.

7. Keep your work area clean and uncluttered.

8. Wear safety goggles in all operations involving drilling, grinding, or use of a chisel.

9. Never use worn tools.

10. Keep a fire extinguisher handy. Be sure that it is rated for gasoline and electrical fires.

CHAPTER TWO

TUNE-UP AND TROUBLESHOOTING

The number of definitions of the term "tune-up" is probably equal to the number of people defining it. For purposes of this book, tune-up will be defined as a general adjustment and/or service of all service items to ensure continued peak operating efficiency of a motorcycle engine.

A maintenance schedule is provided in **Table 1**.

SERVICE OPERATIONS

As part of a proper tune-up, some service procedures are essential. The following paragraphs discuss details of these procedures.

Compression Test

An engine needs 3 basics to develop full power — adequate compression, proper fuel mixture, and a properly timed spark. If for any reason compression is low, the engine will not develop full power. A compression test, or even better, a series of them over the life of the bike will tell much about engine condition.

To make a compression test, proceed as follows.

1. Start the engine, then ride the bike long enough to warm it thoroughly.
2. Remove the spark plug.
3. Screw the compression gauge into the spark plug hole, or if a press-in type gauge is used, hold it firmly in position (**Figure 1**).
4. With the ignition switch OFF and throttle fully open, crank the engine briskly with the kickstarter several times; the compression gauge indication will increase with each kick. Continue to crank the engine until the gauge indicates no more increase, then record the compression gauge reading.

Example:

1st kick	90 psi
2nd kick	130 psi
3rd kick	135 psi
4th kick	140 psi
5th kick	140 psi

A series of measurements made over a period of time may reveal trouble ahead, long before

Table 1   MAINTENANCE SCHEDULE

Service Item	300 (500)	1,000 (1,500)	2,000 (3,000)	3,000 (4,500)	4,000 (6,000)	5,000 (7,500)	6,000 (9,000)	7,000 (10,500)	8,000 (12,000)	9,000 (13,500)	10,000 (15,000)	11,000 (16,500)	12,000 (18,000)
Change engine oil	X	X	X	X	X	X	X	X	X	X	X	X	X
Adjust ignition timing				X			X			X			X
Adjust valve clearance	X			X			X			X			X
Adjust clutch		X		X			X			X			X
Adjust carburetor				X			X			X			X
Adjust drive chain	X	X	X	X	X	X	X	X	X	X	X	X	X
Adjust front and rear brakes		X	X	X	X	X	X	X	X	X	X	X	X
Replace spark plug				X			X			X			X
Clean oil filter	X						X			X			X
Clean fuel strainer				X			X			X			X
Clean muffler							X						X
Check spokes		X					X						X
Tighten nuts and bolts		X					X						X
Adjust headlight				X			X			X		X	X
Check battery water	X	X	X	X	X	X	X	X	X	X	X	X	X

Table 2 COMPRESSION PRESSURE

Mileage	Compression Pressure
New	130
2,000	125
4,000	125
6,000	120
8,000	95

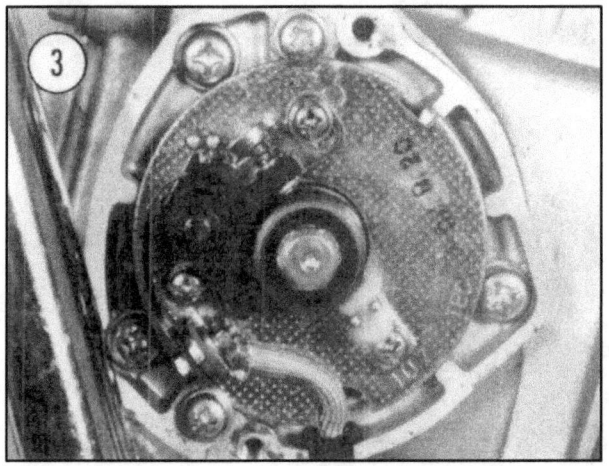

the engine exhibits serious symptoms. For example, a difference of 20 percent between successive readings on any engine, if made under identical conditions, should be taken as an indication that service is required. An example is given in **Table 2**. Note that a one-time compression test taken at 8,000 miles might be considered normal, but compared with the engine's past history, it is an indication of trouble.

It is for the reasons outlined in the foregoing paragraphs that the serious motorcycle hobbyist will want to own and use his own compression gauge, and also keep a permanent record of its findings. It should be pointed out, however, that readings taken under different conditions are not necessarily conclusive, because of production tolerances, calibration errors, and other factors.

Possible causes of low compression are listed below.

a. Burned valves

b. Valves adjusted too tight

c. Worn, stuck, or broken piston rings

d. Leaking head gasket

If compression is low, adjust valves first, then again measure compression pressure. Cylinder disassembly will be required to correct causes other than valve misadjustment.

Servicing Breaker Points

Figure 2 illustrates typical breaker points on a bike with magneto igniton; points on battery-ignition models are shown in **Figure 3**. Service procedures are identical for both types, with the exception that the flywheel must be removed before servicing points on magneto-equipped models.

Normal use of the motorcycle causes the breaker points to burn and pit gradually. If they are not too pitted, they can be dressed with a few strokes of a clean point file. Do not use emery cloth or sandpaper, as particles can remain on the points and cause arcing and burning. If a few strokes of the file do not smooth the points completely, replace them.

Oil or dirt may get on the points, resulting in premature failure. Common causes for this condition are defective crankshaft seals, improper breaker cam lubrication, or lack of care when the breaker point or crankcase cover is removed.

Points should be cleaned and regapped every 1,500-2,000 miles. To clean the points, dress them lightly with a point file, then remove all residue with lacquer thinner. Close the points on a piece of clean white paper such as a business card. Continue to pull the card through the closed points until no discoloration or residue remains on the card. Finally, rotate the engine and observe the points as they open and close. If they do not meet squarely, replace them.

Replacing Points (Battery Ignition Models)

1. Remove the breaker cover (**Figure 4**).

2. Disconnect the wire from the points (**Figure 5**), then remove both attaching screws (A).

3. Install new points in the same position as those removed, then connect the wire, being sure that the wire terminal is clean and the connection is tight. Tighten both point attaching screws only enough so that the stationary member can be moved, but does not slip, for the points must be adjusted after installation.

Point Adjustment (Battery Ignition Models)

1. Remove the alternator cover, then turn the engine over, using a wrench on the crankshaft nut, until points are open to their maximum gap.

2. Measure point gap (**Figure 6**), using a clean feeler gauge. If gap is 0.012-0.016 inch (0.30-0.40 millimeter), tighten both attaching screws, then go on to Step 4. If adjustment is necessary, continue with Step 3.

3. Insert a screwdriver into the pry slots provided for the purpose, then move the stationary contact as required (**Figure 7**).

4. Tighten both attaching screws, then recheck point gap. Readjust if necessary.

5. Apply a very small quantity of distributor cam lubricant to the breaker cam.

6. Adjust ignition timing.

Replacing Points (Magneto Models)

Smaller engines are equipped with magneto ignition. It is necessary to remove the flywheel before the breaker points may be removed.

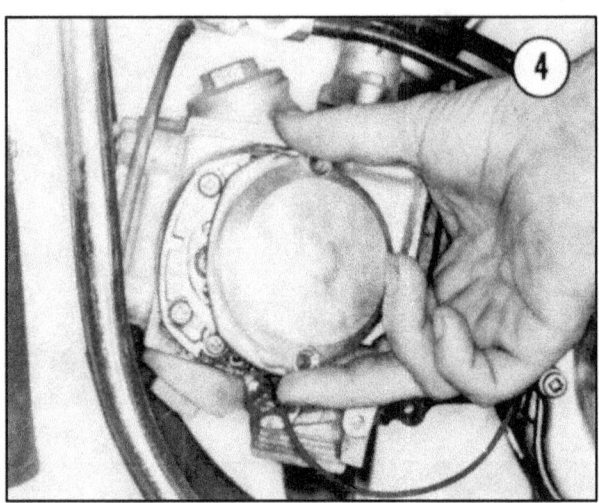

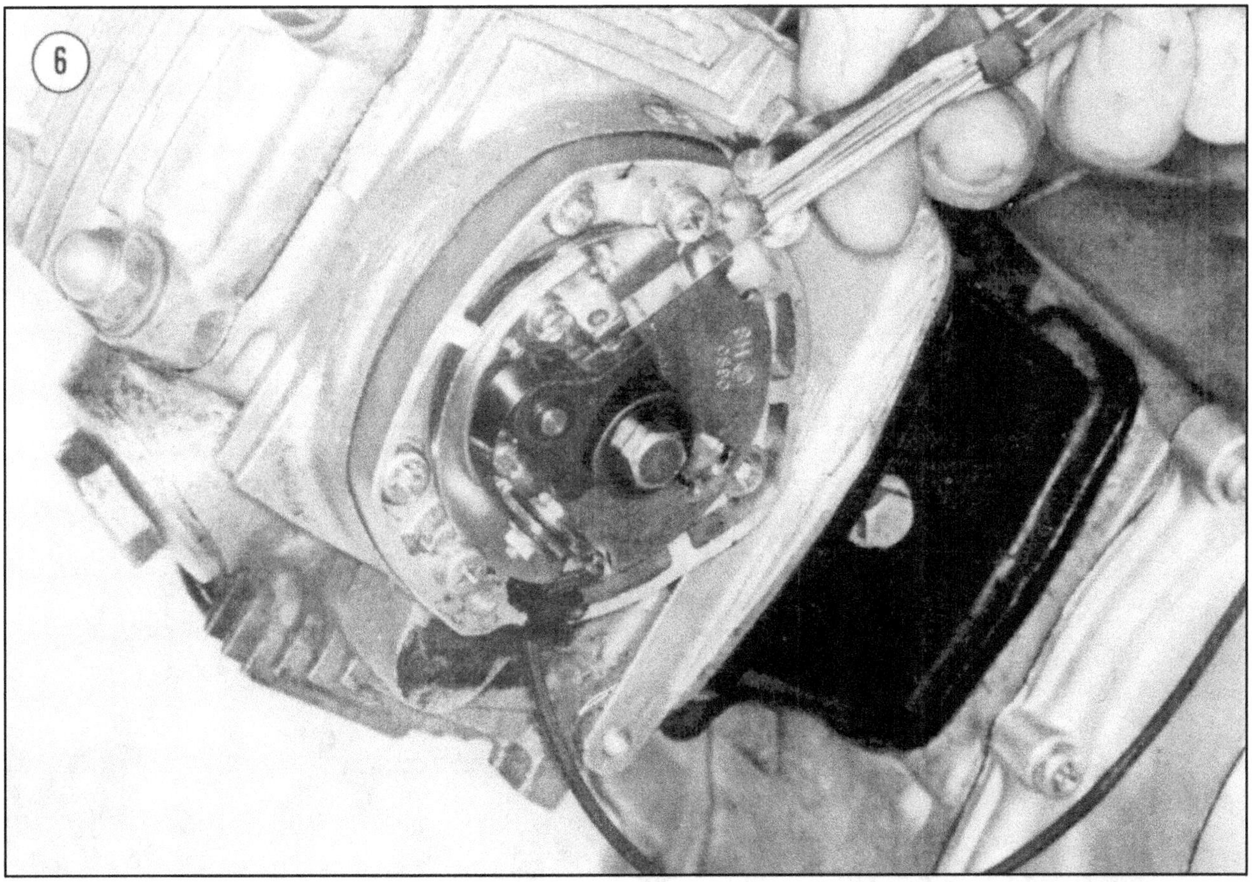

6

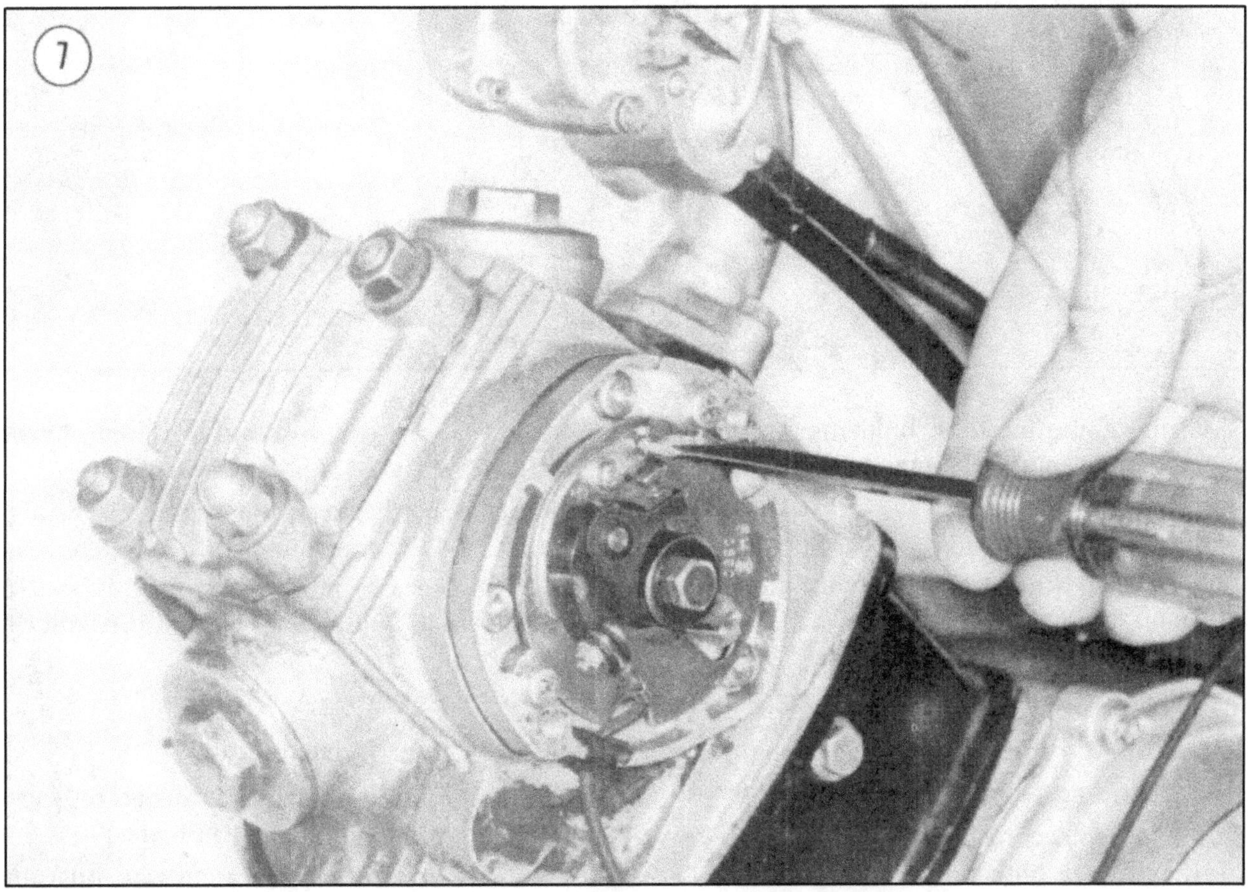

7

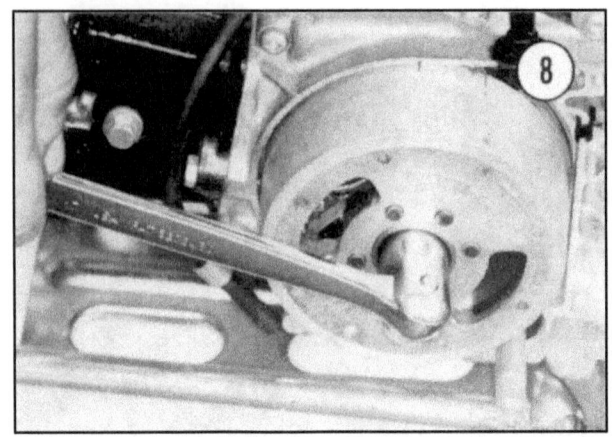
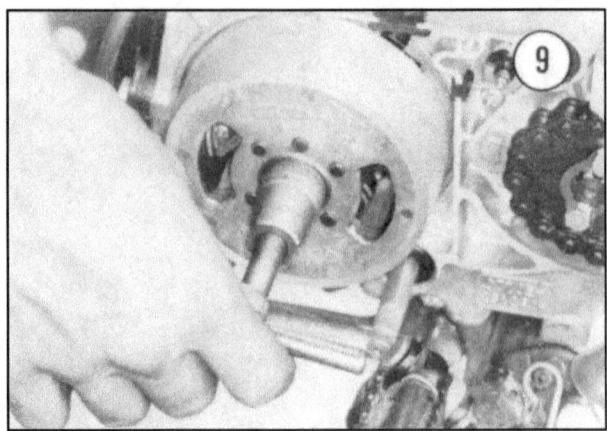

1. Using a suitable tool, hold the flywheel in position and remove the retaining nut (**Figure 8**) and washer.

2. Screw a flywheel puller to its full depth into the flywheel. Note that the flywheel hole has a left-hand thread.

3. Turn the puller screw clockwise to remove the flywheel (**Figure 9**).

4. Disconnect the wire on the points, then remove the point attachment screw (**Figure 10**).

5. Install replacement breaker points by reversing the foregoing steps.

6. Apply a very small quantity of distributor cam lubricant to the breaker cam.

7. Replace the flywheel, then tighten its retaining nut to 24-27 foot-pounds (32-36 N•m).

8. Adjust breaker point gap to 0.012-0.016 inch (0.30-0.40 millimeter), and adjust ignition timing.

Ignition Timing (Magneto Models)

Timing on these models is adjusted by varying breaker point gap. Refer to **Figure 11**.

1. With the magneto cover removed, turn the

engine until the "F" mark on the flywheel aligns with its index mark (**Figure 12**).

2. Connect a suitable timing tester across the breaker points (following instructions supplied with the tester). Be sure ignition switch is ON.

3. Slightly loosen screw (A), then insert a screwdriver into pry slots (B) and move the stationary contact until the points just open. (**Fig. 11**).

4. Tighten screw (A), then check the adjustment by turning the engine. The points should open just as the "F" mark aligns with its index pointer.

5. Finally, turn the engine over until the points are open to their maximum gap. Using a clean feeler gauge, check that point gap is 0.012-0.016 inch (0.30-0.40 millimeter). If point gap is not within tolerance, replace the points.

Ignition Timing (Battery Ignition Models)

1. Remove the breaker point cover and alternator cover.

2. Connect a timing tester or other continuity indicator between the terminal on the points and a good ground. If an ohmmeter is used, disconnect the wire which runs from the points to the alternator.

3. Slowly turn the engine over in its normal running direction (counterclockwise). The "F" mark on the alternator rotor should align with the index on the stator (**Figure 13**) just as the points open.

13

14

12

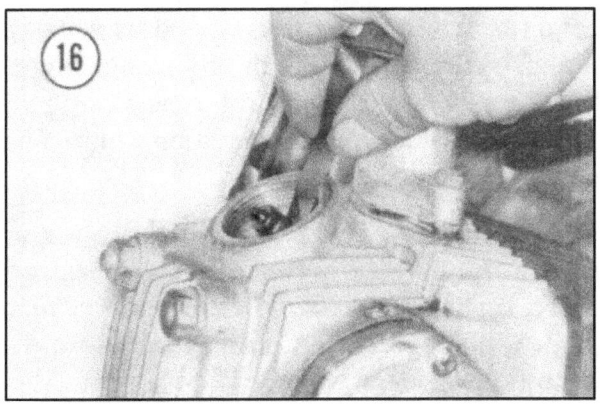

4. If adjustment is required, turn the engine *counterclockwise* until the "F" mark and index are in alignment.

5. Refer to **Figure 14**. Loosen both timing plate screws (A), then turn the timing plate until the points just open.

6. Tighten both screws, then again check timing by repeating Step 3. Adjust as required.

VALVE ADJUSTMENT

Proper valve adjustment is vital to engine performance. If valve clearance is too small, poor performance and short valve life will result. On the other hand, if there is too much clearance, valves will be noisy and the engine will not develop full power.

Inspection and adjustment must be performed with the engine cold.

1. Remove both tappet covers and the alternator cover.

2. Turn the engine over counterclockwise until the "T" mark on the rotor or flywheel aligns with its index (**Figure 15**). If one valve is open, turn the engine counterclockwise one more turn.

3. Measure clearance at each valve, using a 0.002 inch (0.05 millimeter) feeler gauge (**Figure 16**).

4. If clearance is incorrect, loosen locknut (A), then turn adjusting screw (B) as required (**Figure 17**).

5. Tighten the locknut and again check clearance. Readjust as necessary.

SPARK PLUG

One of the most important steps to be done during any tune-up is to remove and examine the spark plug. If the spark plug is still good, it

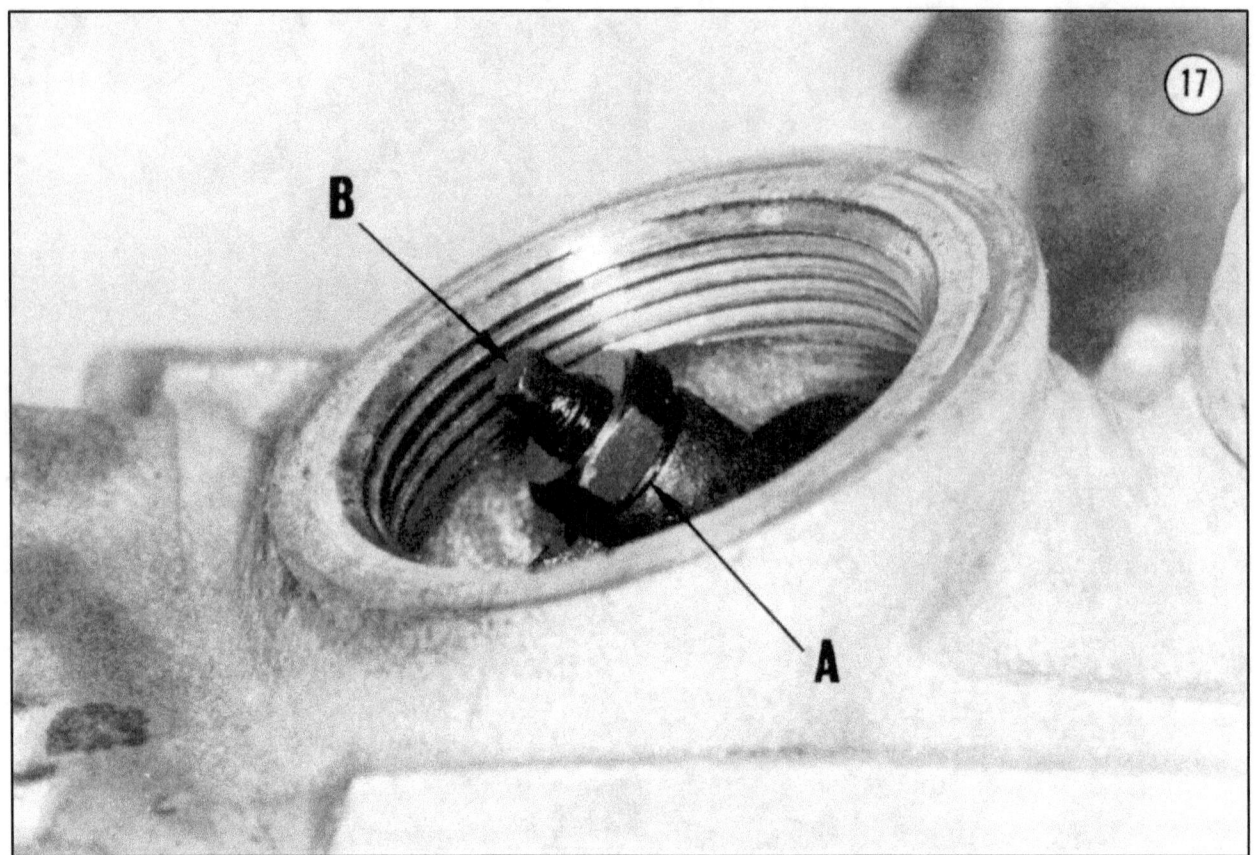

may be serviced and reused. If not, the cause of its failure should be determined and corrected before returning the bike to service.

To remove the spark plug, first clean the area around its base to prevent dirt or other foreign material from entering the cylinder. Then unscrew the spark plug, using a suitable deep socket. If difficulty is encountered removing a spark plug, apply penetrating oil to its base and allow some 20 minutes for the oil to work in. It may also be helpful to rap the cylinder head lightly with a rubber or plastic mallet; this procedure sets up vibrations which help the penetrating oil to work in.

Figure 18 illustrates various conditions which might be encountered upon plug removal.

1. *Normal condition* — If plug has a light tan or gray colored deposit and no abnormal gap wear or erosion, good engine, carburetion, and ignition condition are indicated. The plug in use is of the proper heat range, and may be serviced and returned to use.

2. *Carbon fouled* — Soft, dry, sooty deposits are evidence of incomplete combustion and can usually be attributed to rich carburetion. This condition is also sometimes caused by weak ignition, retarded timing, or low compression. Such a plug may usually be cleaned and returned to service, but the condition which caused fouling should be corrected.

3. *Oil fouled* — This plug exhibits a black insulator tip, damp oily film over the firing end, and a carbon layer over the entire nose. Electrode will not be worn. Common causes for this condition are listed below.

   a. Worn piston rings
   b. Worn valve guides
   c. Crankcase overfill
   d. Wrong spark plug (too cold)

An oil-fouled spark plug may be cleaned, but it is better to replace it. It is important to correct the cause of fouling before the engine is returned to service.

4. *Gap bridging* — A plug with this condition will have the gap shorted out by combustion chamber deposits fused between electrodes. On four-stroke engines, the usual cause is poor oil control resulting from worn piston rings or

SPARK PLUG CONDITION

NORMAL USE

OIL FOULED

CARBON FOULED

OVERHEATED

GAP BRIDGED

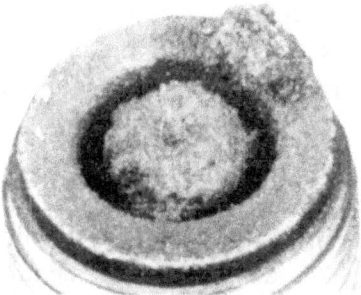

SUSTAINED PREIGNITION

WORN OUT

Photos courtesy of Champion Spark Plug Company.

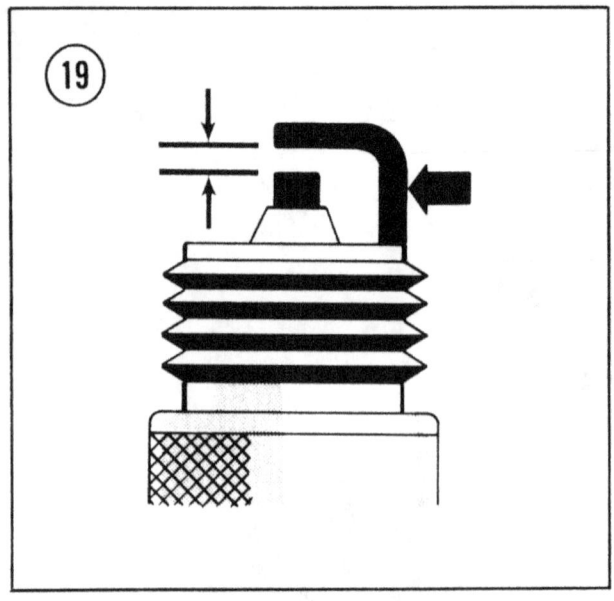

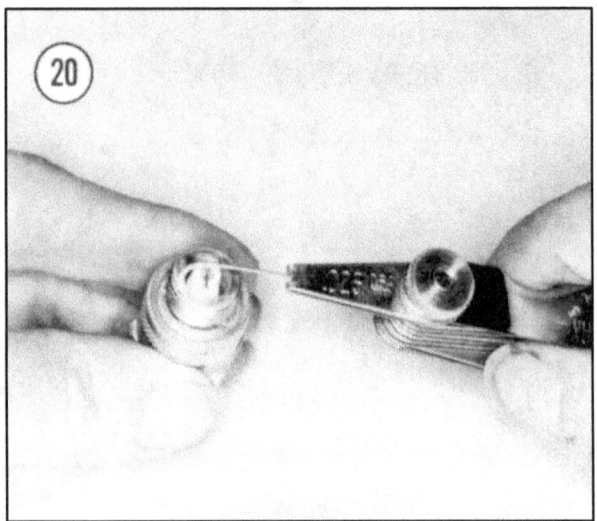

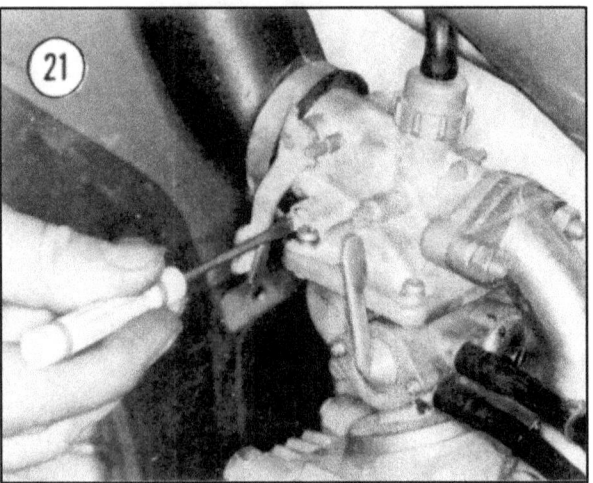

valve guides, or possibly from an overfilled crankcase. Be sure to locate and correct the cause of this spark plug condition. Such a plug must be replaced with a new one.

5. *Overheated* — An overheated spark plug exhibits a burned electrode. The insulator tip will be light gray or even chalk white. The most common cause for this condition is using a spark plug of the wrong heat range (too hot). If it is known that the correct plug is used, other causes are lean fuel mixture, engine overloading or lugging, loose carburetor mounting, or timing advanced too far. Always correct the fault before putting the bike back into service. Such a plug cannot be salvaged; replace with a new one.

6. *Worn out* — Corrosive gases formed by combustion and high voltage sparks have eroded the electrode. A spark plug in this condition requires more voltage to fire under hard acceleration; often more than the ignition system can supply. It should be replaced with a new plug of the same heat range.

7. *Preignition* — If electrodes are melted, preignition is almost certainly the cause. Check for carburetor mounting or intake manifold leaks, also overadvanced ignition timing. It is also possible that a plug of the wrong heat range (too hot) is being used. Find the cause of preignition before placing the engine back into service.

A spark plug may usually be cleaned and re-gapped, which will restore it to near new condition. Since the effort involved is considerable, such service may not be worth it, since a new spark plug is relatively inexpensive.

For those who wish to service the used plug, the following procedure is recommended.

1. Clean all oily deposits from the spark plug with cleaning solvent, then blow dry with compressed air. If this precaution is not taken, oily deposits will cause gumming or caking of the sandblast cleaner.

2. Place the spark plug in a sandblast cleaner and blast 3 to 5 seconds, then turn on air only to remove particles from the plug.

3. Repeat Step 2 as required until the plug is cleaned. Prolonged sandblasting will erode the insulator and make the plug much more susceptible to fouling.

4. Bend the side electrode up slightly, then file the center electrode so that it is no longer rounded, and the side electrode so that edges

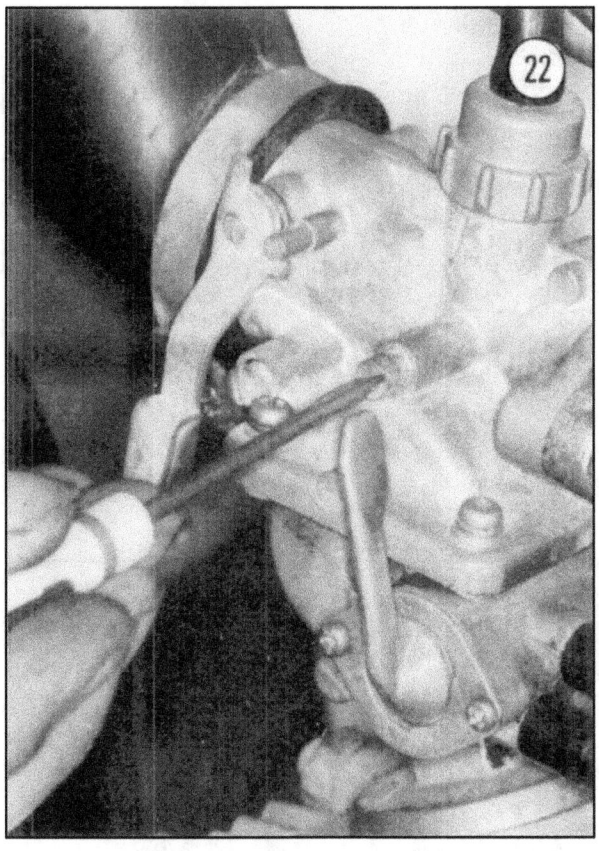

are not rounded. The reason for this step is that less voltage is required to jump between sharp corners than between rounded edges.

5. Adjust the spark plug gap to 0.024-0.028 inch (0.6-0.7 millimeter) for all models, using a round wire gauge for measurement (**Figure 19**). Always adjust spark plug gap by bending the outer electrode only. A spark plug gapping tool does the best job, if one is available. See **Figure 20**.

AIR CLEANER

As part of any tune-up, the air cleaner should be cleaned or replaced, as required. A clogged air cleaner results in an overrich mixture, which causes loss of power and poor gas mileage. Be sure that the air cleaner element is not torn and that it fits so that no dirt can leak past its edges. Clean foam elements in cleaning solvent and re-oil with SAE 80-SAE 90 gear oil.

BATTERY SERVICE

Complete battery service information is contained in Chapter Five. Briefly, the following items should be attended to regularly.

1. Test state of charge. Recharge if at half charge (1.220 specific gravity) or less.
2. Add distilled water if required.
3. Clean battery top.

FUEL STRAINER

The fuel strainer filters out particles which might otherwise get into the carburetor and cause the float needle to remain open. Such particles might also get into the engine and cause damage. Remove the fuel strainer, located at the fuel petcock, and clean it at each tune-up. Many carburetors also have a fuel strainer at the fuel inlet fitting. Clean the fuel filter in solvent; blow dry with compressed air.

CARBURETOR ADJUSTMENT

Carburetor adjustment is left as the last step to be done on the engine, because it cannot be done accurately unless all other adjustments are correct. Although carburetor adjustment is discussed in detail in Chapter Four, an abbreviated procedure is described here.

1. Turn the air screw in (clockwise) until it seats lightly, then back it out 1½ turns (**Figure 21**).
2. Start the engine, then ride the bike long enough to warm it thoroughly.
3. Turn the idle speed screw (**Figure 22**) until the engine runs slower and begins to falter.
4. Turn the idle air screw in or out as required to make the engine run smoothly.
5. Repeat Steps 3 and 4 to achieve the lowest stable idle speed.
6. Adjust idle speed as desired, using the idle speed screw.
7. Check that there is a small amount of slack in the throttle cable when the throttle is fully closed.

OIL AND FILTER CHANGE

While the engine is warm, drain and refill the crankcase, transmission, and clutch. Be sure to use a recommended type and grade of lubricant. Do not use any of the honey-type lubricants in those motorcycles which share a common oil supply for clutch and transmission. Such lubricants may cause clutch slippage.

Remove and clean the oil filters at this time also. It is necessary to first remove the right crankcase cover, then remove the filters (**Figures 23 A and B**) for service. Be sure to note how they fit so that they can be replaced in the proper position.

ELECTRICAL EQUIPMENT

Check lights, horn, and turn signals. Be sure that stoplight switches are adjusted so that the stoplight goes on before braking action begins.

DRIVE CHAIN

Remove and service the chain. To do so, proceed as follows:

1. Disconnect the master link. It may be necessary to turn the rear wheel to position the master link for convenient removal. Upon installation, be sure that the master link clip is installed as shown in **Figure 24**.
2. The chain should be cleaned with solvent and a stiff bristle brush.
3. Rinse thoroughly in clean solvent, then blow dry with compressed air.

After cleaning, examine the chain carefully for wear or damage. Replace it if there is any doubt about its condition (see Chapter Six). If its condition is good, lubricate it by soaking in oil or melted grease, or use one of the special chain lubricants sold by any motorcycle shop. Follow the instructions on the container.

CAM CHAIN TENSIONER

The cam chain is driven by the crankshaft. It runs between the crankshaft and camshaft on the right-hand side of the engine. *Disassembly/Assembly* procedures are found in Chapter Three.

Adjustment

Although the cam chain adjustment is automatic, it does have a manual adjuster. Should the chain become noisy after continual use, adjust as described in the following steps.

1. Place the bike on the centerstand, with the engine running.

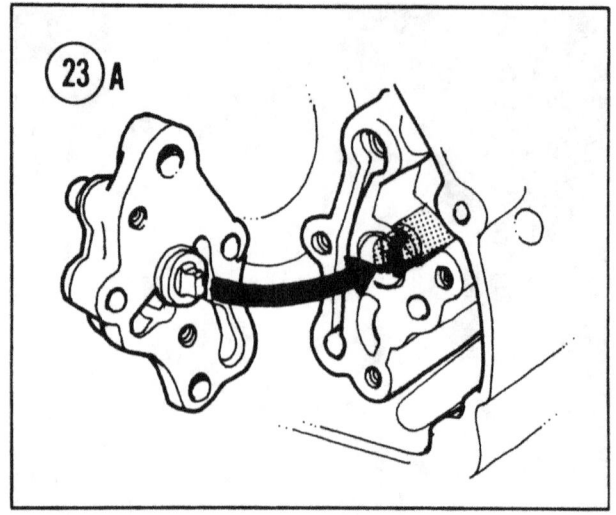

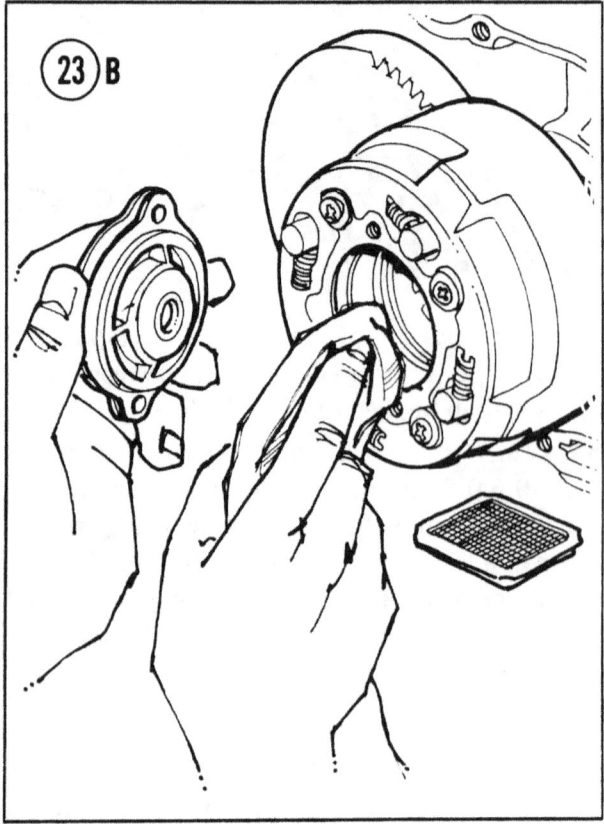

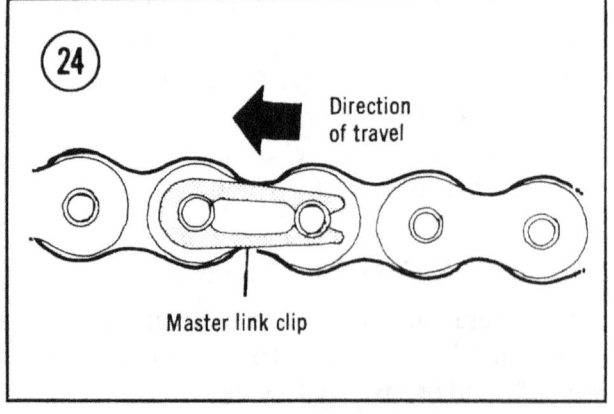

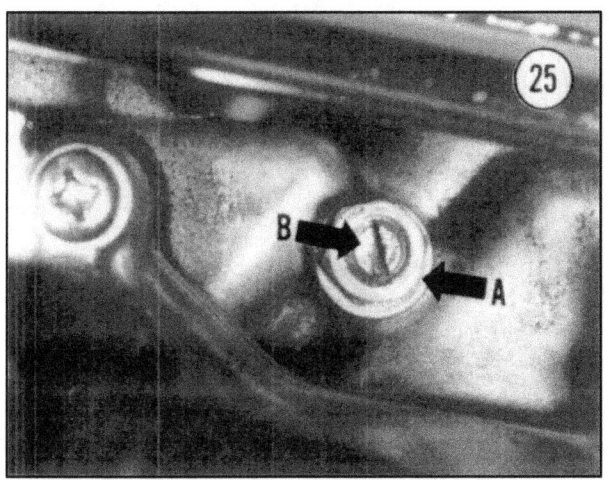

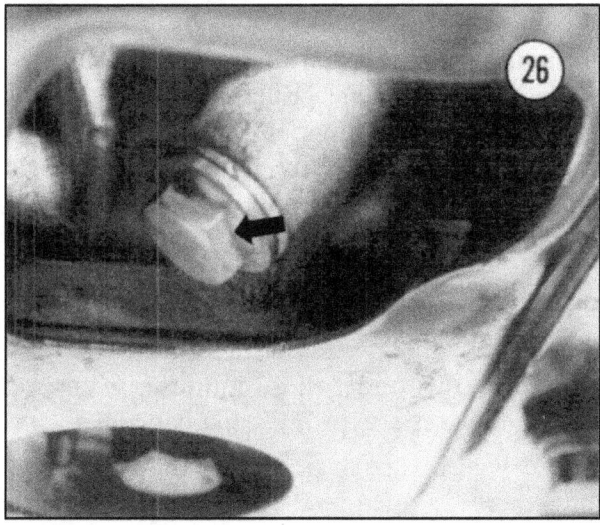

2. Loosen the locknut (A, **Figure 25**), then loosen the adjusting bolt (B) approximately 1½ turns. The chain should automatically adjust by the force of the tensioner spring.

3. If the chain is now quiet, tighten the adjusting bolt and locknut. If the chain is still noisy, follow Step 4.

4. Remove the tensioner bolt (**Figure 26**) and, with a screwdriver, turn the adjusting bolt (which will be found inside) clockwise until the chain is no longer noisy. At this point, stop the adjustment. Install the tensioner bolt, and tighten the adjusting bolt and locknut (B and A, **Figure 25**).

TROUBLESHOOTING

Diagnosing motorcycle ills is relatively simple if you use orderly procedures and keep a few basic principles in mind.

Never assume anything. Don't overlook the obvious. If you are riding along and the bike suddenly quits, check the easiest, most accessible problem spots first. Is there gasoline in the tank? Is the gas petcock in the ON or RESERVE position? Has the spark plug wire fallen off? Check the ignition switch. Sometimes the weight of keys on a key ring may turn the ignition off suddenly. Above all, remember that a bike almost never quits because of misadjustment, so don't start turning screws in the hope of improving matters.

If nothing obvious turns up in a cursory check, look a little further. Learning to recognize and describe symptoms will make repairs easier for you or a mechanic at the shop. Describe problems accurately and fully. Saying that "it won't run" isn't the same as saying "it quit on the highway at high speed and wouldn't start," or that "it sat in my garage for three months and then wouldn't start."

Gather as many symptoms together as possible to aid in diagnosis. Note whether the engine lost power gradually or all at once, what color smoke (if any) came from the exhaust, and so on. Remember that the more complex a machine is, the easier it is to troubleshoot because symptoms point to specific problems.

You don't need fancy equipment or complicated test gear to determine whether repairs can be attempted at home. A few simple checks could save a large repair bill and time lost while the bike sits in a dealer's service department. On the other hand, be realistic and don't attempt repairs beyond your abilities. Service departments tend to charge heavily for putting together a disassembled engine that may have been abused. Some won't even take on such a job. So use common sense — don't take on more than you can handle.

Operating Requirements

An engine needs three basics to run properly: correct gas/air mixture, compression, and a spark at the right time. If one or more are missing, the engine won't run. The electrical system is the weakest link of the three. More problems result from electrical breakdowns than from any other source. Keep that in mind before tampering with carburetor adjustments and the like.

If a bike has been sitting for any length of time and refuses to start, check the battery for a charged condition first, and then look at the gasoline delivery system. This system includes the tank, fuel petcock, fuel line, and carburetor. Rust may have formed in the tank, obstructing fuel flow. Gasoline deposits may have gummed up carburetor jets and air passages. Gasoline tends to lose its potency after standing for long periods. Condensation may contaminate it with water. Drain old gas from the tank and carburetor and try starting with a fresh tankful.

Compression, or the lack of it, usually enters the picture only in the case of older machines. Worn or broken pistons, rings, or cylinder bores could prevent starting. Generally, a gradual power loss and harder and harder starting will be readily apparent in this case.

Starting Difficulties

Check gas flow first. Remove the gas cap and look into the tank. If gas is present, pull off the fuel line at the carburetor and see if gas flows freely. If none comes out, the fuel tap may be shut off, blocked by rust or foreign matter, or the fuel line may be stopped up or kinked. If the carburetor is getting usable fuel, turn to the electrical system next.

Check that the battery is charged by turning on the lights or by beeping the horn. Refer to your owner's manual for starting procedures with a dead battery. Have the battery recharged if necessary.

Pull off the spark plug cap, remove the spark plug, and reconnect the cap. Lay the plug against the cylinder head so its base makes a good connection, and turn the engine over briskly with the kickstarter. A fat, blue-white spark should jump across the electrodes. If there is no spark, or only a weak one, there is electrical system trouble. Check for a defective plug by replacing it with a known good one. Don't assume a plug is good just because it's new. Remember that a faulty spark plug is the greatest single cause of failure to start.

Once the plug has been proven good, but there's still no spark, start backtracking through the system. If the contact at the end of the spark plug wire can be exposed, it can be held about 1/8 inch from the head while the engine is turned over to check for a spark. Remember to hold the wire only by its insulation to avoid a nasty shock. If the plug wire is dirty, greasy, or wet, wrap a rag around it so you don't get shocked. If you do feel a shock or see sparks along the wire, clean or replace the wire and/or its connections.

If there's no spark at the plug wire, look for loose connections at the coil, battery, or magneto. If all seems in order there, check next for oily or dirty contact points. Clean points with electrical contact cleaner or a strip of paper. On battery ignition models, with ignition on, open and close the points manually with a screwdriver.

No spark at the points with this test indicates a failure in the ignition system. Refer to Chapter Five for checkout procedures for the entire system and individual components.

Note that a spark plug of the incorrect heat range (too cold) may cause hard starting. Set gap to specifications. If you have just ridden through a puddle or washed the bike and it won't start, dry off the plug and plug wire. Water may have entered the carburetor and fouled the fuel under these conditions, but wet plugs and wires are the more likely problem.

If a healthy spark occurs at the right time, and there is adequate gas flow to the carburetor, check the carburetor itself at this time. It frequently happens that dirt lodges in the float needle valve, causing the carburetor to flood. The resulting overrich mixture can prevent starting, or may cause the bike to quit. As a temporary cure, rap the carburetor smartly with any convenient object to dislodge the dirt, then crank the engine with the throttle wide open.

If the foregoing procedure didn't fix the trouble, and it has definitely been determined that carburetion is the trouble, it will be necessary to disassemble and check the carburetor. Make sure all jets and air passages are clean, check float level, and adjust if necessary. Shake the float to check for gasoline inside it, and replace or repair as indicated. Check that the carburetor is mounted snugly. Check for a clogged air filter.

Compression may be checked in the field by turning the kickstarter by hand and noting that adequate resistance is felt, or by removing the spark plug and placing a finger over the plug hole and feeling for pressure.

Poor Idling

Poor idling may be caused by incorrect carburetor adjustment, incorrect timing, or ignition system defects. Check the gas cap vent for an obstruction. Check carburetor mounting.

Misfiring

Misfiring can be caused by a weak spark or dirty plugs. Check for fuel contamination. Run the machine at night or in a darkened garage to check for spark leaks on plug wires or under the spark plug cap. If misfiring occurs only at certain throttle settings, refer to the carburetor chapter for the specific carburetor circuits involved. Misfiring under heavy load, as when climbing hills or accelerating, is usually caused by bad spark plugs.

Flat Spots

If the engine seems to die momentarily when the throttle is opened and then recovers, check for a dirty main jet in the carburetor, water in the fuel, or an excessively lean mixture.

Power Loss

Poor condition of rings, pistons, or cylinders will cause a lack of power and speed. Ignition timing should be checked.

Overheating

If the engine seems to run too hot all the time, be sure you are not idling it for long periods. Air-cooled engines are not designed to operate at a standstill for any length of time. Heavy stop-and-go traffic is hard on a motorcycle engine. Spark plugs of the wrong heat range can burn pistons. An excessively lean gas mixture may cause overheating. Check ignition timing. Don't ride in too high a gear. Broken or worn rings may permit compression gases to leak past them, heating heads and cylinders excessively. Check oil level and use the proper grade lubricants.

Backfiring

Check that ignition timing is not advanced too far. Check fuel for contamination.

Lighting Problems

Bulbs which continuously burn out may be caused by excessive vibration, loose connections that permit sudden current surges, poor battery connections, or use of the wrong type bulb.

A dead battery, or one which discharges quickly, may be caused by a faulty generator or rectifier. Check for loose or corroded terminals. Shorted battery cells or broken terminals will keep a battery from charging. Low water level will decrease a battery's capacity. A battery left uncharged after installation will sulphate, rendering it useless.

A majority of light and horn or other electrical accessory problems are caused by loose or corroded ground connections. Check those first, and then substitute known good units for easier troubleshooting.

CHAPTER THREE

ENGINE, TRANSMISSION, AND CLUTCH

This chapter describes removal, disassembly, service, and reassembly of the engine, transmission, and clutch. Although major service requires engine removal, work on the clutch, shifter, magneto or alternator, and cam chain tensioner may be performed with the engine in place.

PREPARATION FOR ENGINE DISASSEMBLY

1. Thoroughly clean the engine exterior of dirt, oil, and foreign material, using one of the cleaners formulated for the purpose.
2. Be sure you have the proper tools for the job. See *General Information* in Chapter One.
3. As you remove parts from the engine, place them in trays in the order of their disassembly. Doing so will make reassembly faster and easier, and will ensure correct installation of all engine parts.
4. Note that disassembly procedures will vary slightly between the various models. Be sure to read the steps carefully and follow those which apply to your engine.

CAUTION
Many engine components are retained by Phillips screws. These screws are very tight, and should only be loosened with an impact driver. Attempts to loosen them with an ordinary Phillips screwdriver will probably result in damaged screw heads and difficult, expensive, professional removal.

ENGINE REMOVAL

Engine removal is generally similar for all models. Detailed procedures for selected models are set forth as a guide.

50cc-70cc Models

1. Warm the engine thoroughly, if possible, then drain the oil.
2. Remove the fairing, if so equipped.
3. Remove the muffler and exhaust pipe, footpeg assembly, and tool box.
4. Remove oil lines on S50 and S65.
5. On C models, remove the carburetor from the cylinder head. On S models, remove the inlet tube. Be sure that no fuel leaks onto the engine. Plug the line if necessary.
6. Disconnect the clutch cable at the engine on models so equipped.
7. Remove the kickstarter and shift levers.
8. Remove the left crankcase cover, then disconnect all wiring. On CL70 and SL70, disconnect the white, yellow, and pink wires under the battery cover.

9. Disconnect the master link, then remove the chain from the engine sprocket.

10. Disconnect the spark plug lead; also, remove its clip from the right crankcase cover.

11. Remove the brake pedal and stoplight switch return springs.

12. Remove the engine mounting bolts, then carefully lower the engine.

13. Reverse this procedure to install.

90cc Models

1. Start the engine and warm it thoroughly, then drain the oil.

2. Remove the engine protection plate on models so equipped.

3. Remove the footpeg assembly, muffler, and chain.

4. Disconnect the clutch cable, if so equipped.

5. Disconnect the intake manifold at the cylinder head.

6. Disconnect the spark plug cable.

7. Disconnect all wiring.

8. Remove kickstarter and shifter pedals.

9. Remove the engine mounting bolts, then carefully lift the engine from the frame.

10. Reverse this procedure to install.

LEFT CRANKCASE COVER

Under the left crankcase cover are the cam chain tensioner, magneto or alternator, and engine sprocket. On CT90 from frame No. 12251, the Posi-torque mechanism is integral with the left crankcase cover, and must be removed before removing the left crankcase cover.

POSI-TORQUE MECHANISM (8-SPEED)

Later CT90 models are equipped with an auxiliary gear reduction system, which makes it unnecessary to replace the rear wheel sprocket for trail use. When in low range, greater driving power is supplied to the rear wheel.

Disassembly/Assembly

Figure 1 shows an exploded view of the reduction gear assembly. Refer to this illustra-

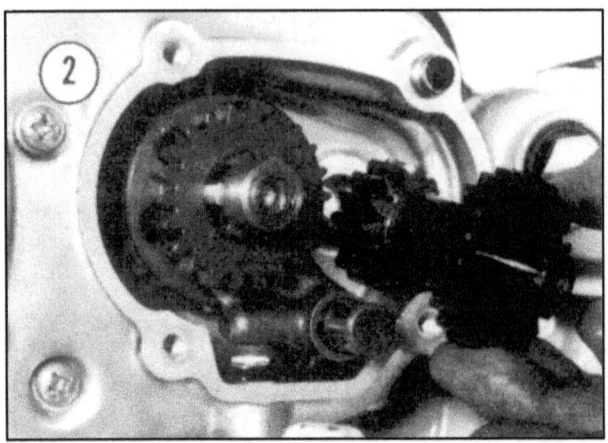

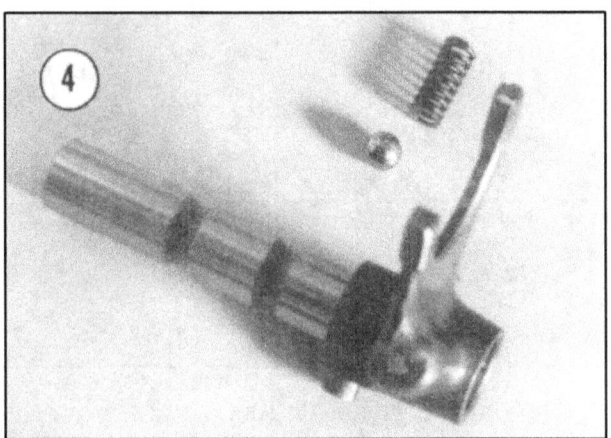

tion during the disassembly and assembly procedures.

1. Remove the 4 screws securing the reduction gear cover, and remove the cover. Note that one screw is longer.

2. Remove the countergear and shaft (**Figure 2**) by pulling it straight out from the cover.

3. Pull out the sliding (lower) gear, selector fork, and shaft. Note that the shaft is located by the selection lever. See **Figure 3**.

4. Remove the selector fork shaft (**Figure 4**). The shaft is retained by a steel ball and spring.

5. Remove the circlip and washer. Pull out the sprocket drive gear. See **Figure 5**.

6. Remove the spring clip securing the selection lever (A, **Figure 5**). There is an O-ring located on the selection lever shaft.

7. Reassemble by reversing the removal procedures.

MAGNETO

Some models are equipped with flywheel magnetos which supply all power for ignition, and also for lights and battery charging on machines so equipped.

Removal

1. Remove the left crankcase cover.

2. Refer to **Figure 6**. Using a suitable flywheel holding tool, remove flywheel retaining nut with a socket wrench.

3. Refer to **Figure 7**. Screw a flywheel puller to its full depth into flywheel, then turn puller screw to remove the flywheel.

4. Remove both base plate mounting screws, then tap the stator plate lightly with a plastic mallet, if necessary, to remove it.

Service

Magneto service is covered in Chapter Five. On models so equipped, be sure that the ignition advance weights inside the flywheel

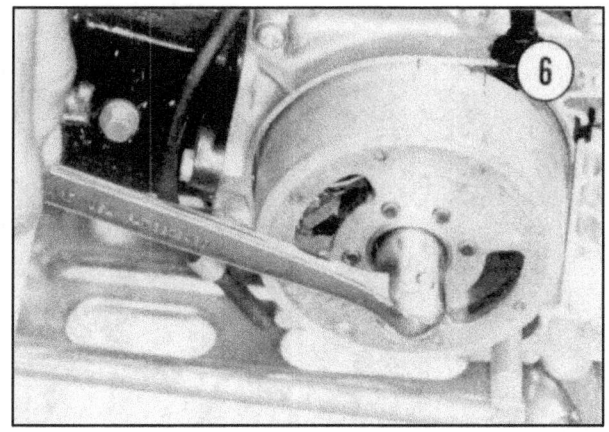

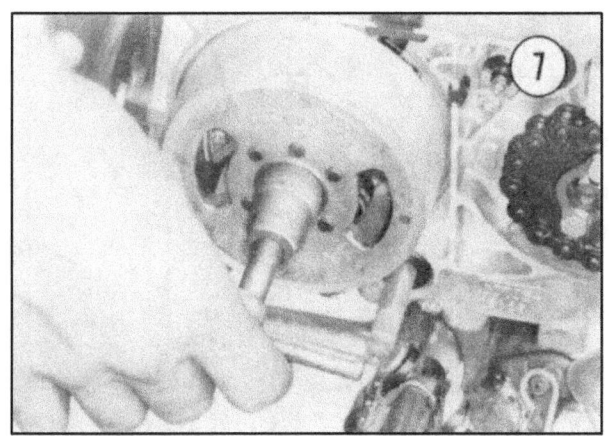

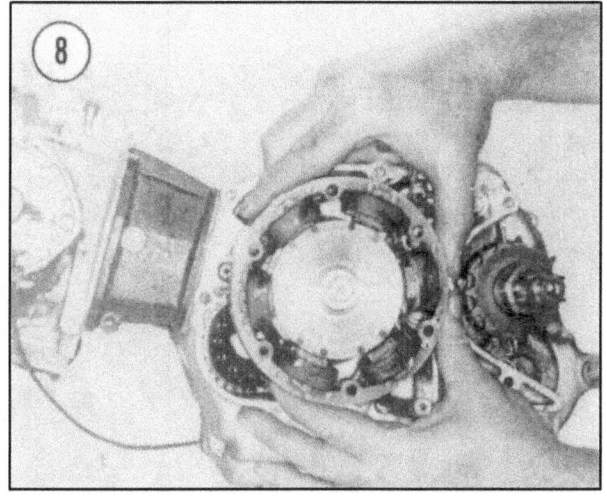

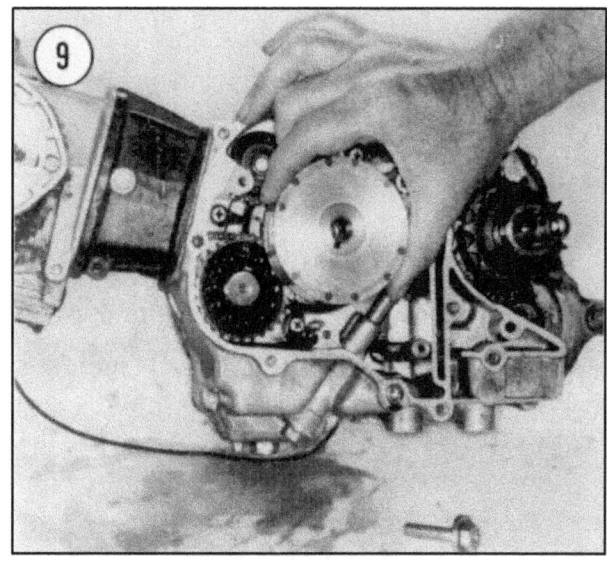

operate freely, and snap back when the mechanism is twisted and then released.

Installation

Reverse the removal procedure to install the magneto. Don't forget to install the crankshaft O-ring, stator plate O-ring, and stator plate screw O-rings. Torque the flywheel nut to 23.9-27.5 foot-pounds (32-37 N•m).

ALTERNATOR

Models with 90cc engines, and smaller models with electric starters are equipped with alternators.

Removal

1. Remove the left crankcase cover.
2. Disconnect all wiring from the alternator.
3. Remove 3 retaining screws, then pull out the stator (**Figure 8**).
4. Remove the rotor retaining bolt, then using a suitable puller, remove the rotor (**Figure 9**).
5. Pull the Woodruff key from the crankshaft.

Service

Alternator service is covered in Chapter Five.

Installation

Reverse the removal procedure to install the alternator. Be sure that no iron filings are attached to the rotor as it is installed. Also be sure that the slot in the rotor aligns with the Woodruff key on the crankshaft. Tighten the retaining bolt to 15.9-21.7 foot-pounds (22-30 N•m).

CYLINDER HEAD

The cylinder head is made of lightweight aluminum alloy, and incorporates the camshaft, cam sprocket, valves, and rocker arms. On 90cc models, breaker points and the ignition

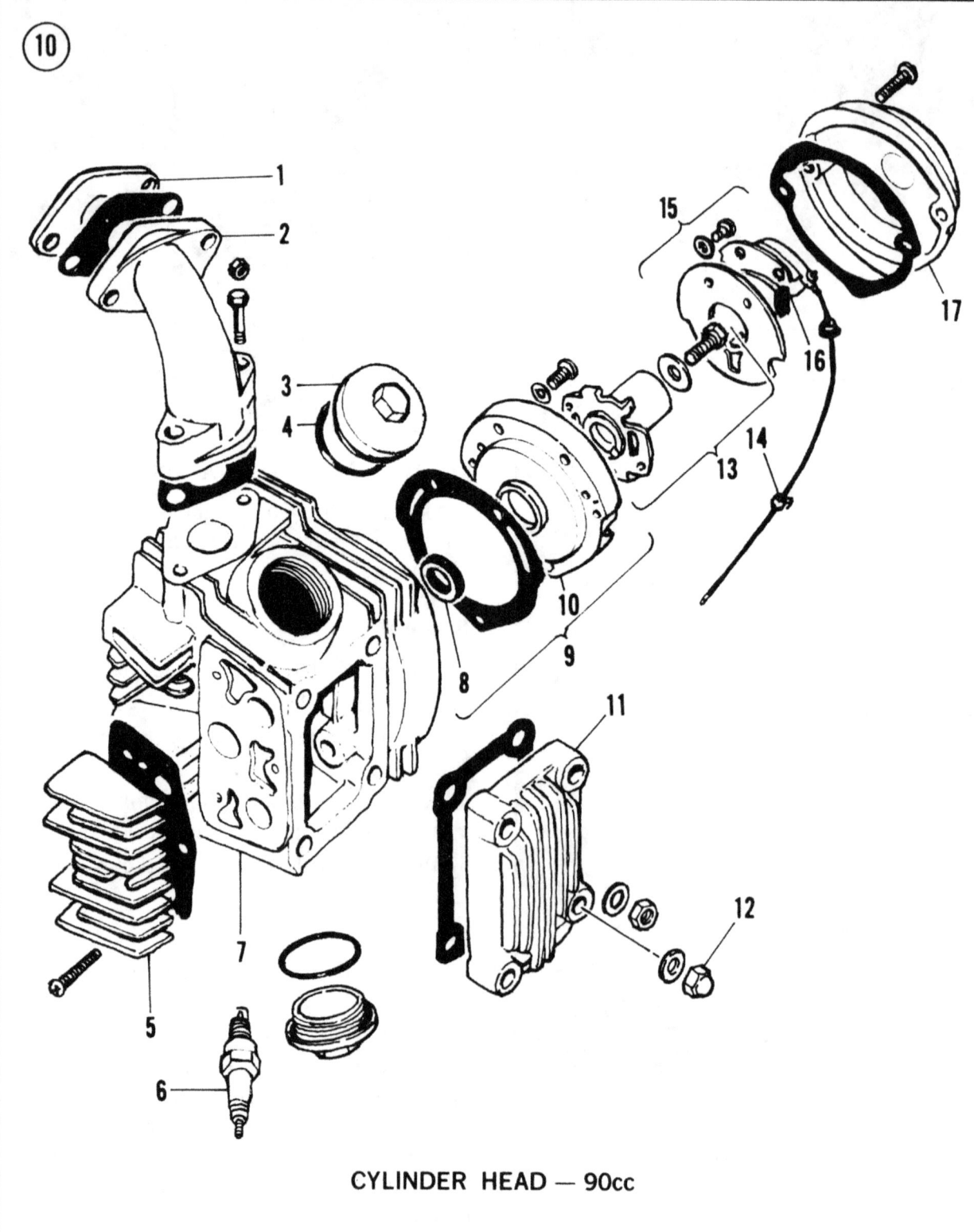

CYLINDER HEAD — 90cc

1. Insulator
2. Intake manifold
3. Tappet cover
4. O-ring
5. Cover
6. Spark plug
7. Cylinder head
8. Spacer
9. Point base assembly
10. Point base
11. Cover
12. Acorn nut
13. Ignition advance assembly
14. Clip
15. Breaker point assembly
16. Breaker points
17. Breaker point assembly cover

advance mechanism are also part of the cylinder head.

Removal (90cc Models)

Figure 10 is an exploded view of a typical 90cc cylinder head. Refer to that illustration during removal and service.

1. Remove the breaker point cover and left crankcase cover.
2. Remove the alternator stator and rotor.
3. Remove 2 retaining screws, then the breaker point base (**Figure 11**).
4. Pull off the advance assembly (**Figure 12**) after removing its retaining bolt.
5. Carefully remove the locating dowel from the camshaft (**Figure 13**).

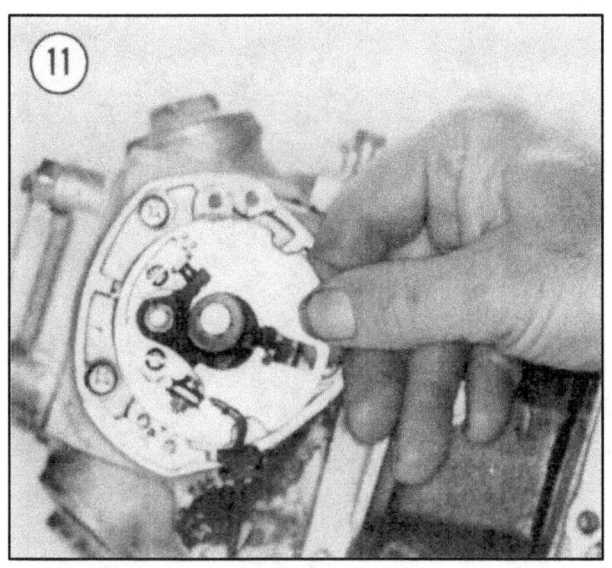

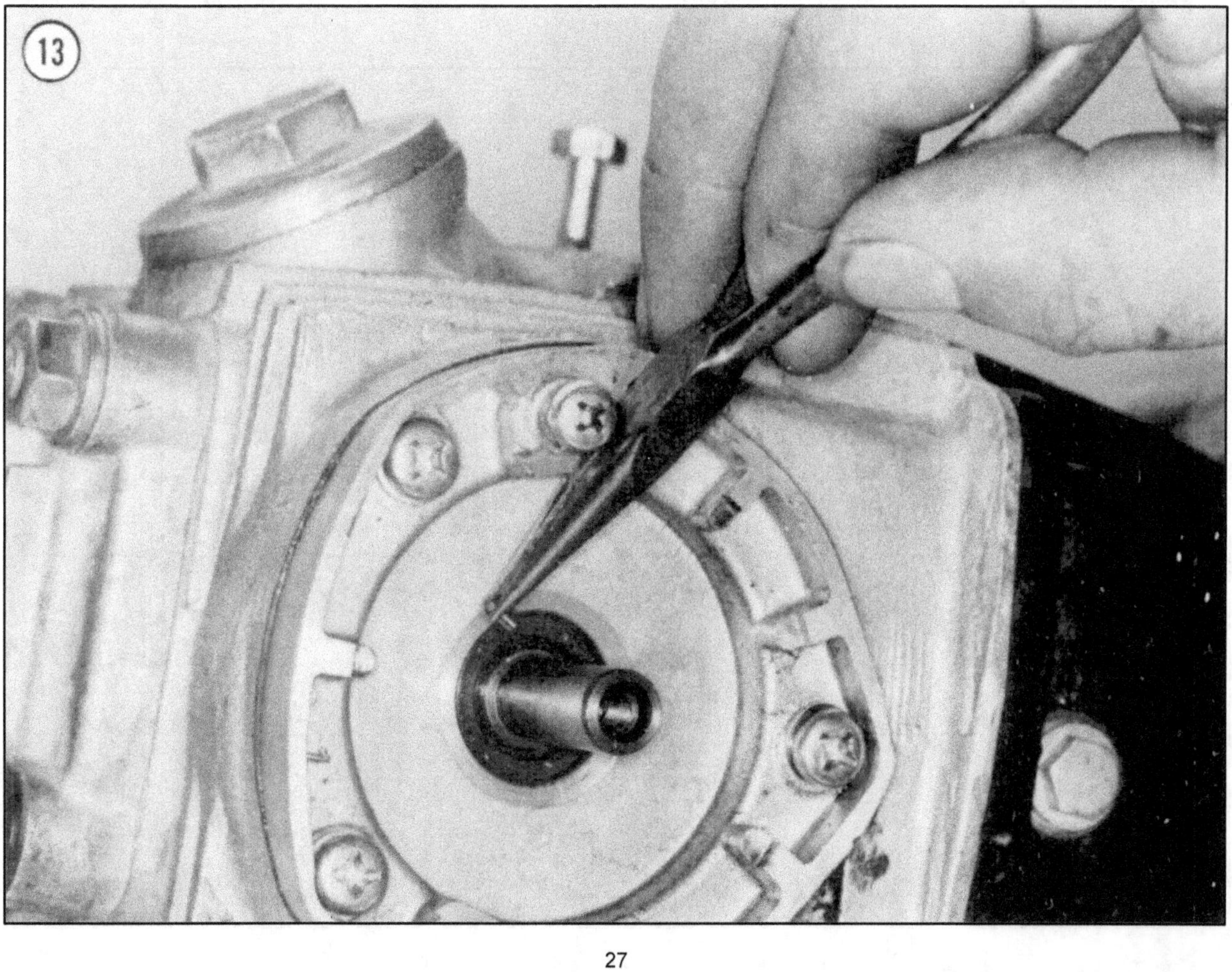

28

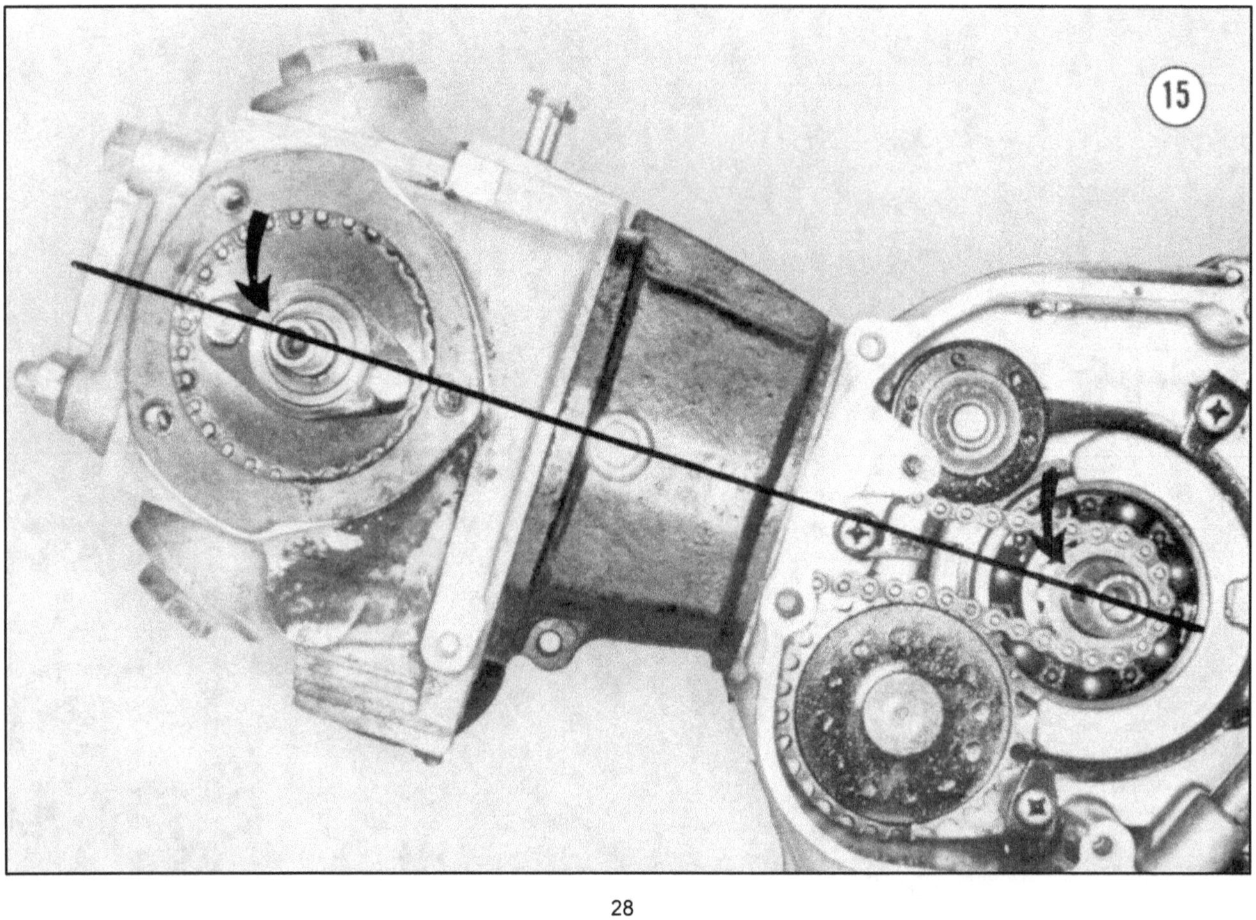

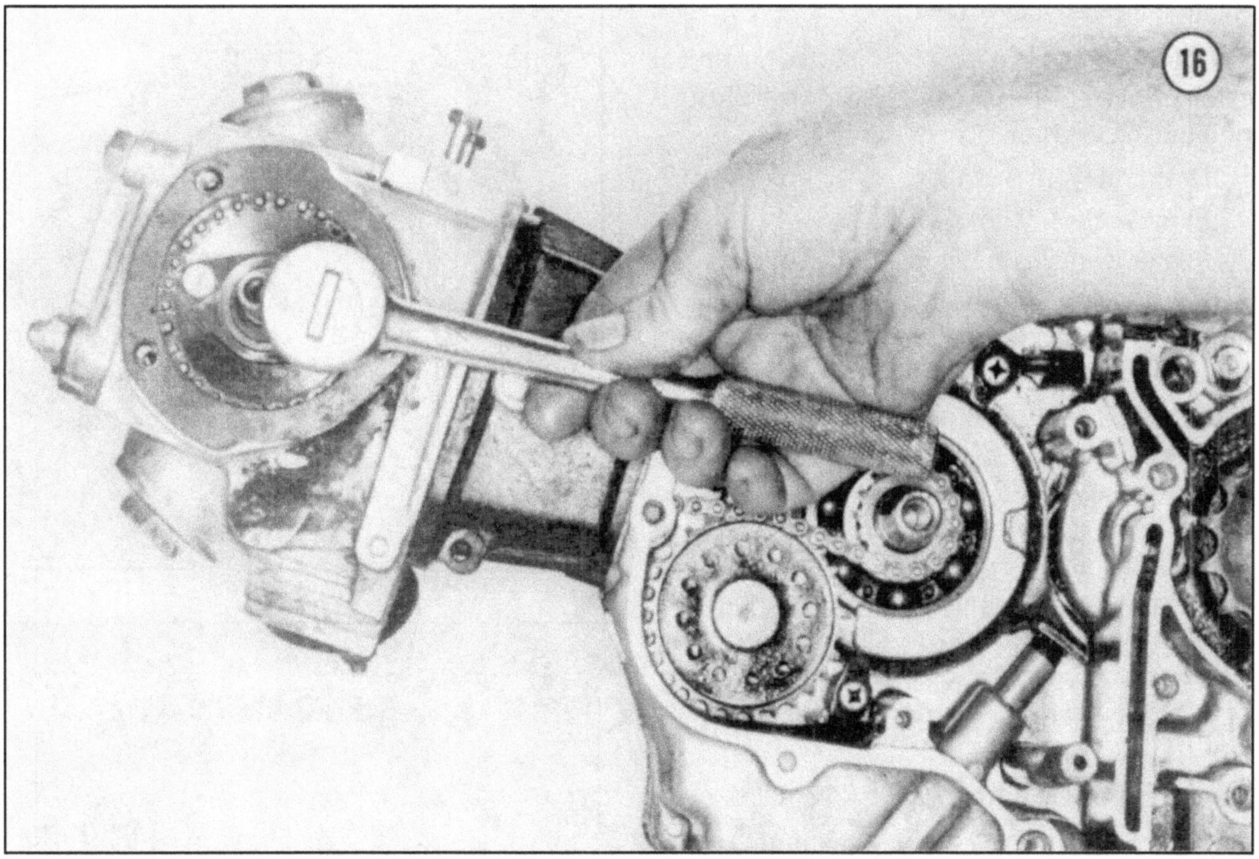

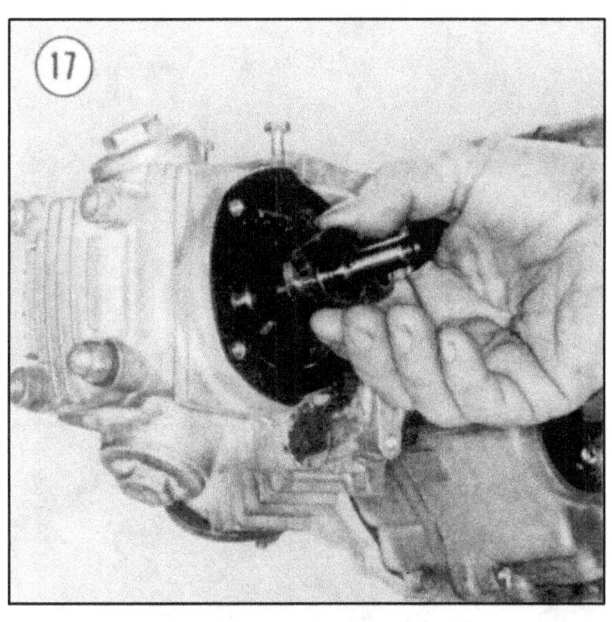

8. Remove 2 retaining bolts (**Figure 16**), then pull out the camshaft (**Figure 17**).

9. Loosen in crisscross order, then remove 4 cylinder head nuts (**Figure 18**). Note that there is one acorn nut; its location is marked by the wrench in the illustration.

10. Carefully pull the cylinder head from the engine (**Figure 19**). It may be necessary to tap it lightly with a plastic or rubber mallet to free it; if so, be careful not to break any cooling fins.

6. Pull off the point base (**Figure 14**) after removing 3 retaining screws.

7. Rotate the engine until the Woodruff key on the crankshaft and the dowel pin hole on the camshaft are aligned, and both pointing toward the cylinder head cover (**Figure 15**). Both valves will be fully closed when these conditions exist, making camshaft removal possible.

Removal (50cc-70cc Models)

Figure 20 is an exploded view of a typical cylinder head of this type. Refer to that illustration during disassembly and service.

1. Drain oil from the engine.
2. Remove the left crankcase cover.
3. Remove both cylinder head side covers.
4. Remove the flywheel and magneto stator plate. On models with electric starters, remove the alternator rotor and stator. Also remove the starter drive chain, starter motor sprocket, and engine sprocket.
5. Refer to **Figure 21**. Remove 3 cam sprocket bolts (2) from cam sprocket (1).
6. Remove 4 cylinder head nuts in crisscross order, and one hex bolt. Pull the cylinder head from the cylinder. It may be necessary to free it with a few taps with a plastic or rubber mallet, but if so, don't break any cooling fins.

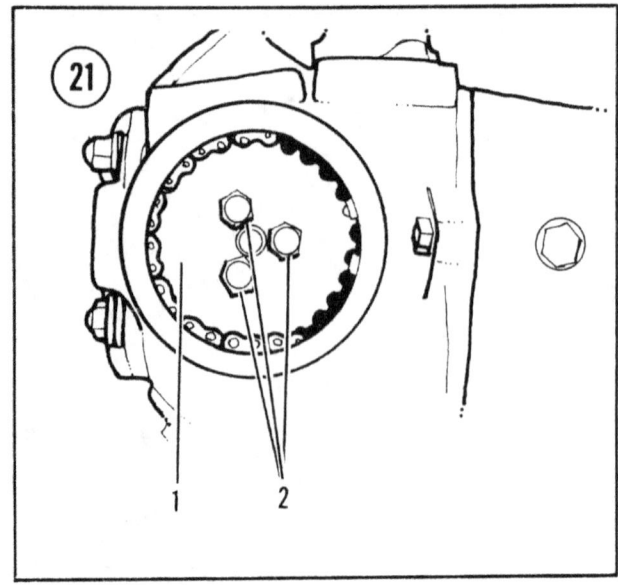

Inspection (All Models)

1. Remove both valves, using a suitable valve lifter (**Figure 22**).
2. Refer to **Figure 23**. Place a straightedge (2) across each pair of mounting holes on machined gasket surface (1). At each location, check that clearance does not exceed 0.002 inch (0.05 millimeter), using a feeler gauge (3).

If warpage exceeds 0.002 inch (0.05 millimeter), place a sheet of fine emery paper on a surface plate, then move the head back and forth until no warpage exists.

3. Measure clearance between the stem and valve guide. Insert each valve into its guide, then measure side play with a dial indicator.

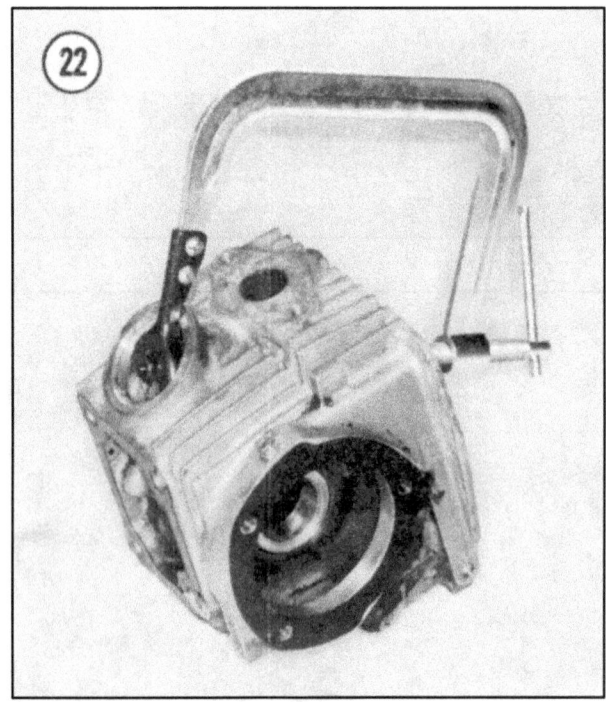

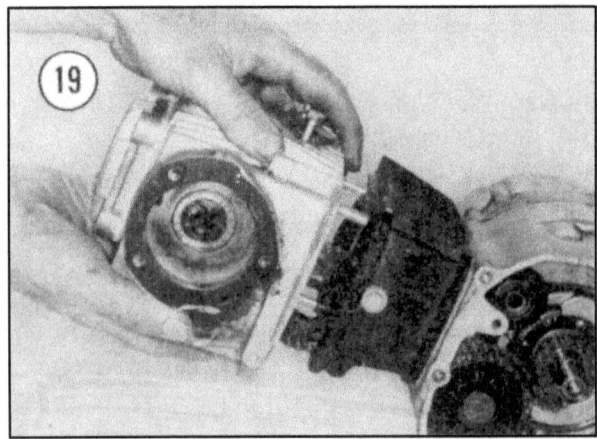

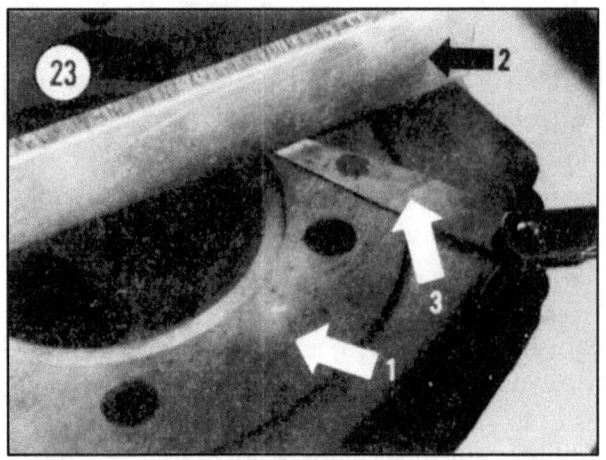

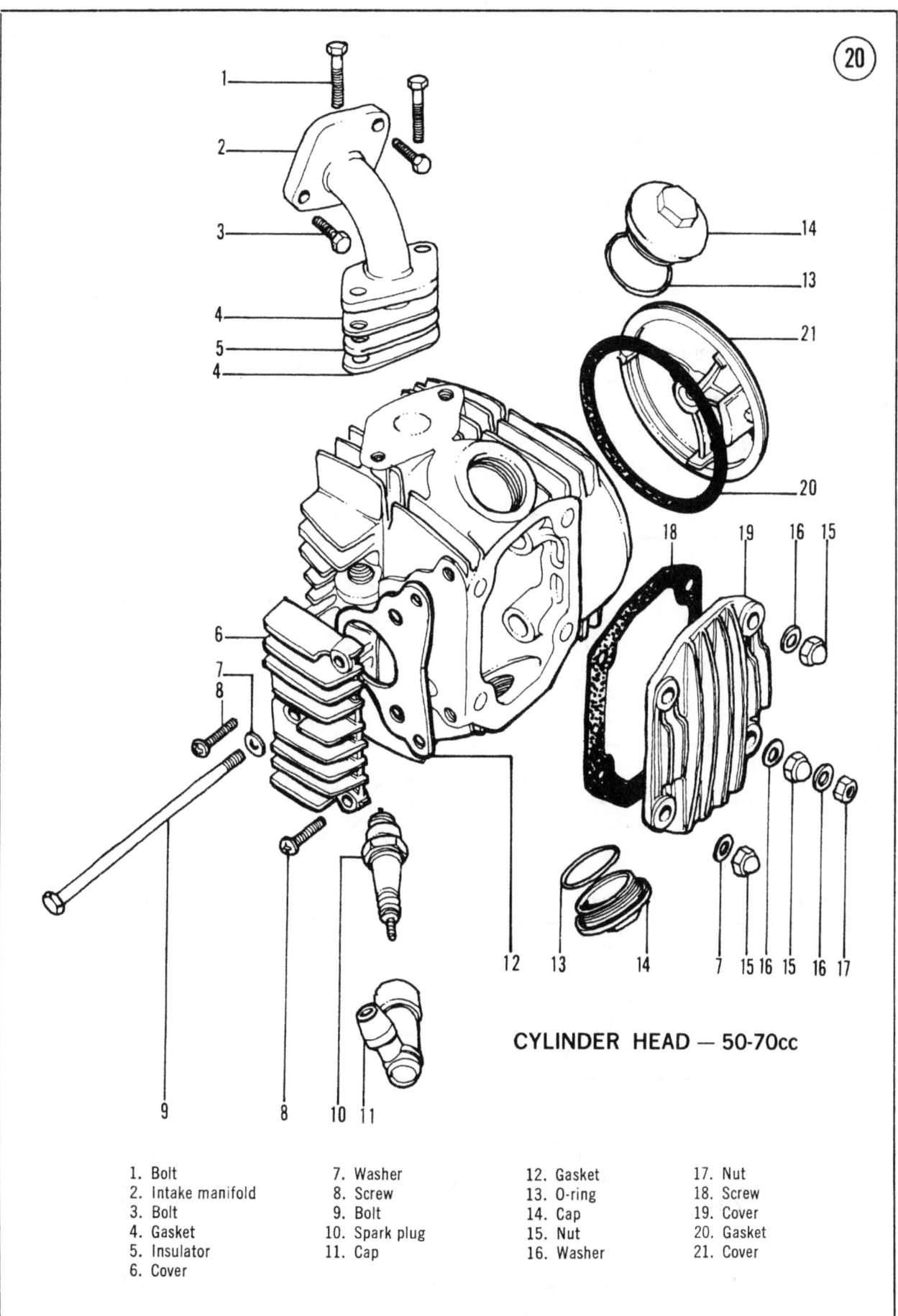

CYLINDER HEAD — 50-70cc

1. Bolt
2. Intake manifold
3. Bolt
4. Gasket
5. Insulator
6. Cover
7. Washer
8. Screw
9. Bolt
10. Spark plug
11. Cap
12. Gasket
13. O-ring
14. Cap
15. Nut
16. Washer
17. Nut
18. Screw
19. Cover
20. Gasket
21. Cover

Replace valves and/or guides if clearance exceeds the service limit given in **Table 1**.

If new valve guides are installed, they must be reamed to provide proper clearance. For all models, valve stem to valve guide clearance should be as specified in **Table 2**.

4. Valve and valve seat refacing is best left to an expert. Seats should be at a 45-degree angle. Seat width should be as specified. Replace valves and resurface the seats if they are leaking or if seat width exceeds the service limit in **Table 3**.

5. Measure free length of each valve spring. Replace springs which are shorter than their service limit. See **Table 4**.

6. Compress each spring to the length specified, then measure its tension. Replace any

Table 1 VALVE-TO-GUIDE CLEARANCE

Model	Service Limit			
	Intake		Exhaust	
	Inch	(Millimeter)	Inch	(Millimeter)
50cc	0.0023	(0.06)	0.0032	(0.08)
65cc	0.0023	(0.06)	0.0032	(0.08)
70cc	0.0032	(0.08)	0.004	(0.10)
90cc	0.0032	(0.08)	0.0032	(0.08)

Table 2 VALVE STEM-TO-GUIDE CLEARANCE (NEW)

Intake		Exhaust	
Inch	(Millimeter)	Inch	(Millimeter)
0.0004-0.0012	(0.01-0.03)	0.0012-0.0020	(0.03-0.05)

Table 3 VALVE SEAT WIDTH

Model	Standard Value		Service Limit	
	Inch	(Millimeter)	Inch	(Millimeters)
50cc	0.040-0.051	(1.0-1.3)	0.08	(2.0)
65cc	0.040-0.051	(1.0-1.3)	0.08	(2.0)
70cc	0.040-0.051	(1.0-1.3)	0.08	(2.0)
90cc	0.028-0.048	(0.7-1.2)	0.08	(2.0)

Table 4 VALVE SPRING FREE LENGTH

Model	Free Length			
	Inner		Outer	
	Standard	Service Limit	Standard	Service Limit
50cc	0.090 in. (25.1mm)	0.094 in. (23.9mm)	1.110 in. (28.1mm)	1.060 in. (26.9mm)
65cc	0.090 in. (25.1mm)	0.094 in. (23.9mm)	1.080 in. (27.4mm)	1.030 in. (26.2mm)
CL70, SL70	1.004 in. (25.5mm)	0.957 in. (24.3mm)	1.106 in. (28.1mm)	1.059 in. (26.9mm)
C70, C70M, CT70, CT70H, ATC70	0.988 in. (25.1mm)	0.941 in. (23.9mm)	1.106 in. (28.1mm)	1.059 in. (26.9mm)
90cc	1.044 in. (26.5mm)	1.005 in. (25.5mm)	1.253 in. (31.8mm)	1.207 in. (30.6mm)

spring with tension less than its specified service limit given in **Table 5**.

7. Measure camshaft diameter at the right-end bearing (**Figure 24**), height of each cam lobe, left-end bearing, and left end. Replace the camshaft if any measurement is less than its specified service limit. See **Table 6**.

Installation (90cc Models)

Reverse the removal procedure to install the cylinder head. Be sure that the acorn nut is in its proper position. Always install a new cylinder head gasket. Torque cylinder head nuts to 14.5-18.1 foot-pounds (20-25 N•m) in the order shown in **Figure 25**.

Do not attempt to install the camshaft until the cylinder head is fully tightened. When installing the camshaft, be sure that its dowel pin hole points directly away from the crankshaft. Before attaching the camshaft sprocket, be sure that the crankshaft Woodruff key and camshaft dowel pin hole are properly aligned; it may be necessary to turn the camshaft sprocket in relation to the cam chain until its holes align with those on the camshaft.

When installing the point base, it is necessary to use an oil seal guide tool. If this precaution is not taken, the oil seal may leak.

Installation (50cc-70cc Models)

Reverse the removal procedure to install the cylinder head. Be sure that the crankshaft Woodruff key and the camshaft "O" mark both point directly toward the cylinder head cover. It may be necessary to turn the camshaft sprocket in relation to its chain until this condition exists.

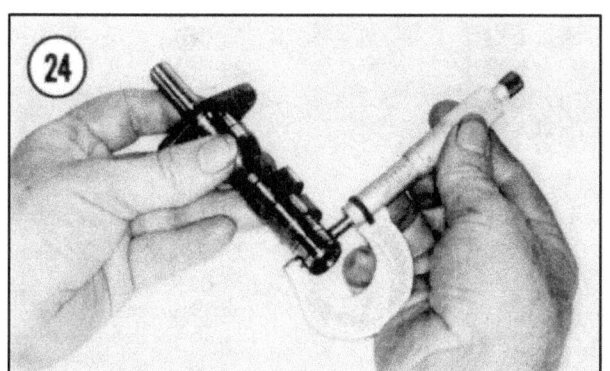

Table 5 VALVE SPRING TENSION

Model	Length Inch	(Millimeters)	Tension Pounds	(Kilograms)
50cc				
Inner	0.690	(17.5)	15.8	(7.2)
Outer	0.980	(24.9)	14.0	(6.4)
65cc				
Inner	0.690	(17.5)	15.8	(7.2)
Outer	0.980	(24.9)	14.0	(6.4)
CL70, SL70				
Inner	0.894	(22.7)	6.84	(3.10)
Outer	0.980	(24.9)	10.14	(4.6)
C70, C70M, CT70, CT70H, ATC70				
Inner	0.894	(22.7)	4.41	(2.0)
Outer	0.980	(24.9)	10.14	(4.6)
90cc	0.942	(23.9)	6.60	(3.0)

Table 6 CAMSHAFT MEASUREMENT

Model	Service Limit Inches	(Millimeters)
50cc		
Left end diameter	1.135	(28.8)
Right end diameter	1.135	(28.8)
Lobe height	0.190	(4.90)
Left end bearing	1.145	(29.06)
Right end bearing	1.145	(29.06)
65cc		
Left end diameter	1.135	(28.8)
Right end diameter	1.135	(28.8)
Lobe height	0.190	(4.90)
Left end bearing	1.145	(29.06)
Right end bearing	1.145	(29.06)
70cc	(Not specified)	
90cc		
Left end diameter	0.991	(25.18)
Right end diameter	0.715	(17.90)
Lobe height	0.968	(24.60)
Left end bearing	1.026	(26.05)
Right end bearing	0.711	(18.05)

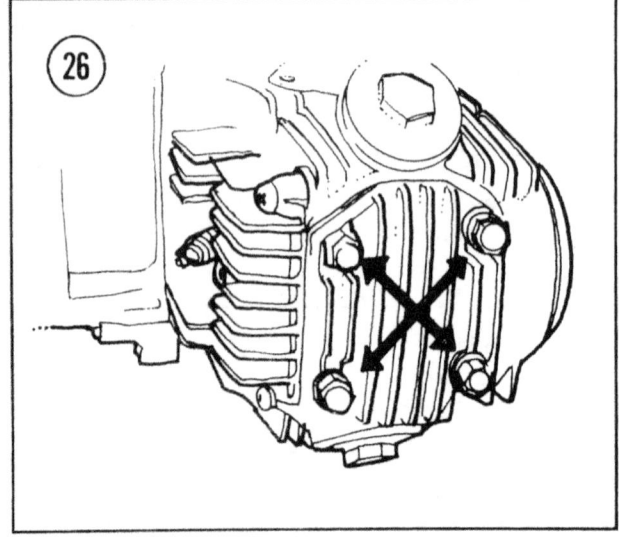

Figure 26 illustrates proper tightening sequence. Torque each nut to 6.5-9.0 foot-pounds (9-12 N•m). Be sure that copper sealing washer is in the proper position under the one plain nut.

CYLINDER

Cylinders are made of cast iron for long wear and good heat dissipation. After long wear or a piston seizure, cylinders may be rebored.

Removal

1. Pull out the cam chain guide roller after removing its shaft bolt (**Figure 27**).

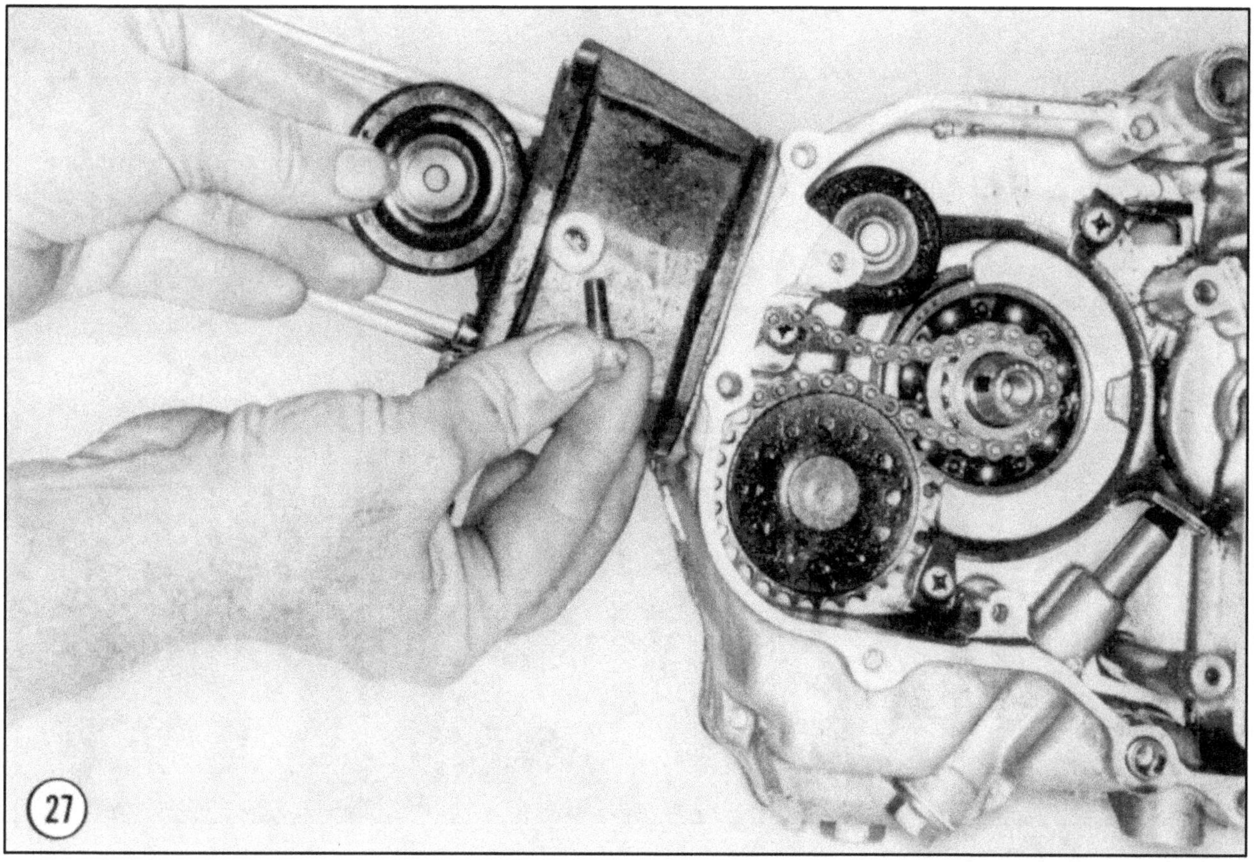

Table 7 CYLINDER DIAMETER

Model	Standard Bore Wear Limit	
	Inches	(Millimeters)
50cc	1.539	(39.1)
65cc	1.736	(44.1)
70cc	1.854	(47.1)
90cc	1.974	(50.1)

2. Carefully remove the cylinder from its studs (**Figure 28**). Carefully note positions of locating dowels and O-rings. It may be necessary to tap the cylinder lightly with a soft mallet to break it loose.

Inspection

1. Measure cylinder diameter at 3 depths parallel and at right angles to the crankshaft. Rebore and hone to the next larger oversize if any measurement exceeds the specified wear limit (**Table 7**), if taper exceeds 0.002 inch (0.05 millimeter), or if the cylinder is out-of-round by 0.002 inch (0.05 millimeter). If reboring, pistons and piston rings are available in oversizes of 0.01, 0.02, 0.03, and 0.04 inch (0.25, 0.50, 0.75, and 1.00 millimeter). Also see *Piston Clearance*.

Installation

Reverse the removal procedure to install the cylinder. It will be necessary to compress each piston ring as it enters the cylinder. A screw-type hose clamp of appropriate size makes a good ring compressor, but it is possible to do the job by hand. Lubricate the cylinder wall liberally with engine oil before installation. Always use new gaskets and seals.

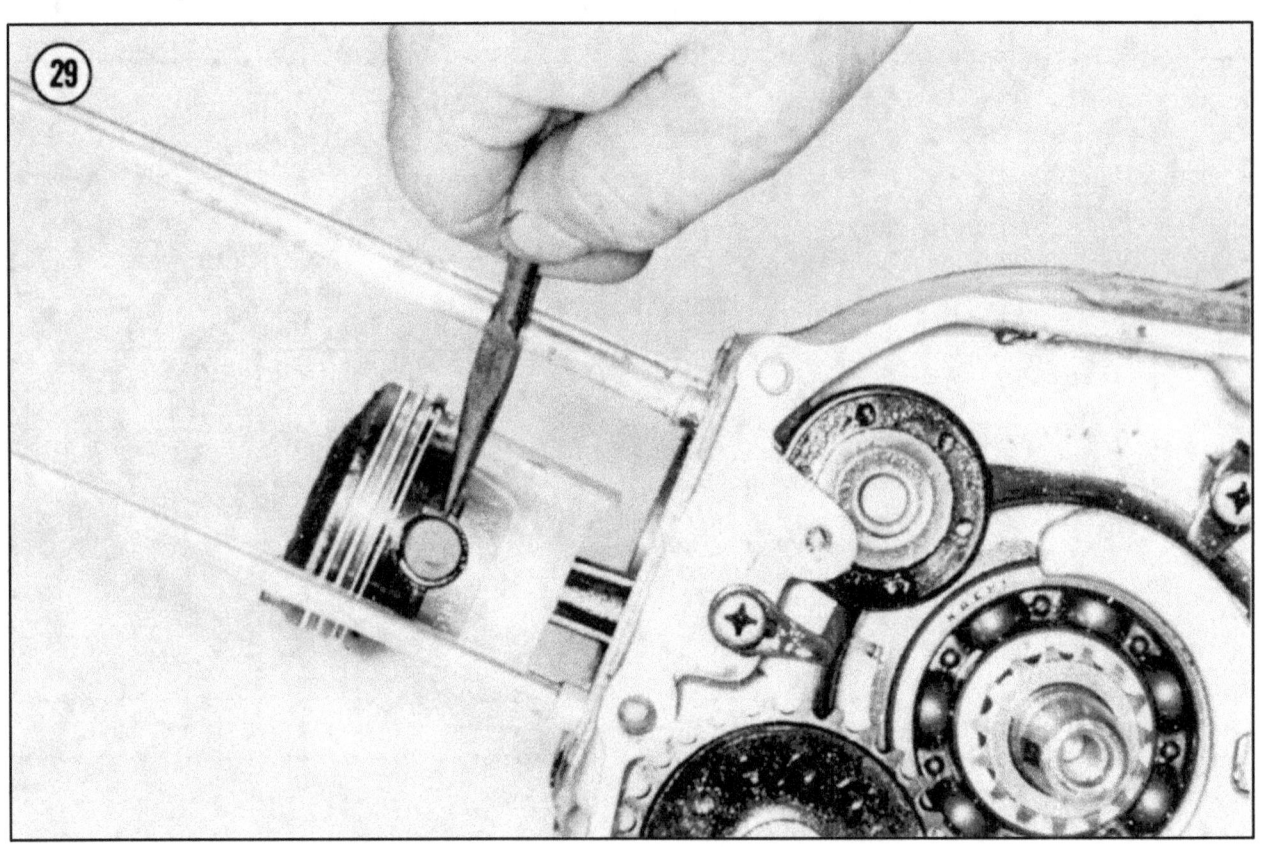

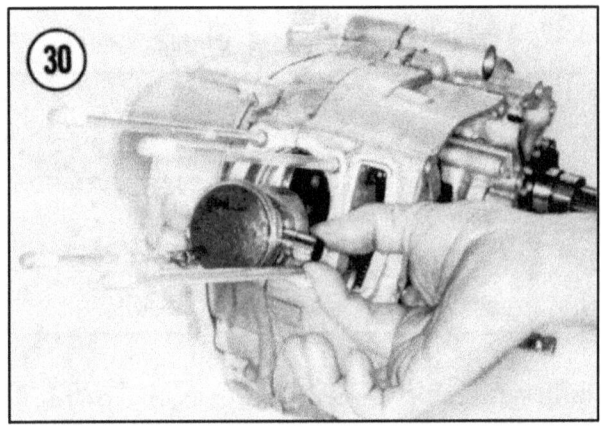

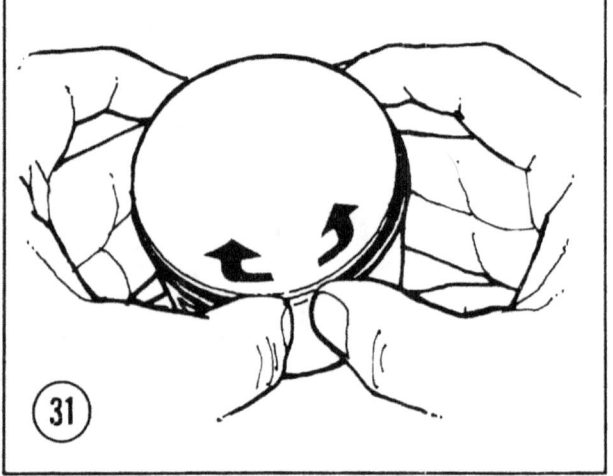

PISTON

Pistons are of aluminum alloy for light weight and good heat dissipation. They are available in oversizes of 0.01, 0.02, 0.03, and 0.04 inch (0.25, 0.50, 0.75, and 1.00 millimeter).

Removal

1. Carefully remove the snap ring from either end of the piston pin hole (**Figure 29**).

> **WARNING**
> *The snap ring is under spring pressure and may fly out. Wear safety goggles to prevent possible eye injury.*

2. Push out the piston pin from the opposite side (**Figure 30**), using any convenient tool. Do not apply any side force to the connecting rod. If the piston pin does not push out easily, heat the piston with a heat lamp or rags soaked in hot water.

3. Remove piston rings by spreading the top ring with a thumb on each end, as shown in **Figure 31**, then remove the ring from the top. Repeat this procedure for each remaining ring. Be careful not to spread the rings any farther than necessary, to avoid breakage.

Table 8 PISTON RING GAP

Model	Standard Ring Gap	
	Inch	(Millimeter)
50cc		
Compression	0.004-0.012	(0.10-0.30)
Oil	0.012	(0.30)
65cc		
Compression	0.006-0.014	(0.15-0.35)
Oil	0.004-0.014	(0.10-0.35)
70cc		
Compression	0.006-0.014	(0.15-0.35)
Oil	0.006-0.016	(0.15-0.40)
90cc		
Compression	0.006-0.014	(0.15-0.35)
Oil	0.006-0.016	(0.15-0.40)

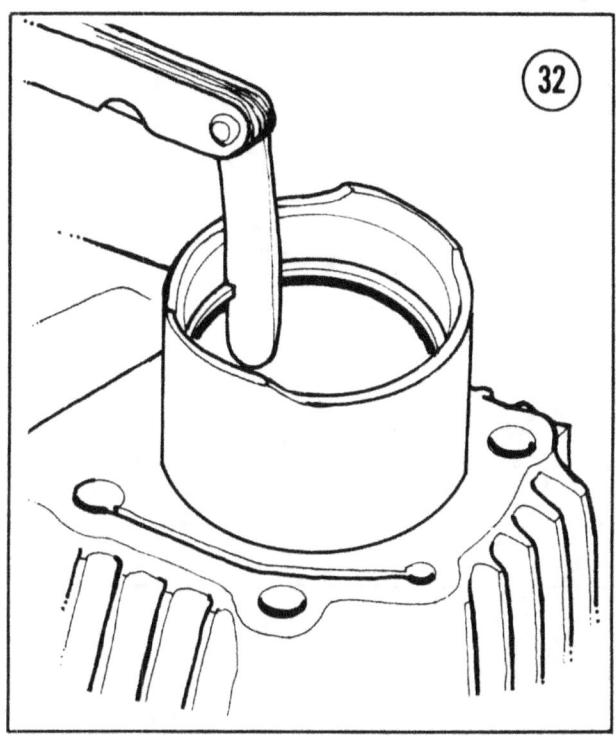

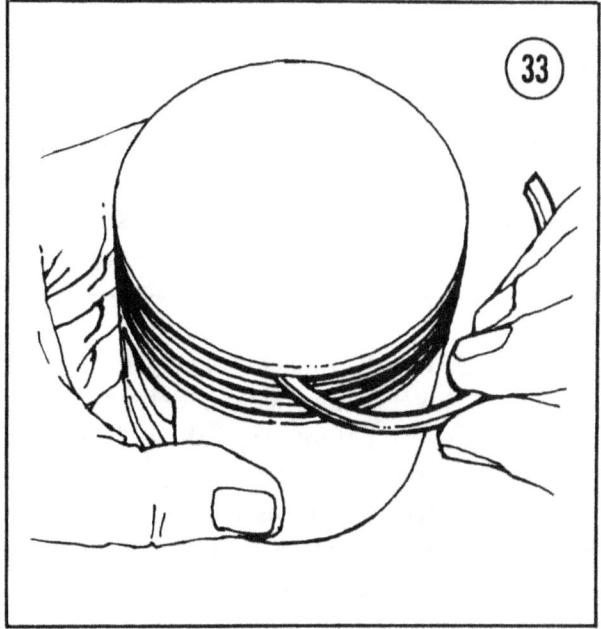

Inspection

Measure each ring for wear as shown in **Figure 32**. Insert the ring approximately 0.2 inch (5 millimeters) into the cylinder, then measure ring gap with a feeler gauge. If any ring gap exceeds 0.02 inch (0.50 millimeter) replace all rings. To ensure that piston rings are square in the cylinder, push them into position with the piston head. When replacing rings, be sure that sufficient gap exists by checking each new ring also. If sufficient gap does not exist, the rings may seize. File the end of each ring, if necessary, to increase the ring gap to the value as specified in **Table 8**.

Clean all carbon from ring grooves, using a ring groove cleaner or a broken piston ring **(Figure 33)**. Any deposits left in ring grooves will result in gas blowby and loss of power. Also clean carbon from the piston head.

Before installing new rings, check their fit by slipping the outer surface of the ring into its

Table 9   PISTON RING CLEARANCE

Model	Wear Limit Inch	(Millimeter)
50cc		
Compression	0.0047	(0.12)
Oil	0.0047	(0.12)
65cc		
Compression	0.0047	(0.12)
Oil	0.0047	(0.12)
70cc		
Compression	0.0047	(0.12)
Oil	0.0047	(0.12)
90cc		
Compression	0.004	(0.10)
Oil	0.004	(0.10)

Table 10   PISTON CLEARANCE

Model	Service Limit Inches	(Millimeters)
50cc	1.531	(38.88)
65cc	1.671	(42.45)
70cc	1.846	(46.90)
90cc	1.964	(49.90)

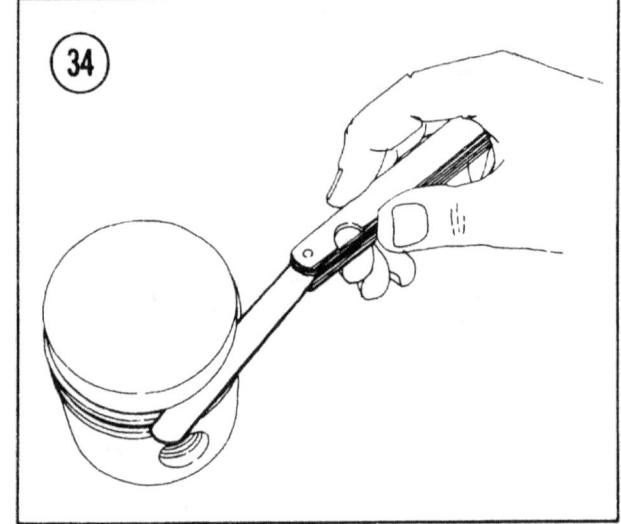

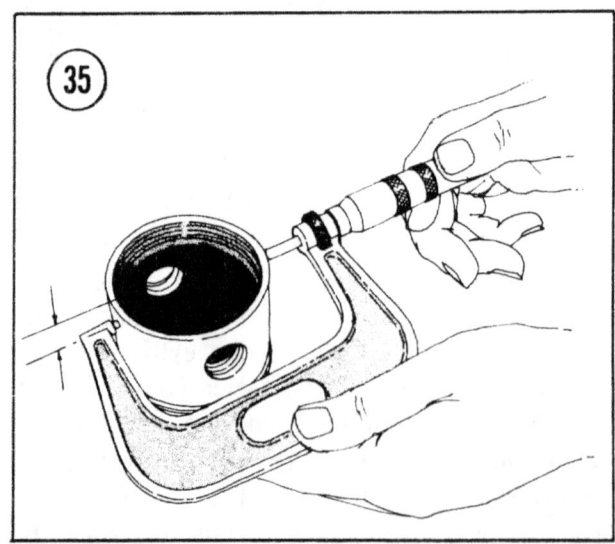

groove, then roll the ring completely around the piston. If any binding occurs, determine and correct the cause before proceeding. After ring installation, measure piston ring groove clearance using a feeler gauge as shown in **Figure 34**. Replace the piston and/or rings if clearance exceeds wear limits **(Table 9)**.

Note that, when installing piston rings, any markings on the ring must be toward the piston crown.

Piston Clearance

Piston clearance is the difference between maximum piston diameter and minimum cylinder diameter, and is dependent on both cylinder wear and piston wear. Measure piston diameter at right angles to the piston pin (**Figure 35**), then subtract this measurement from the minimum cylinder diameter determined earlier. Replace any piston worn beyond its specified service limit. If piston clearance exceeds 0.004

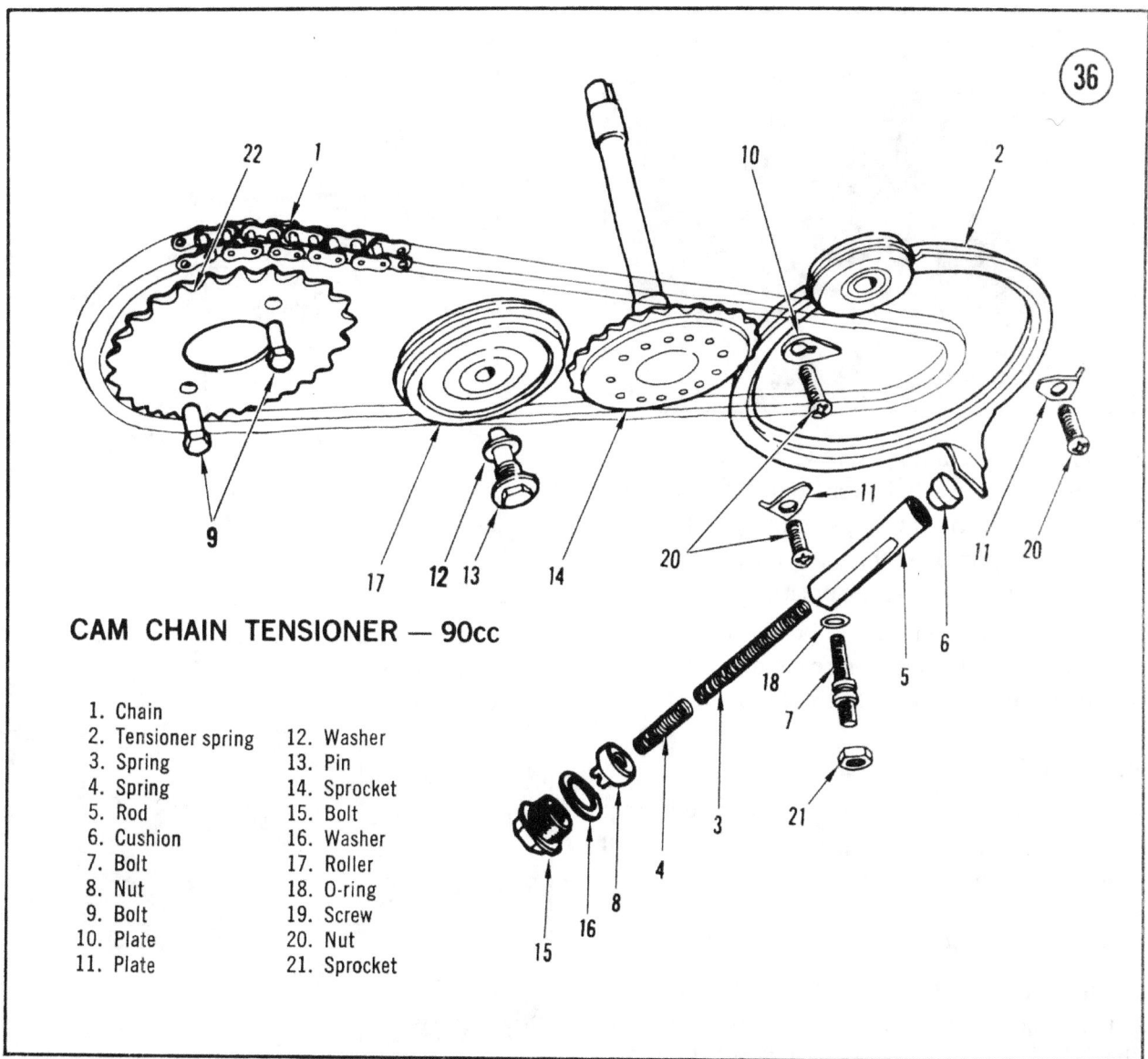

CAM CHAIN TENSIONER — 90cc

1. Chain
2. Tensioner spring
3. Spring
4. Spring
5. Rod
6. Cushion
7. Bolt
8. Nut
9. Bolt
10. Plate
11. Plate
12. Washer
13. Pin
14. Sprocket
15. Bolt
16. Washer
17. Roller
18. O-ring
19. Screw
20. Nut
21. Sprocket

inch (0.10 millimeter) it may be necessary to bore and hone the cylinder to the next oversize. See **Table 10**.

Piston Pin

The piston pin should be a light press fit in the piston and upper end of the connecting rod at room temperature. Replace it and/or the piston if any looseness exists. In extreme cases, it may be necessary to replace the crankshaft assembly.

Piston Installation

Reverse the removal procedure to install the piston. Be sure that piston ring gaps are staggered at approximately 120 degree intervals around the piston. Because the piston pin hole is offset, it is important that the piston be installed with the proper side up. On 90cc models, letters IN should go toward the top of the engine. On smaller models, the arrow on the piston head must point downward. Always use new piston pin retaining clips on installation.

CAM CHAIN TENSIONER

Valve timing (and ignition timing on 90cc models) is dependent on maintaining proper camshaft drive chain tension. The cam chain tensioner performs this task.

Removal (90cc Models)

Figure 36 is a diagram of this mechanism.

1. Remove the cam chain guide sprocket (**Figure 37**).

2. Remove 3 retaining screws and clips, then pull off the cam chain tensioner (**Figure 38**). Note that one of the clips is longer than the other two; upon assembly, the longer clip goes in approximately 9 o'clock position.

3. Remove the tensioner bolt, spring, and pushrod (**Figure 39**). Upon reassembly, the rubber tip on the rod goes into the engine first.

Removal (50cc-70cc Models)

Figure 40 illustrates the cam chain tensioner on these models. Disassembly is similar to that described for 90cc models.

Inspection (All Models)

Check all parts for wear, in particular the guide rollers. On models with check valves, check for oil leaks. Clean check valves by blowing out with compressed air.

Installation (All Models)

Reverse the removal procedure to install the cam chain tensioner.

RIGHT CRANKCASE COVER

The right crankcase cover houses the clutch, oil pump, oil filter screen, primary reduction gears, and shifter linkage. Cover removal is necessary to service any of these components.

CLUTCH

Honda motorcycles are either equipped with manual or automatic clutches. Automatic clutches are engaged by centrifugal force and disengaged by gearshift pedal motion.

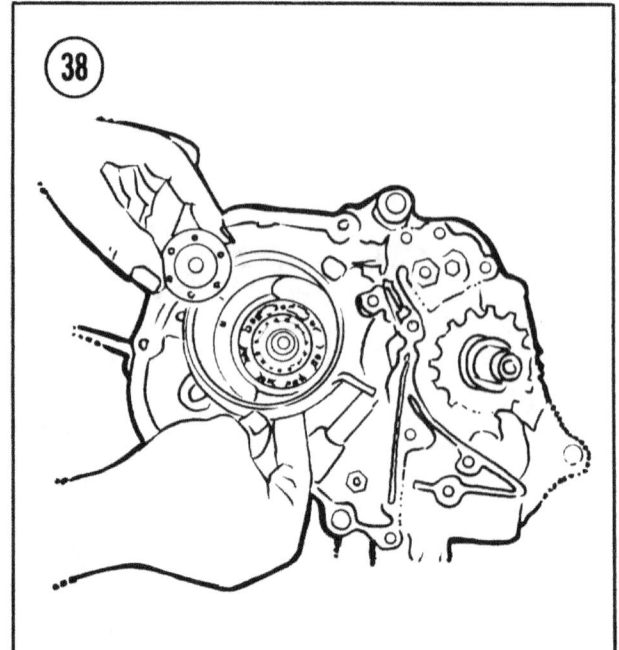

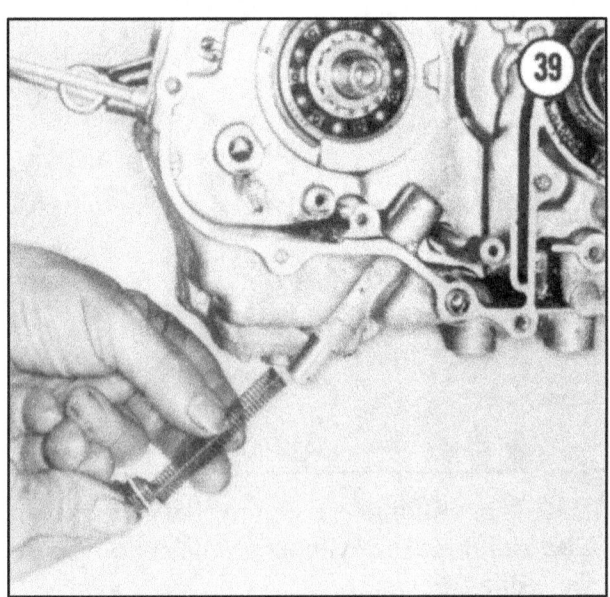

Automatic Clutch Removal

Figures 41 and 42 illustrate typical clutches and release mechanisms of this type. Refer to those illustrations during disassembly. Take careful note of how each component is installed.

1. Remove the right crankcase cover. Be prepared to catch oil as it drains out.
2. Remove the clutch lever.
3. Remove the clutch cam plate (**Figure 43**).
4. Remove the bearing (**Figure 44**).
5. Remove 2 retaining screws, then the clutch outer cover (**Figure 45**).

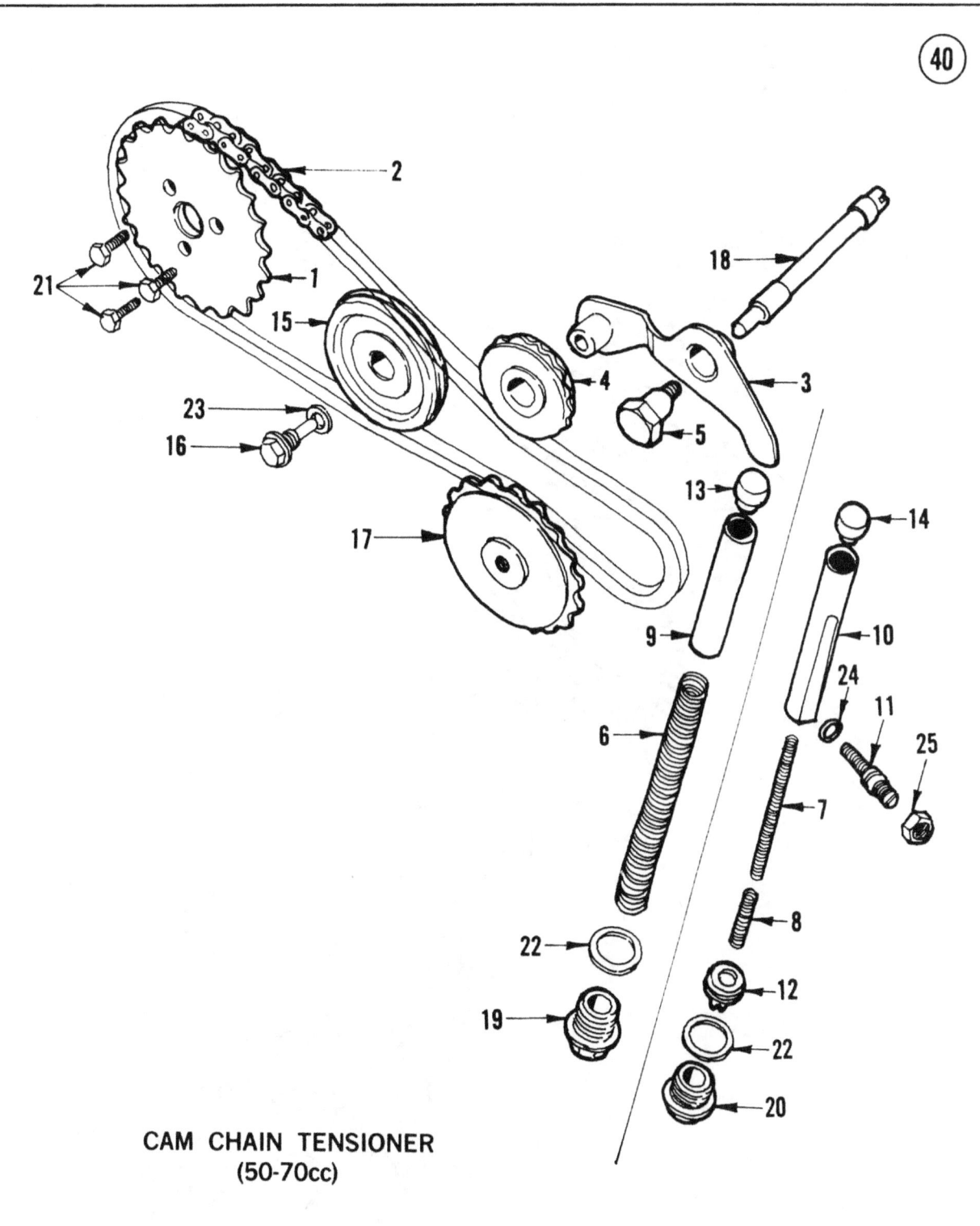

CAM CHAIN TENSIONER
(50-70cc)

1. Sprocket
2. Chain
3. Arm
4. Roller
5. Pivot
6. Spring
7. Spring
8. Spring
9. Rod
10. Rod
11. Bolt
12. Nut
13. Pushrod cushion
14. Pushrod cushion
15. Roller
16. Pin
17. Sprocket
18. Shaft
19. Bolt
20. Bolt
21. Bolt
22. Washer
23. Washer
24. Washer
25. Nut

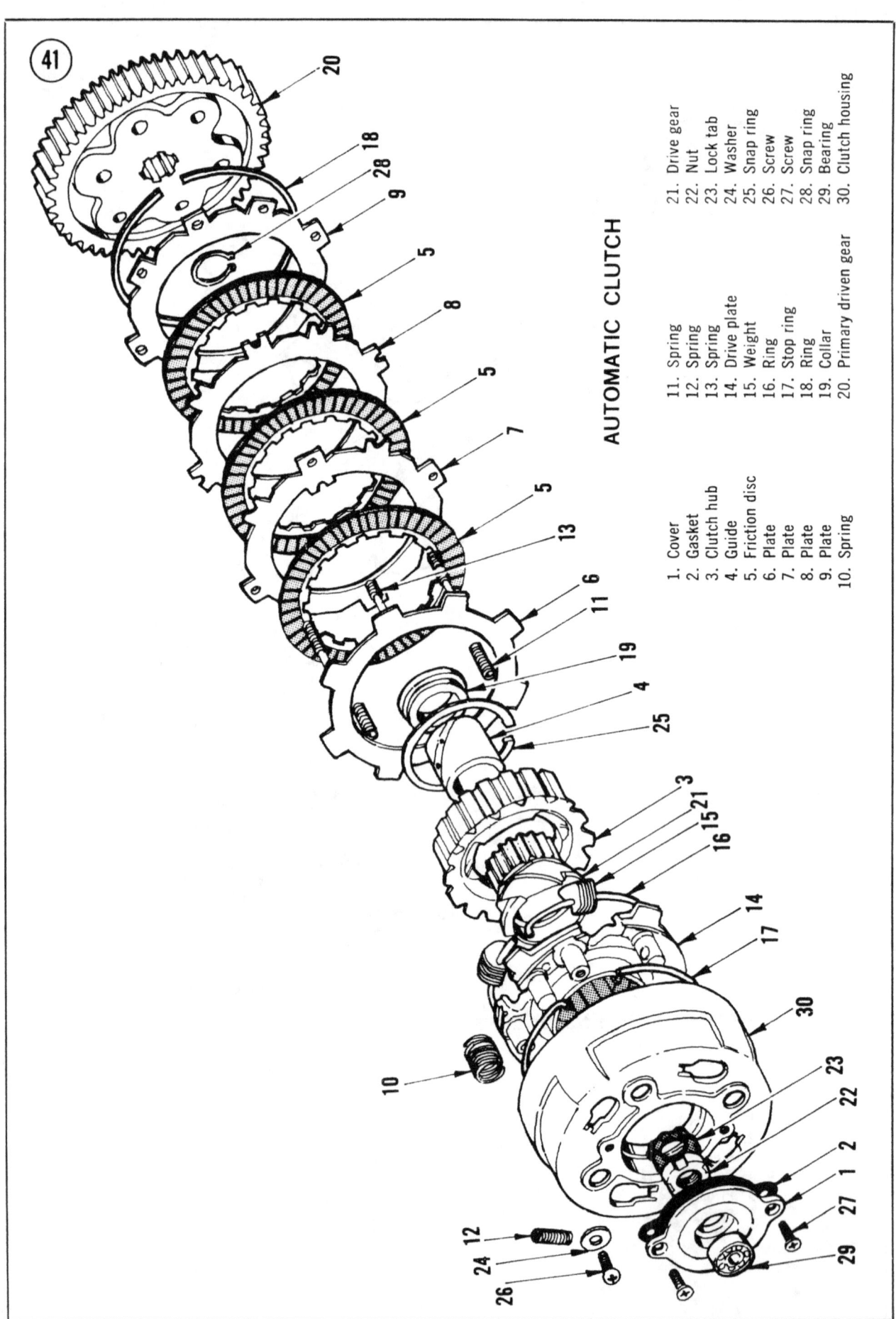

AUTOMATIC CLUTCH

1. Cover
2. Gasket
3. Clutch hub
4. Guide
5. Friction disc
6. Plate
7. Plate
8. Plate
9. Plate
10. Spring
11. Spring
12. Spring
13. Spring
14. Drive plate
15. Weight
16. Ring
17. Stop ring
18. Ring
19. Collar
20. Primary driven gear
21. Drive gear
22. Nut
23. Lock tab
24. Washer
25. Snap ring
26. Screw
27. Screw
28. Snap ring
29. Bearing
30. Clutch housing

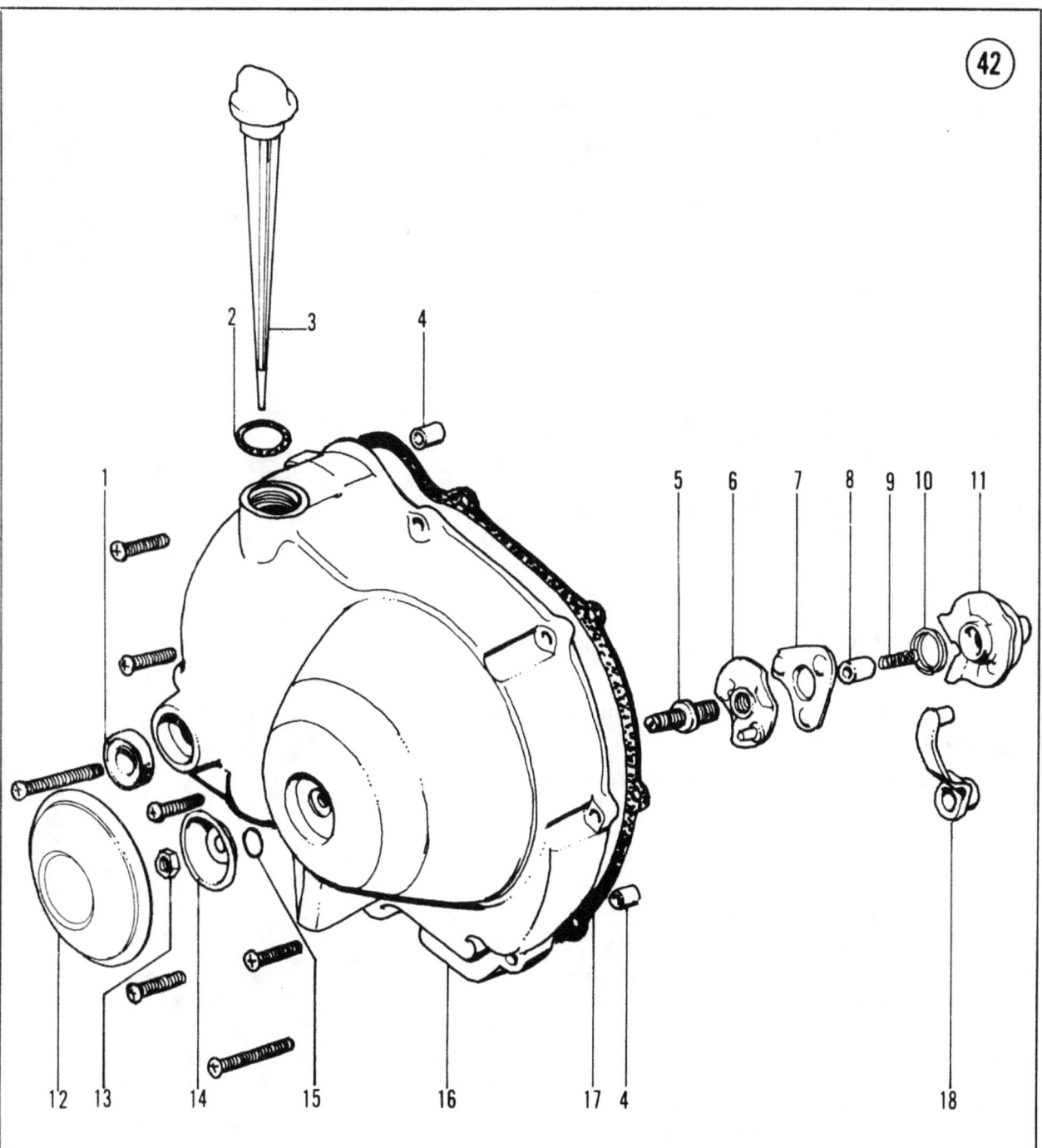

RIGHT CRANKCASE — AUTOMATIC CLUTCH LIFTER

1. Oil seal
2. O-ring
3. Dipstick
4. Dowel
5. Adjusting screw
6. Cam plate
7. Ball retainer
8. Oil guide
9. Spring
10. Spring
11. Cam plate assembly
12. Cover
13. Nut
14. Washer
15. O-ring
16. Crankcase cover
17. Gasket
18. Clutch release lever

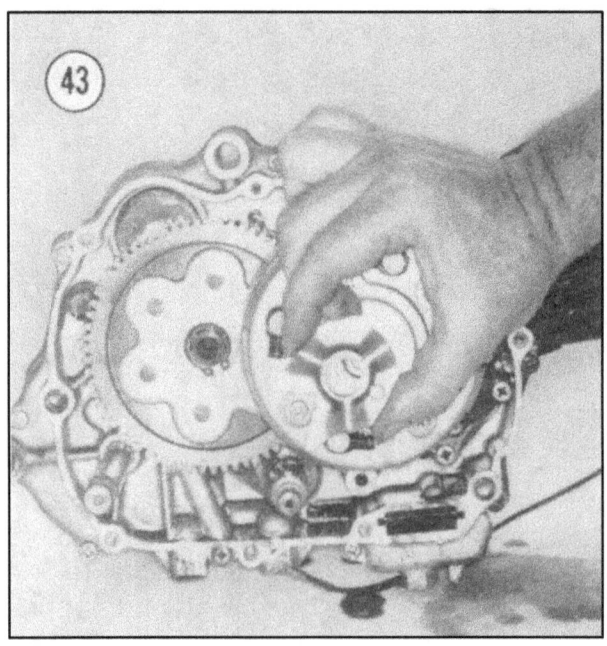

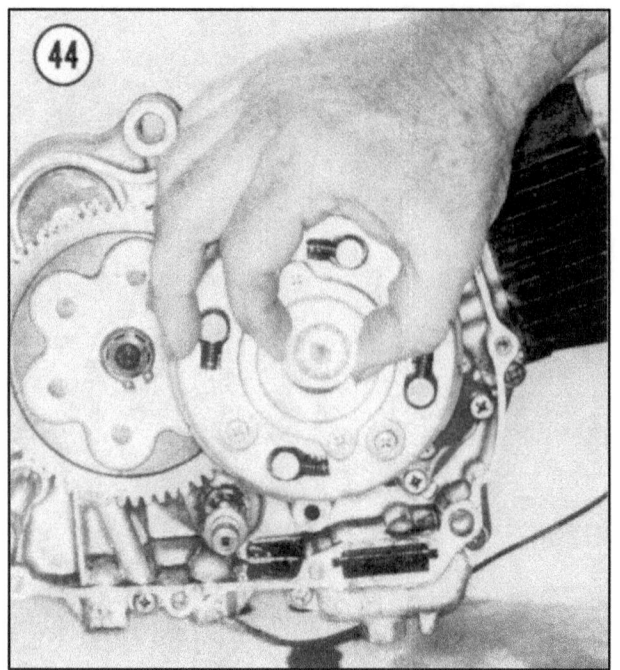

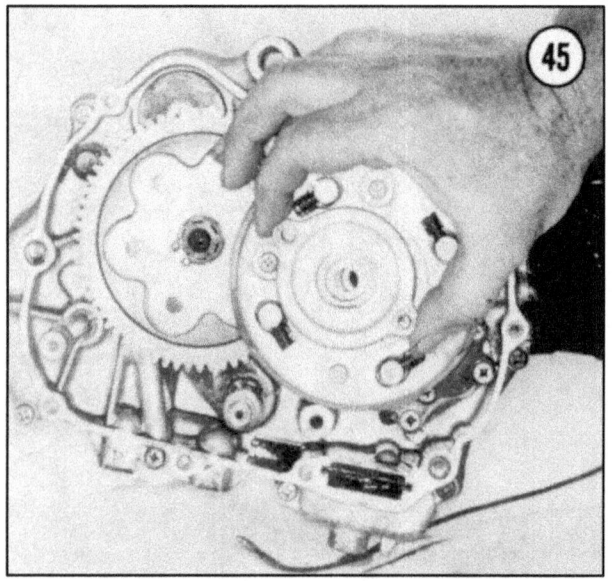

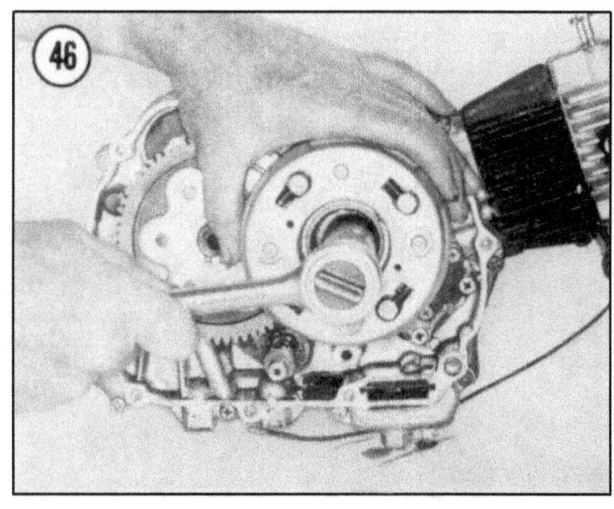

6. Flatten the lockwasher tab, then remove the clutch retaining nut (**Figure 46**). This nut requires a special wrench; it may be possible to have a Honda dealer do this job.

7. Pull the clutch assembly from the crankshaft (**Figure 47**).

8. Remove the center guide bushing from the crankshaft (**Figure 48**).

Manual Clutch Removal

Figure 49 (page 46) is an exploded view of a typical manual clutch, and **Figure 50** (page 47) shows its release mechanism. Removal procedures are similar to those for automatic clutches.

Clutch Inspection

Refer to **Figure 51**. A clutch disassembly tool is available to compress the assembly, making disassembly easier. A suitable substitute may be fabricated locally. Compress the clutch assembly, avoiding the drive plate and damper spring, then remove the snap ring. Release the tool, then pull out each clutch plate, friction disc, and spring.

Clean all parts, except for friction discs, in solvent, then blow dry with compressed air.

If any of the plates or discs are worn, burned, or scored, replace the entire set. Measure thickness of plates and discs, using a micrometer or vernier calipers. Replace the set if any is worn beyond its wear limit. See **Table 11**.

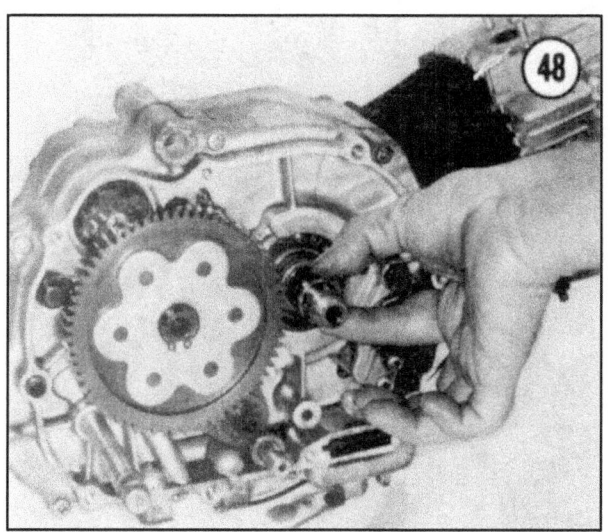

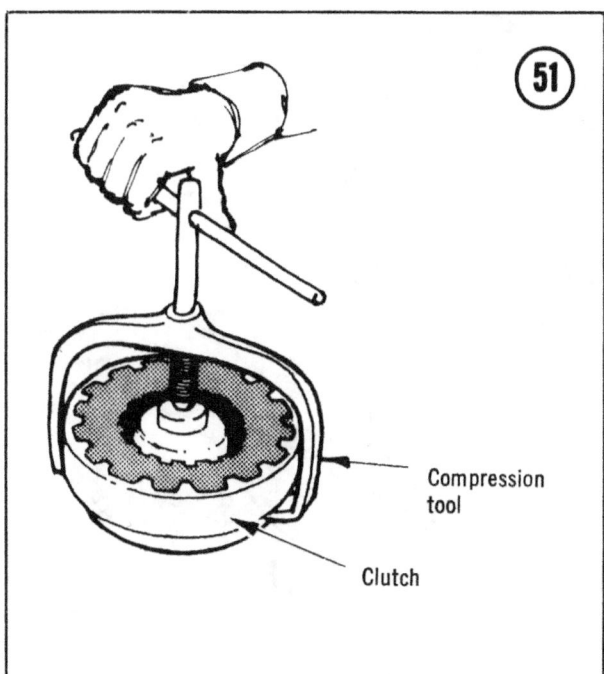

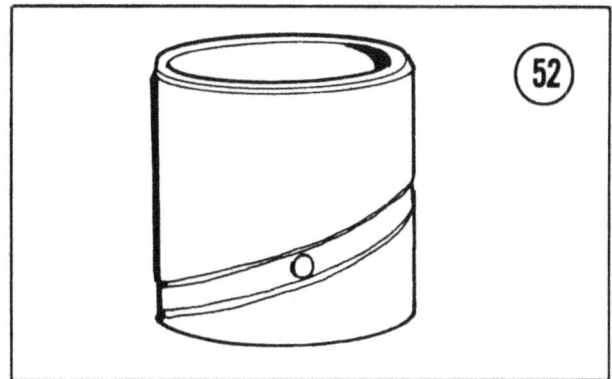

**Table 11
CLUTCH PLATE AND DISC WEAR LIMITS**

Model	Wear Limit Inch	(Millimeters)
50cc		
Disc	0.122	(3.1)
Plate	0.059	(1.5)
65cc		
Disc	0.122	(3.1)
Plate	0.059	(1.5)
70cc		
Disc	0.122	(3.1)
Plate	0.059	(1.5)
90cc		
Disc	0.094	(2.4)
Plate	0.073	(1.8)

Table 12   CLUTCH SPRING LENGTH

Model	Service Limit Inches	(Millimeters)
50cc	0.72	(18.2)
65cc	0.72	(18.2)
CL70, SL70	0.75	(19.0)
C70, C70M, CT70, ATC70	0.83	(20.4)
90cc	1.02	(26.0)

Measure each plate for warpage by placing it on a flat surface, then measuring warp with a feeler gauge. Replace set if warp exceeds 0.02 inch (0.5 millimeter).

Measure length of each clutch spring, using calipers. Replace all springs if any is shorter than its service limit. See **Table 12**.

Measure clearance between the clutch center guide bushing (**Figure 52**) and crankshaft.

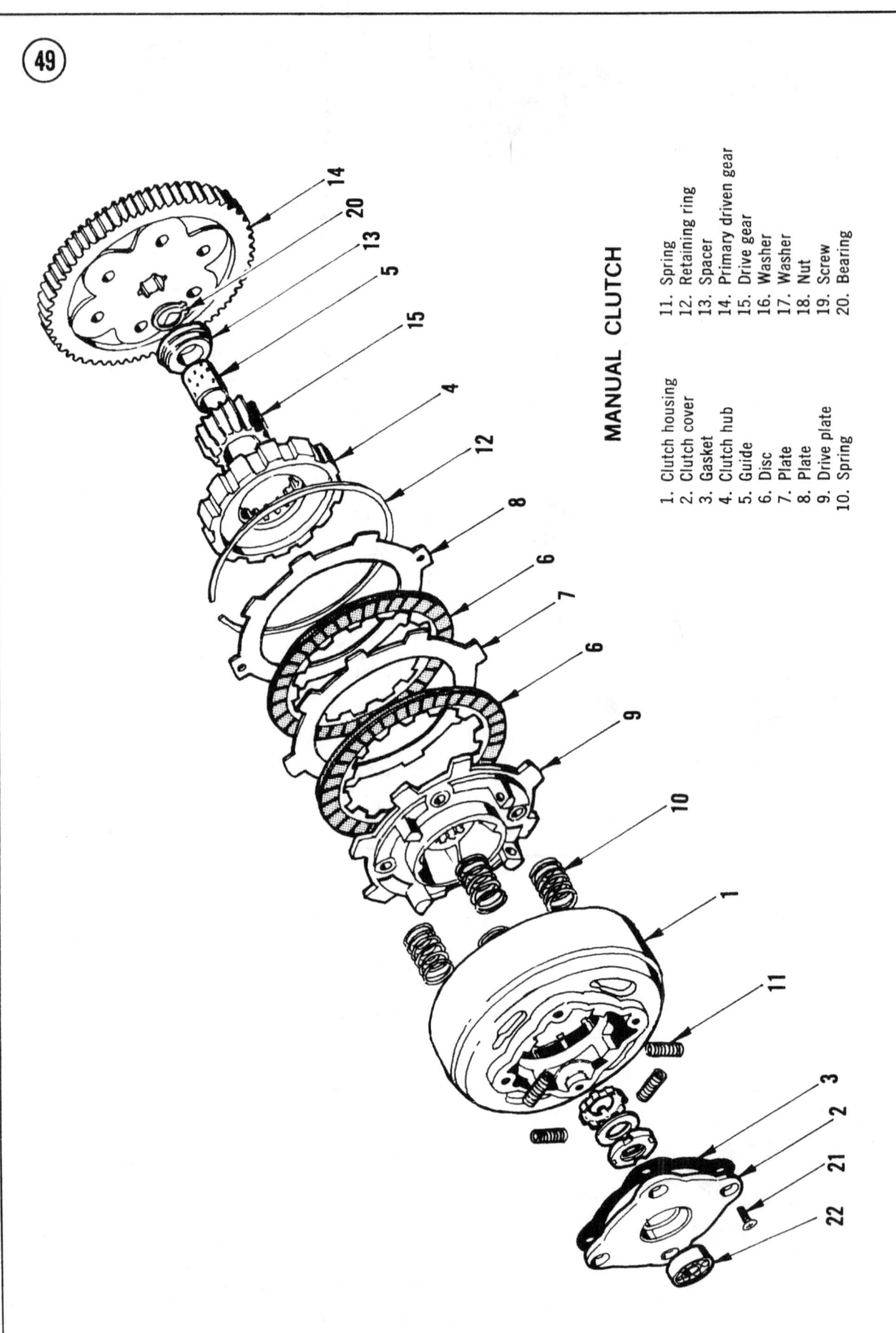

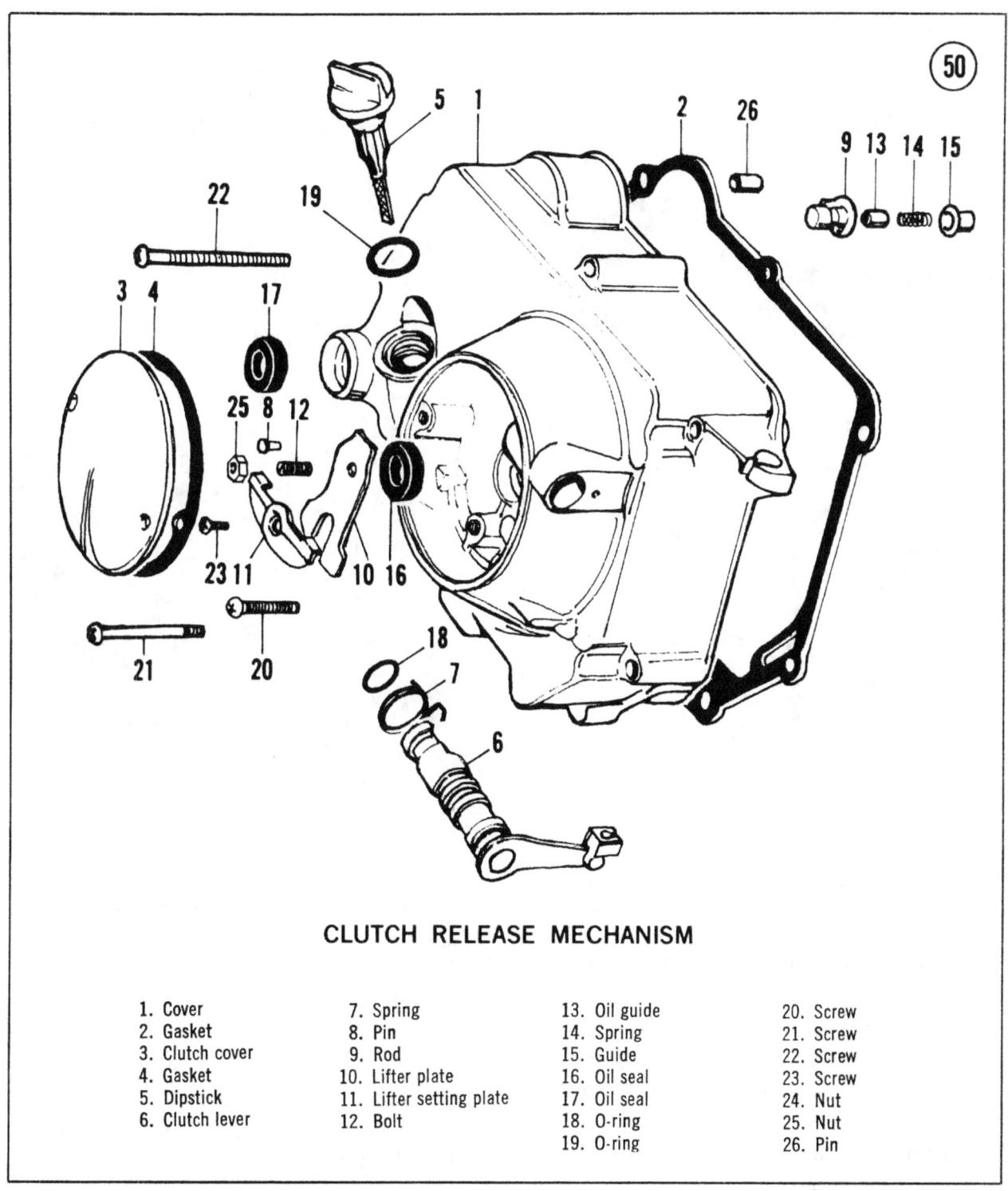

CLUTCH RELEASE MECHANISM

1. Cover
2. Gasket
3. Clutch cover
4. Gasket
5. Dipstick
6. Clutch lever
7. Spring
8. Pin
9. Rod
10. Lifter plate
11. Lifter setting plate
12. Bolt
13. Oil guide
14. Spring
15. Guide
16. Oil seal
17. Oil seal
18. O-ring
19. O-ring
20. Screw
21. Screw
22. Screw
23. Screw
24. Nut
25. Nut
26. Pin

Replace the bushing if clearance exceeds 0.060 inch (0.15 millimeter).

Check the primary drive gear for burrs or excessive wear. It may be possible to smooth minor burrs with an oilstone.

Clutch Installation

Reverse the disassembly procedure to install the clutch. Torque the retaining nut to 54-64 foot-pounds (43-87 N•m). If a tab on the lockwasher does not line up, tighten the nut slightly, but do not back it off.

Manual Clutch Adjustment (50cc-70cc Models)

Adjust clutch whenever it begins to drag or slip, or at each 3,000 miles (4,500 kilometers).

1. Loosen the locknut at the clutch hand lever,

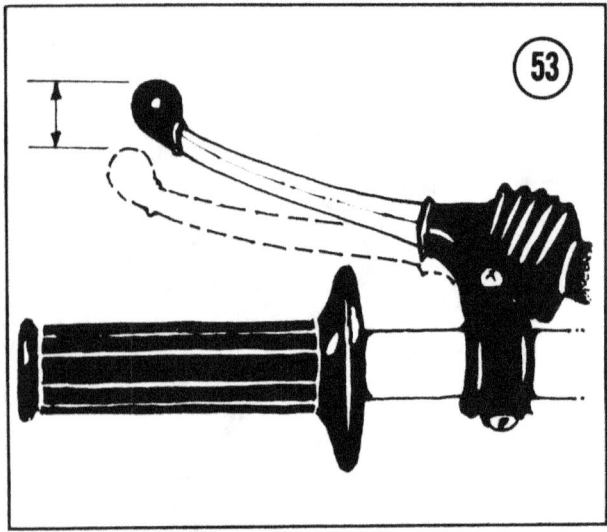

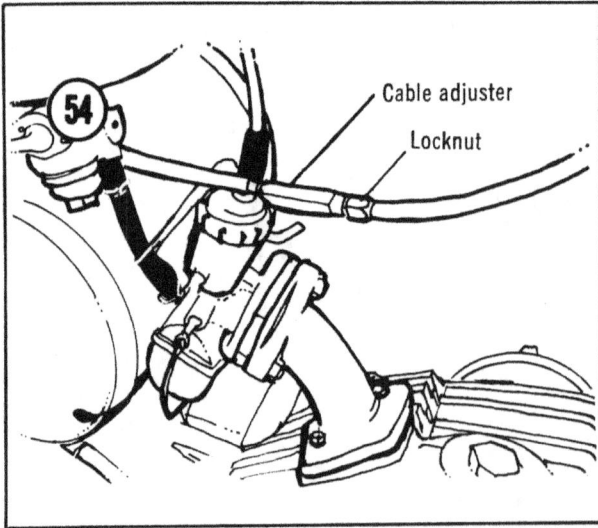

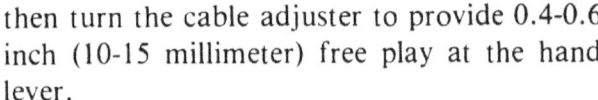

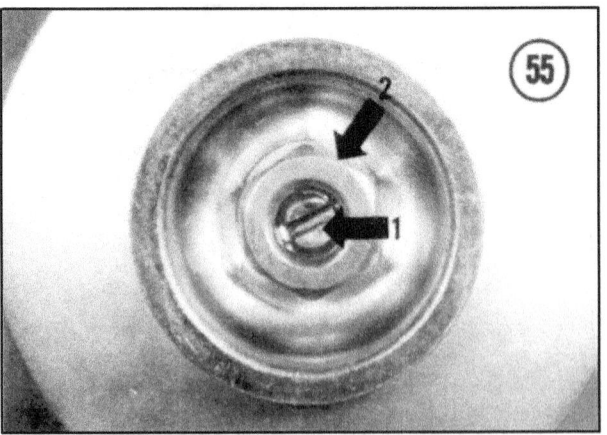

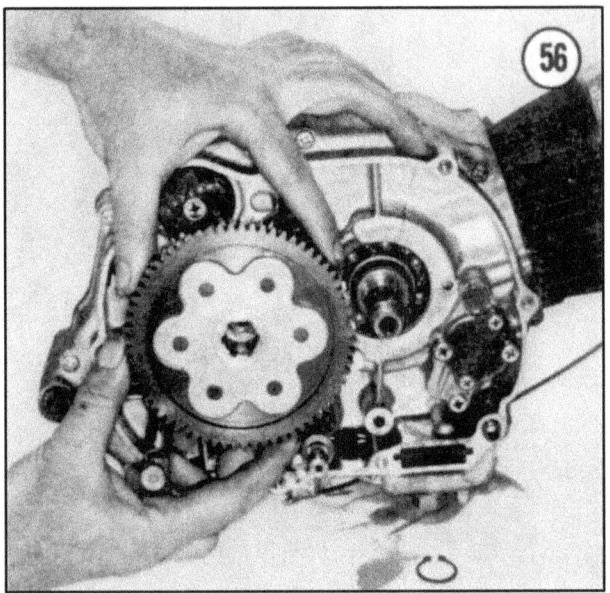

then turn the cable adjuster to provide 0.4-0.6 inch (10-15 millimeter) free play at the hand lever.

2. Tighten the locknut.

3. Check clutch operation with the engine running. If clutch operation is not satisfactory, go on to Step 4.

4. Remove the clutch cover.

5. Loosen the adjusting screw locknut.

6. Turn the adjusting screw clockwise until it seats, then back it out 1/8-1/4 turn.

7. Hold the adjusting screw in this position, then tighten the locknut.

8. Repeat Steps 1 and 2.

Manual Clutch Adjustment (90cc Models)

Adjust clutch whenever it begins to drag or slip, or at each 3,000 miles (4,500 kilometers).

1. Loosen the locknut at the clutch hand lever (**Figure 53**), then turn the cable adjuster to provide 0.4-0.6 inch (10-15 millimeters) free play at the hand lever.

2. Tighten the locknut.

3. Start engine, then check clutch operation.

4. On some models, there is a cable adjuster at the midpoint of the clutch cable, near the carburetor (**Figure 54**).

Automatic Clutch Adjustment

Adjust clutch whenever it begins to drag or slip, or at each 3,000 miles (4,500 kilometers).

1. Refer to **Figure 55**. Loosen locknut (2), then turn adjusting screw (1) counterclockwise until it drags, then turn it back 1/8 turn. Hold the screw in that position, then tighten the locknut.

2. Check the adjustment with the engine running. Make small corrections as required.

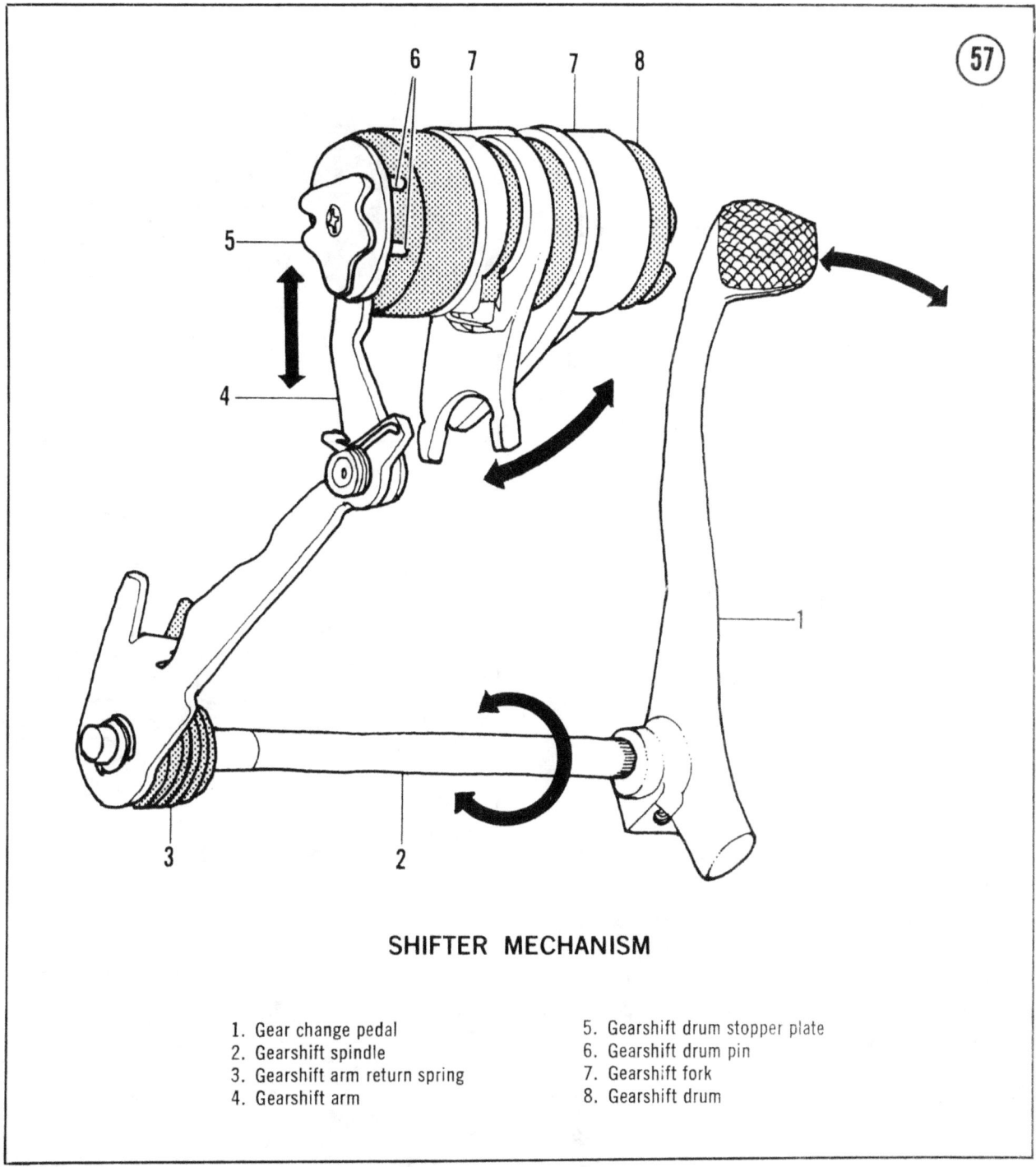

SHIFTER MECHANISM

1. Gear change pedal
2. Gearshift spindle
3. Gearshift arm return spring
4. Gearshift arm
5. Gearshift drum stopper plate
6. Gearshift drum pin
7. Gearshift fork
8. Gearshift drum

PRIMARY DRIVEN GEAR

To remove the primary driven gear, it is only necessary to remove one snap ring, then pull the gear from its shaft (**Figure 56**). Note carefully which side of the gear goes out. Reverse this procedure for installation.

SHIFTER LINKAGE

Figure 57 illustrates a typical shifter mechanism. When the rider presses lever (1), shaft (2) moves arm (4) to the left or right. Teeth on this arm engage pins (6) on shift drum cam (8), turning the cam one step at a time. Grooves in the cam move shift forks (7), which in turn move sliding gears within the transmission. Stopper plate (5) engages a spring-loaded stopper pawl (not shown) which holds the shift drum in position at each step.

Shifter linkage can be removed for service without engine removal.

1. Remove the stopper pawl (**Figure 58**).

2. Disconnect the shifter arm from the shift drum, then pull it and its attached linkage and shaft from the engine (**Figure 59**).

Check springs for cracks or fatigue. Be sure that the shaft is not bent, and that linkage is not worn excessively. Also check each pin on the shift drum.

Reverse the removal procedure to install the shifter.

OIL PUMP

Figure 60 illustrates oil flow through a typical engine. Oil pressure is supplied by an oil pump, which is driven by a sprocket from the cam chain.

Should oil pump service be required, refer to **Figure 61**. Remove screws (1) and one bolt (2).

SPLITTING CRANKCASE HALVES

It is necessary to split the crankcase to service the transmission, kickstarter, and crankshaft.

90cc Models

1. Remove any remaining spacers, etc.
2. Remove all crankcase screws.
3. Remove the shift drum retaining bolt (**Figure 62**).
4. Hold the engine by the right crankcase half, with that half upward. Alternately tap the transmission input shaft and right end of the crankshaft with a soft mallet to split both crankcase halves.

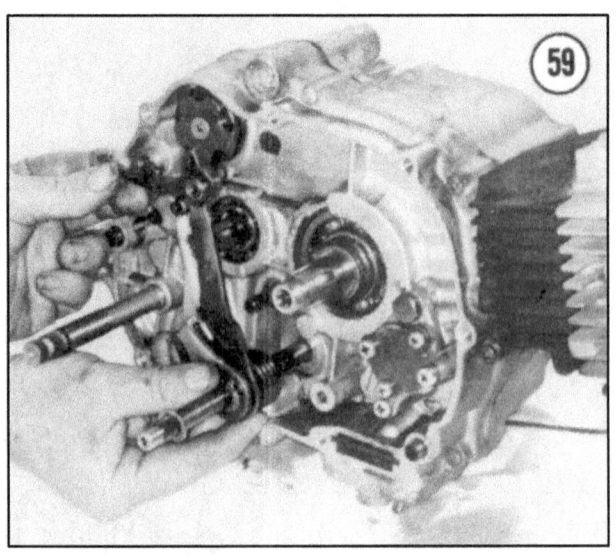

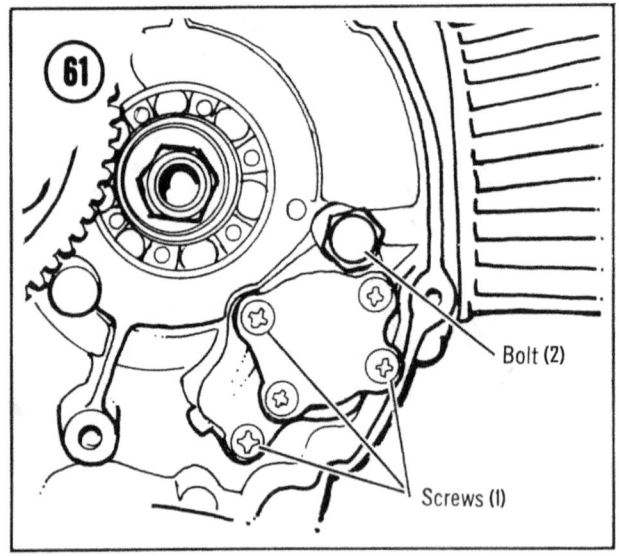

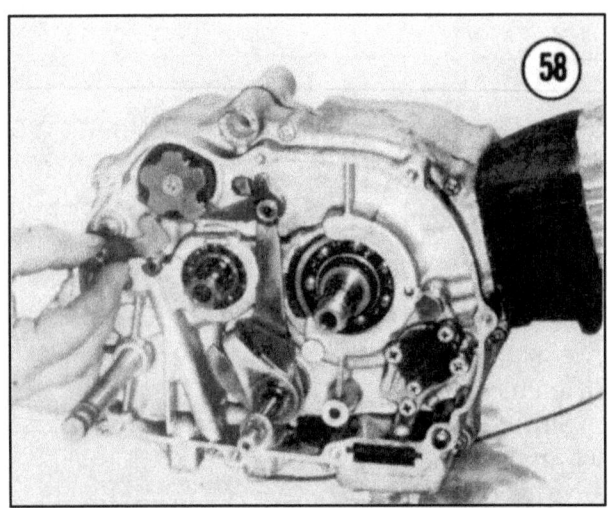

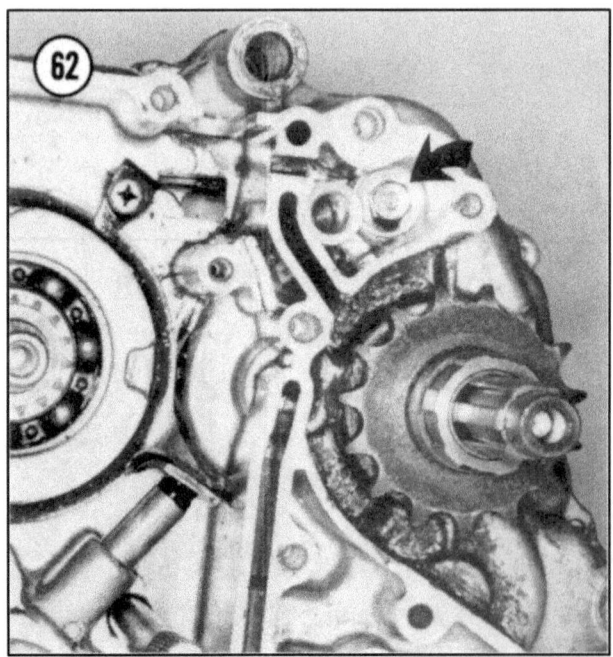

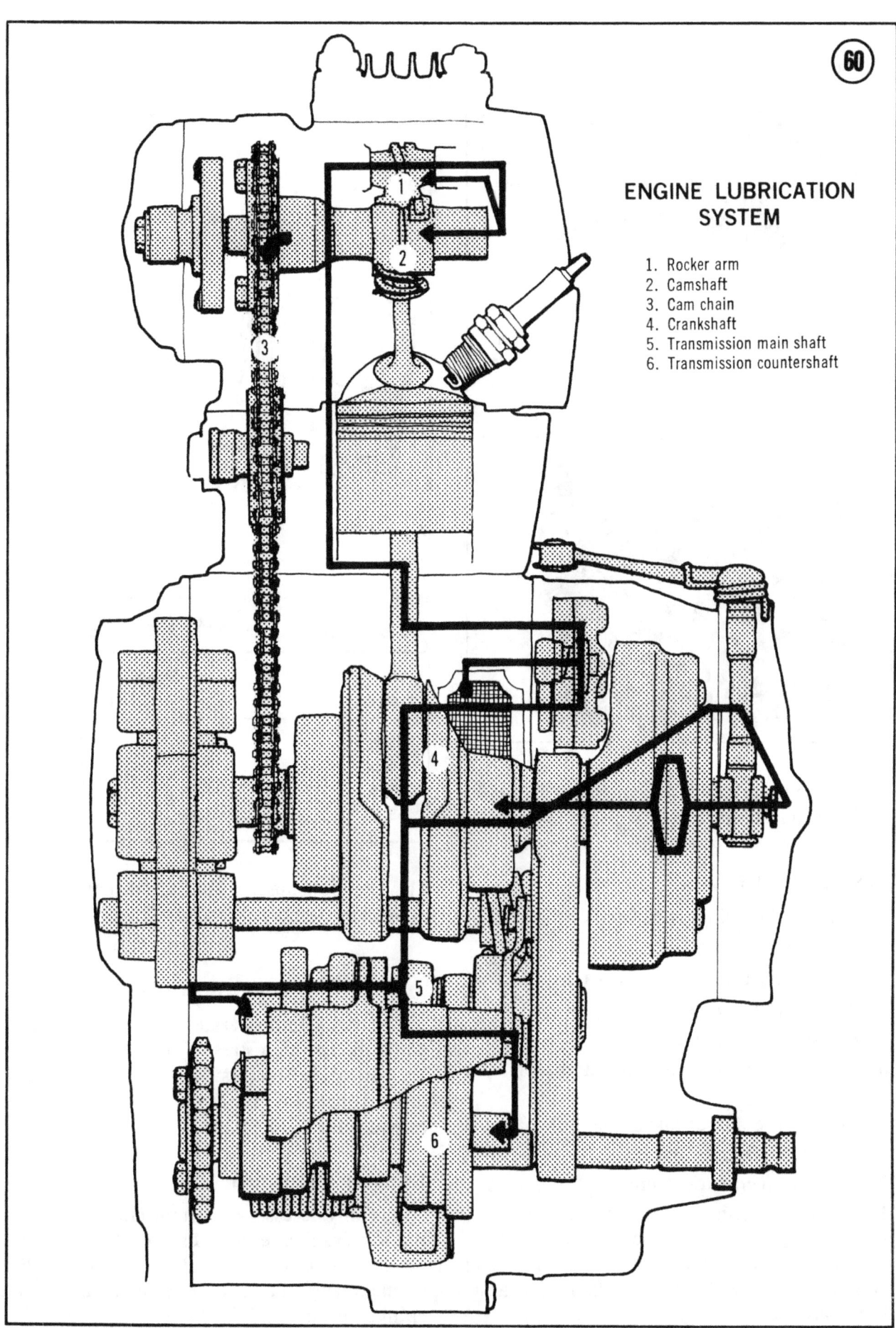

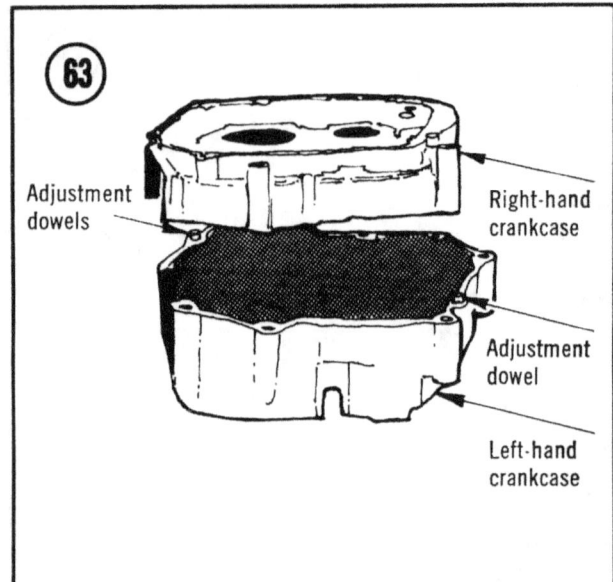

Table 13   CRANKSHAFT RUNOUT

Model	Service Limit Inch	(Millimeter)
50cc	0.0020	(0.05)
65cc	0.0020	(0.05)
70cc	0.0020	(0.05)
90cc	0.0040	(0.10)

5. The crankshaft and transmission will remain in the left half (**Figure 63**).

50cc-70cc Models

1. Remove the cylinder head and cylinder.
2. Remove the clutch.
3. Remove the primary driven gear.
4. Remove the kickstarter spring.
5. Remove the oil pump.
6. Remove the magneto (or alternator) and cam chain.
7. Remove the shift drum stopper bolt.
8. Remove the engine sprocket.
9. Remove all crankcase screws.
10. Hold the engine by the right crankcase half with the right crankcase half turned upward. Tap the transmission input shaft and right crankshaft end with a soft mallet to separate both halves.
11. The transmission and crankshaft will remain in the left crankcase half.

CRANKSHAFT

The crankshaft operates at high speed, under conditions of high stress. Dimension tolerances are critical. It is necessary to correct crankshaft discrepancies as soon as possible to avoid catastrophic failure later.

Removal/Installation

It is only necessary to lift the crankshaft from the left crankcase half (**Figure 64**). Take care not to drop it as it is handled. When installing it, make sure that it is fully seated in the left crankcase half.

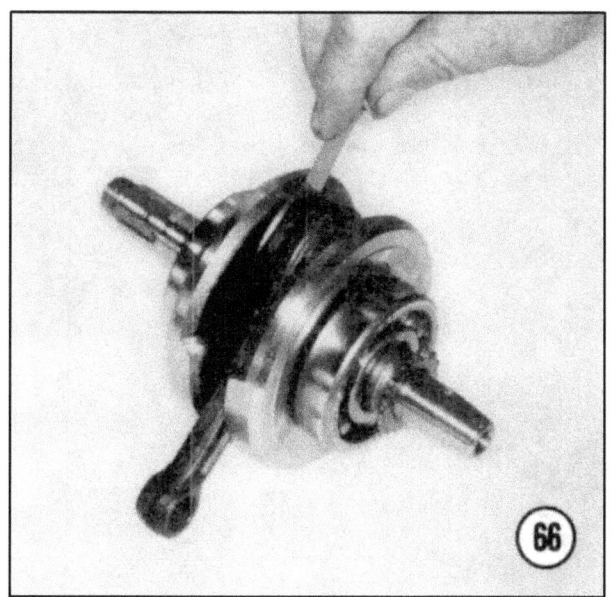

Table 14 CONNECTING ROD SIDE CLEARANCE

Model	Service Limit Inch	(Millimeter)
50cc	0.004	(0.10)
65cc	0.004	(0.10)
70cc	0.004	(0.10)
90cc	0.032	(0.80)

Inspection

Refer to **Figure 65**. Mount crankshaft (1) in a pair of V-blocks (2), then rotate it slowly through several revolutions. Measure runout, using dial gauge (3) at each end. Replace the entire assembly if runout exceeds service limits given in **Table 13**.

Measure connecting rod side clearance, using a feeler gauge as shown in **Figure 66**. Replace the crankshaft if side clearance exceeds service limits. See **Table 14**.

Measure clearance between the connecting rod and crankpin, using the setup shown in **Figure 67**. Replace the crankshaft if clearance exceeds 0.002 inch (0.05 millimeter) for all models.

KICKSTARTER

All models are equipped with kickstarters. Their mechanisms are simple and reliable, and when service is required, any cause for malfunction will be obvious.

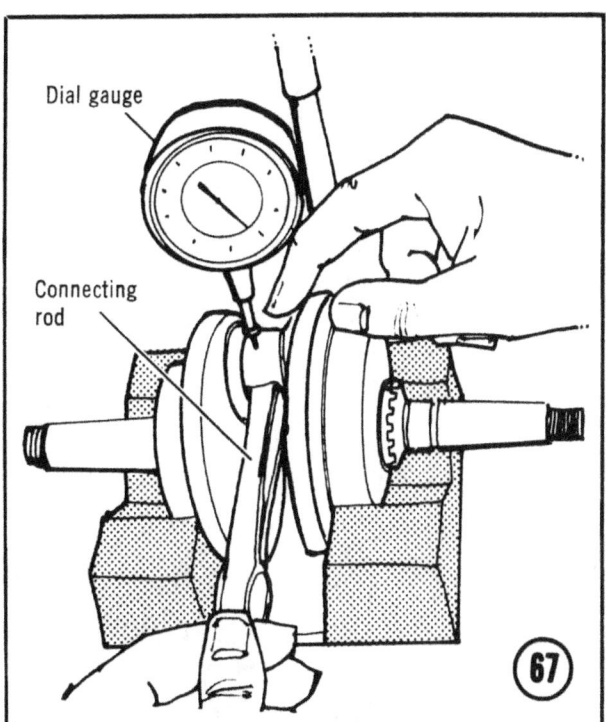

Removal/Installation (50cc-70cc Models)

Figure 68 is an exploded view of a typical kickstarter on these models. Refer to that illustration during disassembly.

After disassembly, check teeth on the kickstarter gear. Be sure that splines on the shaft and gear are not worn. Always use new snap rings upon reassembly.

Removal/Installation (90cc Models)

To remove the kickstarter, pull it out from the left crankcase (**Figure 69**).

Disassemble the kickstarter and check for worn gear teeth, weak springs, and wear on the ratchet pawl. Be sure to assemble the gear with its large diameter outward (**Figure 70**).

TRANSMISSION

Honda motorcycles are either equipped with 3- or 4-speed transmissions. Service procedures are similar for both types.

Operation

The following paragraphs discuss operation of a typical 4-speed transmission. Operation of 3-speed transmission is similar.

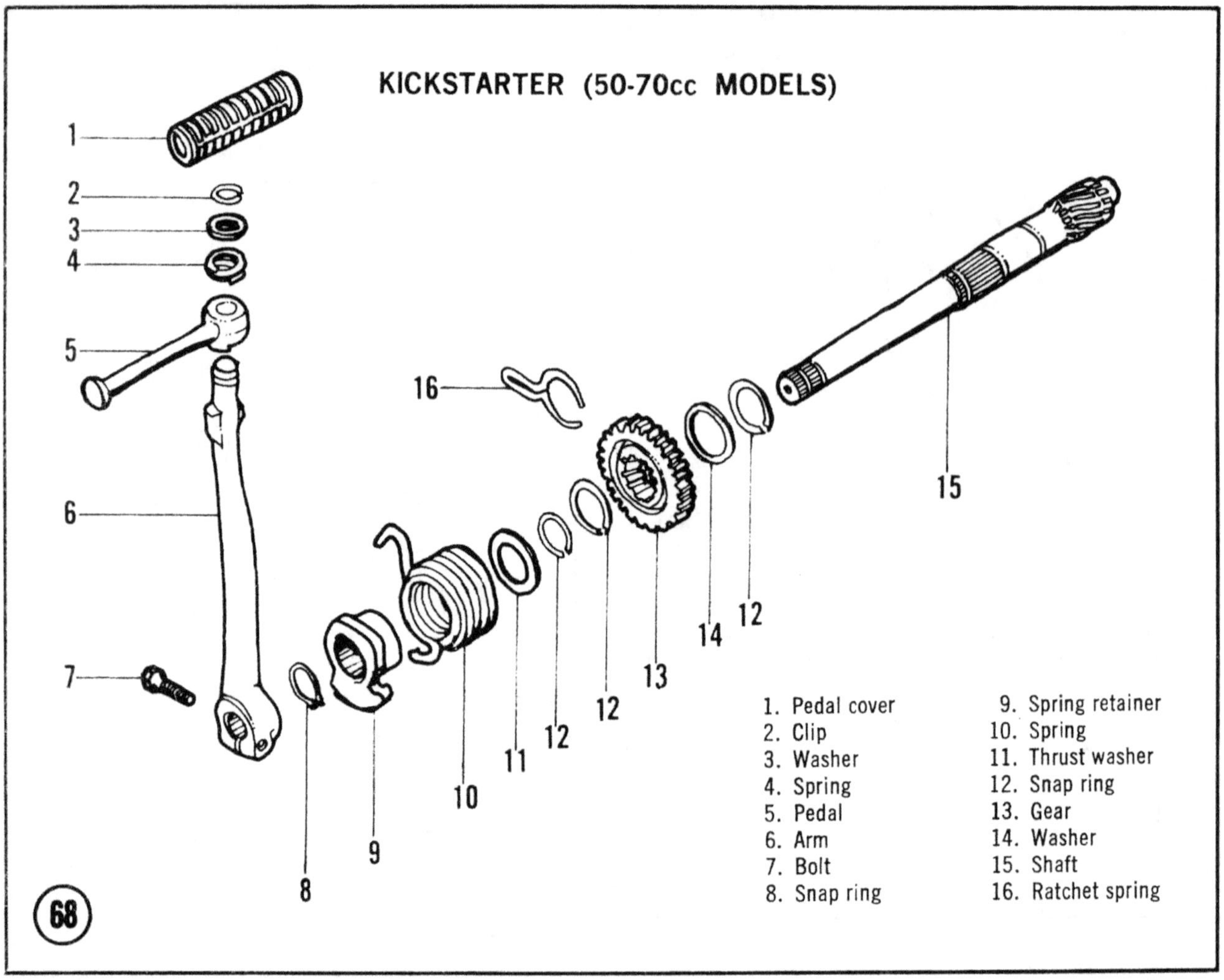

KICKSTARTER (50-70cc MODELS)
68
1
2
3
4
5
6
7
8
9
10
11
12
13
14
15
16
1. Pedal cover
2. Clip
3. Washer
4. Spring
5. Pedal
6. Arm
7. Bolt
8. Snap ring
9. Spring retainer
10. Spring
11. Thrust washer
12. Snap ring
13. Gear
14. Washer
15. Shaft
16. Ratchet spring

Figure 71 illustrates 1st gear operation. Power flows from the clutch through main shaft (1) and fixed gear (2). Low driven gear (4) is normally free to rotate on output shaft (3). Sliding gear (5) is splined to output shaft (3). Dog teeth on the right side of gear (5) engage gear (4), thereby causing it to be locked to output shaft (3) as well.

Operation of 2nd gear is illustrated in **Figure 72**. Input power from main shaft (1) flows through fixed 2nd input gear (2), through 2nd driven gear (5), which is splined to output shaft (4). Sliding gear (3), which is splined to input shaft (1), is not in mesh.

Figure 73 illustrates 3rd gear operation. Power from main shaft (1) flows through sliding 3rd input gear (2), which is splined to the input shaft. Gear (2) is meshed with 3rd output shaft (3). But dog teeth on sliding 2nd output gear (5), which is splined to output shaft (3), engage 3rd driven gear (4), forcing gear (4) to turn the output shaft.

69

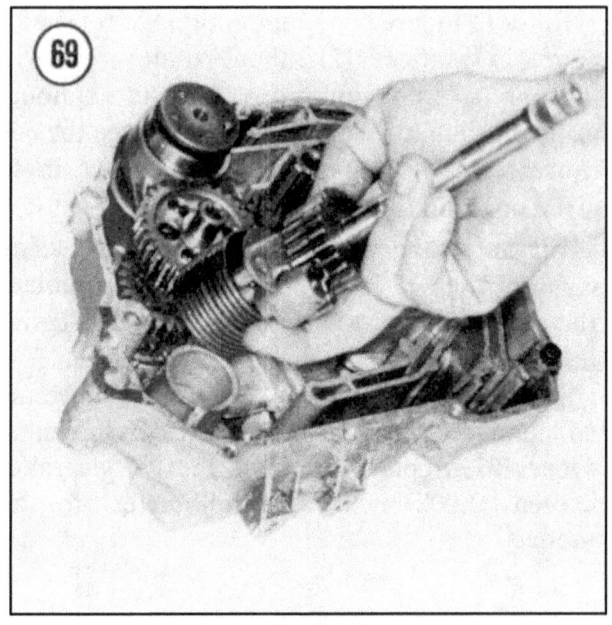

Operation in 4th gear is illustrated in **Figure 74**. Power from input shaft (1) flows from sliding 3rd input gear (3) to 4th input gear (2), which is normally free to rotate on its shaft.

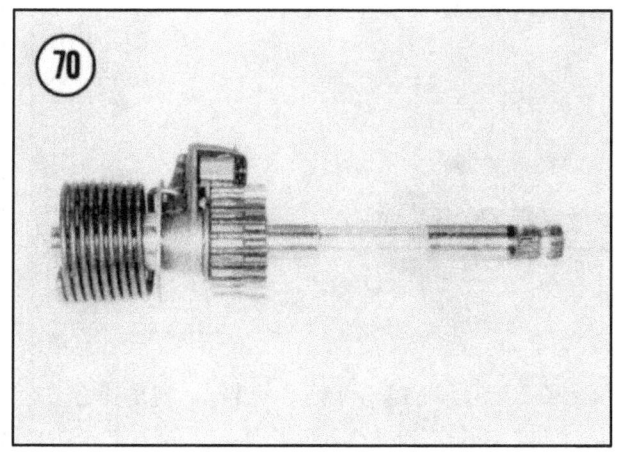

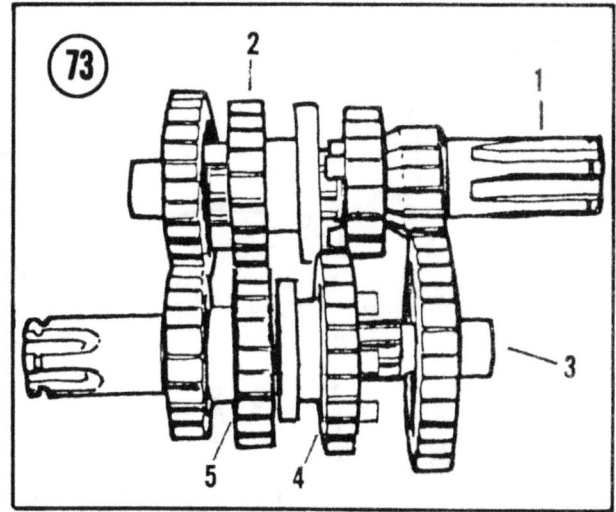

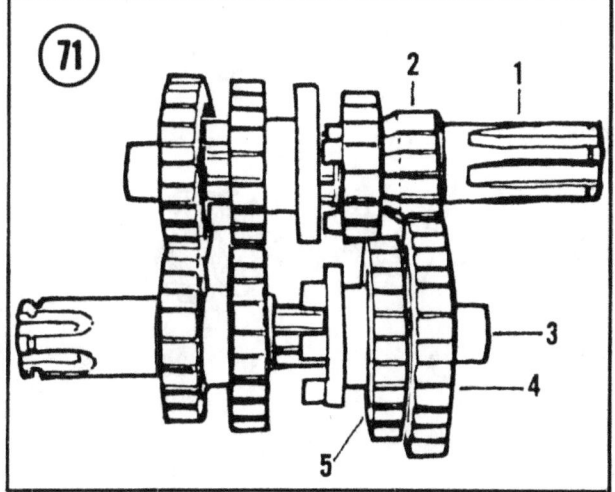

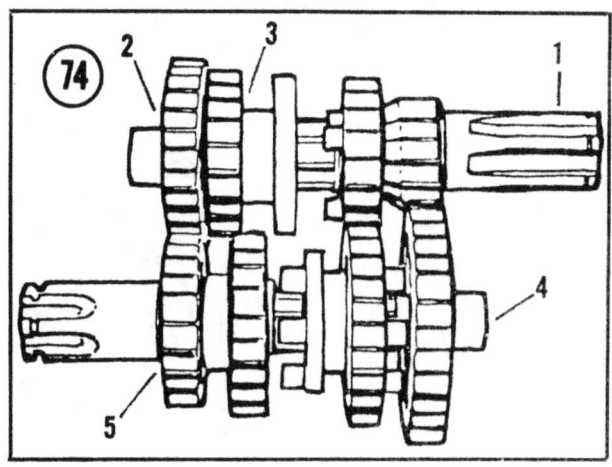

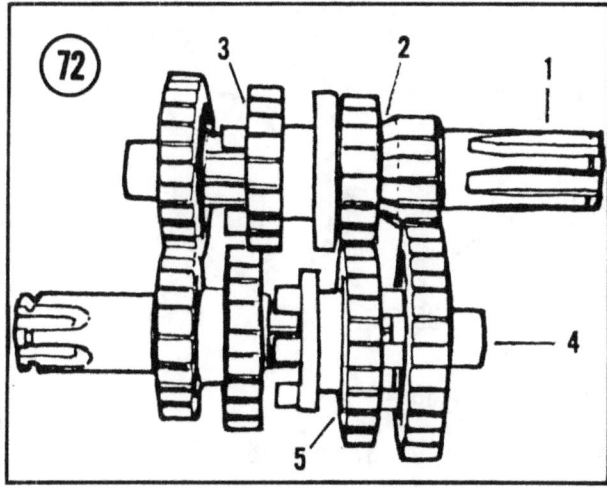

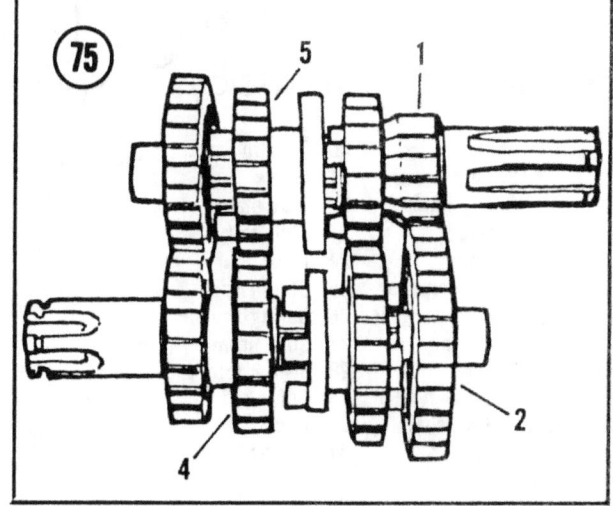

However, dog teeth on gear (3) engage gear (2), forcing it to turn with input shaft (1). Power then flows from 4th input gear (2) through fixed 4th driven gear (5).

Neutral operation is shown in **Figure 75**. All gears are meshed, but since input gears (1) and (3) are meshed with freely rotating gears (2) and (4) on the output shaft, no power is transmitted through the transmission.

Transmission Removal

Although it is possible to remove the transmission as a unit, a step-by-step procedure

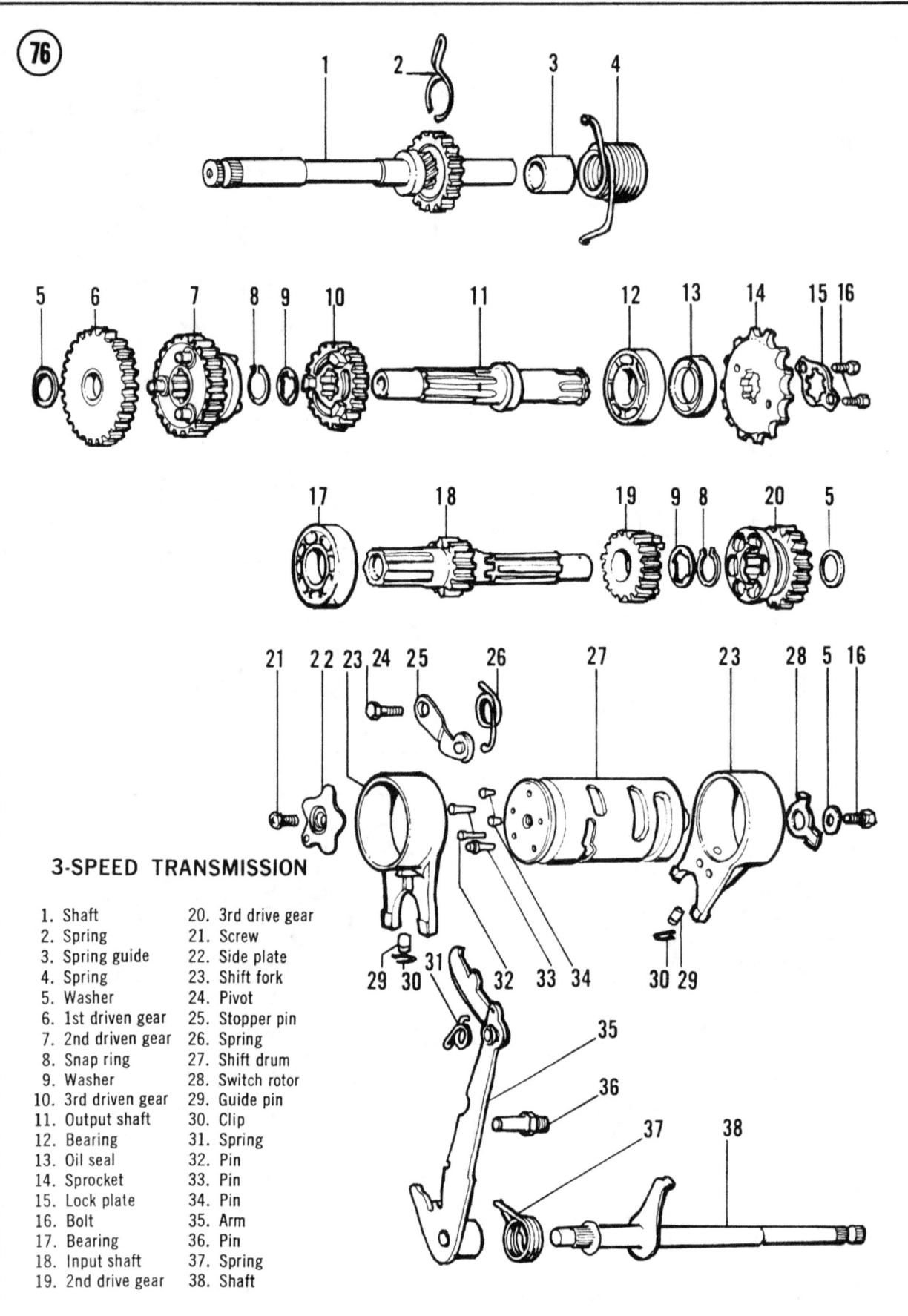

3-SPEED TRANSMISSION

1. Shaft
2. Spring
3. Spring guide
4. Spring
5. Washer
6. 1st driven gear
7. 2nd driven gear
8. Snap ring
9. Washer
10. 3rd driven gear
11. Output shaft
12. Bearing
13. Oil seal
14. Sprocket
15. Lock plate
16. Bolt
17. Bearing
18. Input shaft
19. 2nd drive gear
20. 3rd drive gear
21. Screw
22. Side plate
23. Shift fork
24. Pivot
25. Stopper pin
26. Spring
27. Shift drum
28. Switch rotor
29. Guide pin
30. Clip
31. Spring
32. Pin
33. Pin
34. Pin
35. Arm
36. Pin
37. Spring
38. Shaft

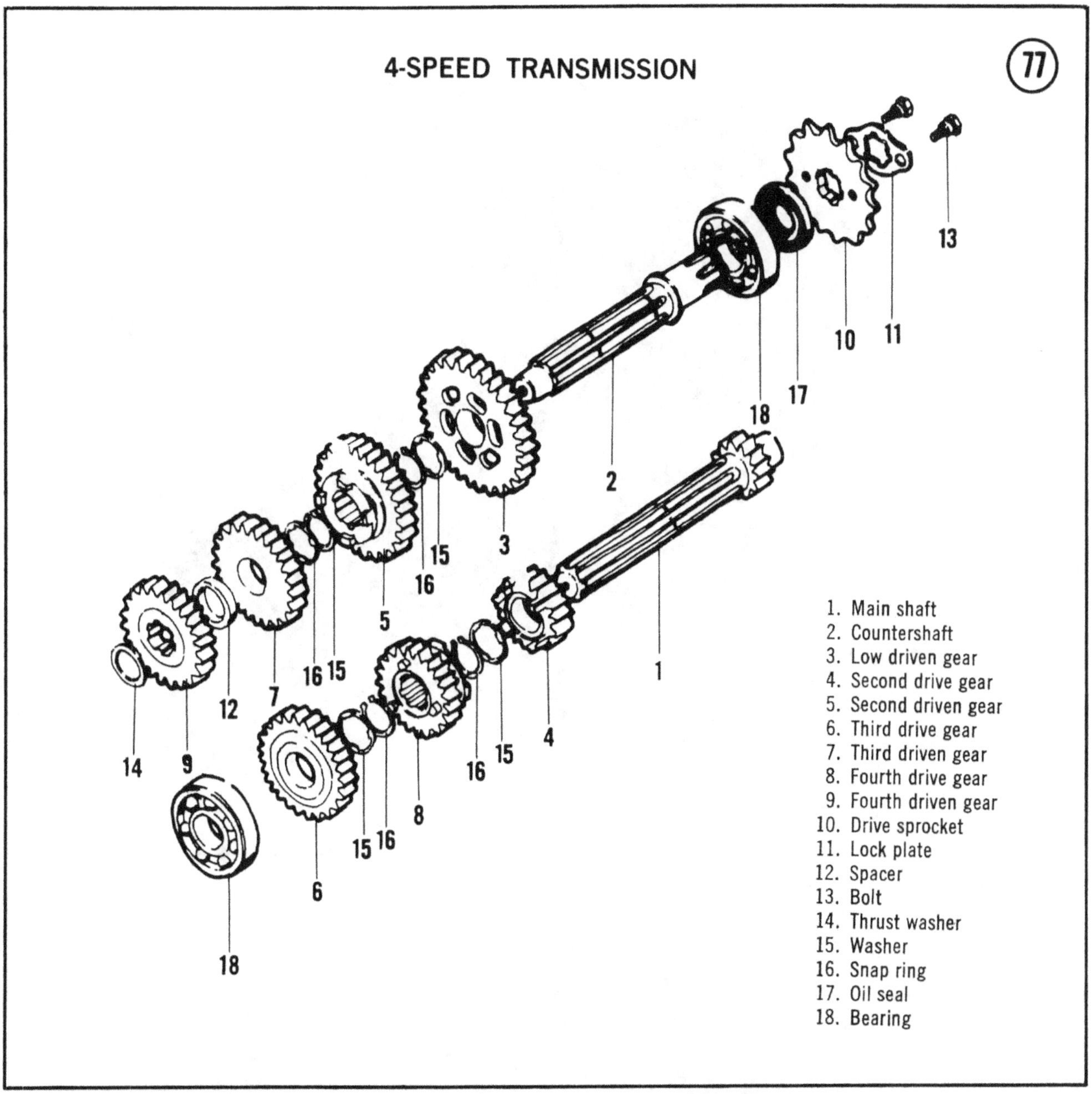

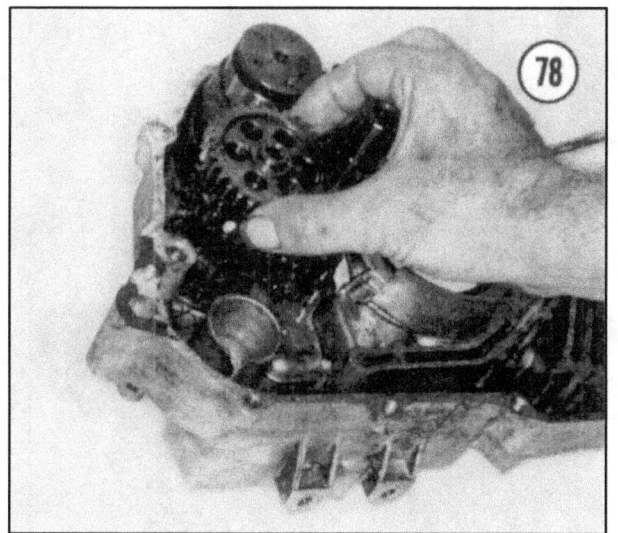

4-SPEED TRANSMISSION
77
1
2
3
4
5
6
7
8
9
10
11
12
13
14
15
16
17
18
1. Main shaft
2. Countershaft
3. Low driven gear
4. Second drive gear
5. Second driven gear
6. Third drive gear
7. Third driven gear
8. Fourth drive gear
9. Fourth driven gear
10. Drive sprocket
11. Lock plate
12. Spacer
13. Bolt
14. Thrust washer
15. Washer
16. Snap ring
17. Oil seal
18. Bearing

78

is set forth to lessen the possibility of errors in disassembly and reassembly. **Figures 76 and 77** are exploded views of typical 3-speed and 4-speed transmissions. Refer to the applicable illustration during service.

> NOTE: *Take careful notice of locations of all small parts such as thrust washers and snap rings.*

A disassembly procedure for a 4-speed transmission is presented in the following paragraphs. Procedures for 3-speed transmissions are similar and will present no difficulty.

1. Pull 1st driven gear from the output shaft (**Figure 78**).

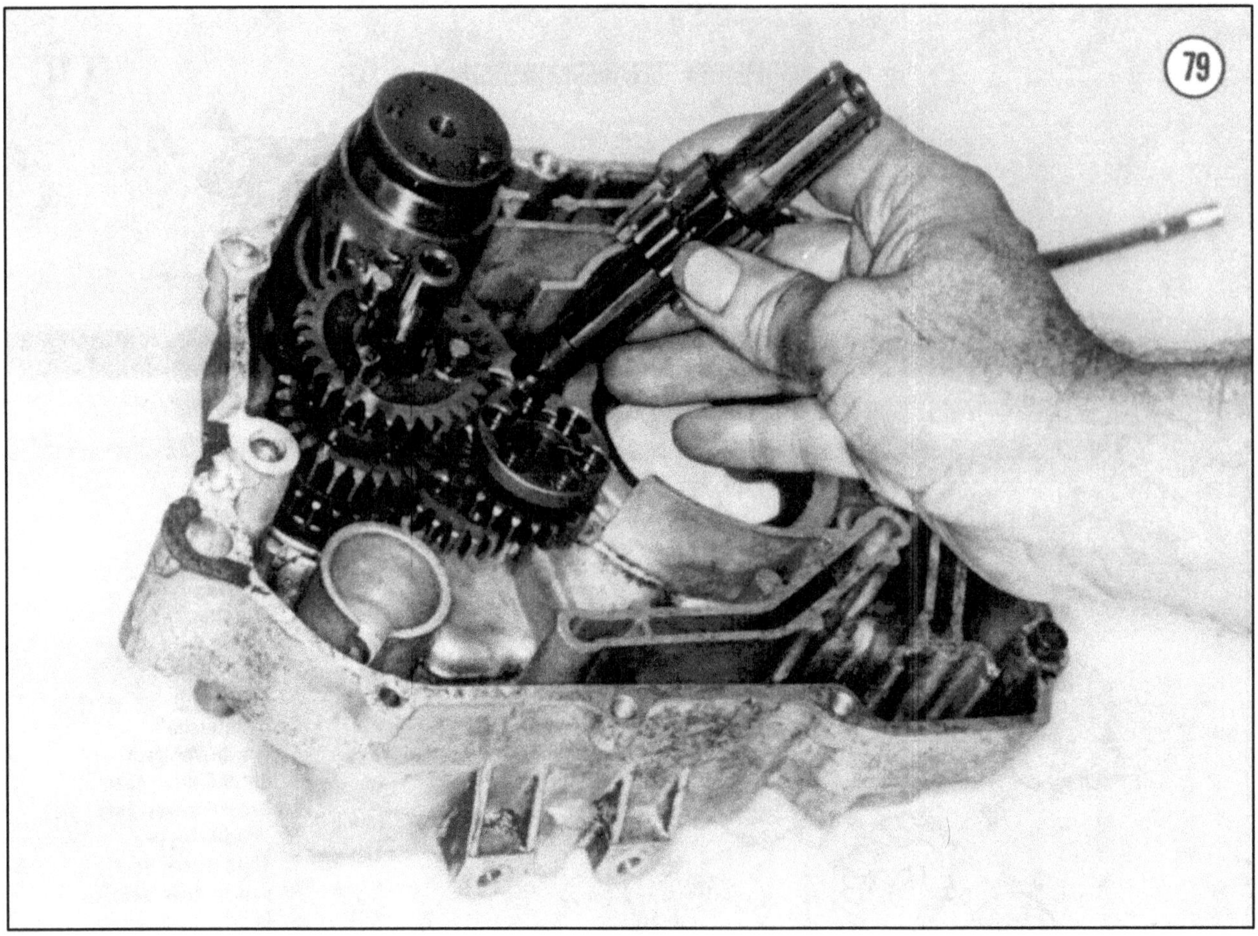

58

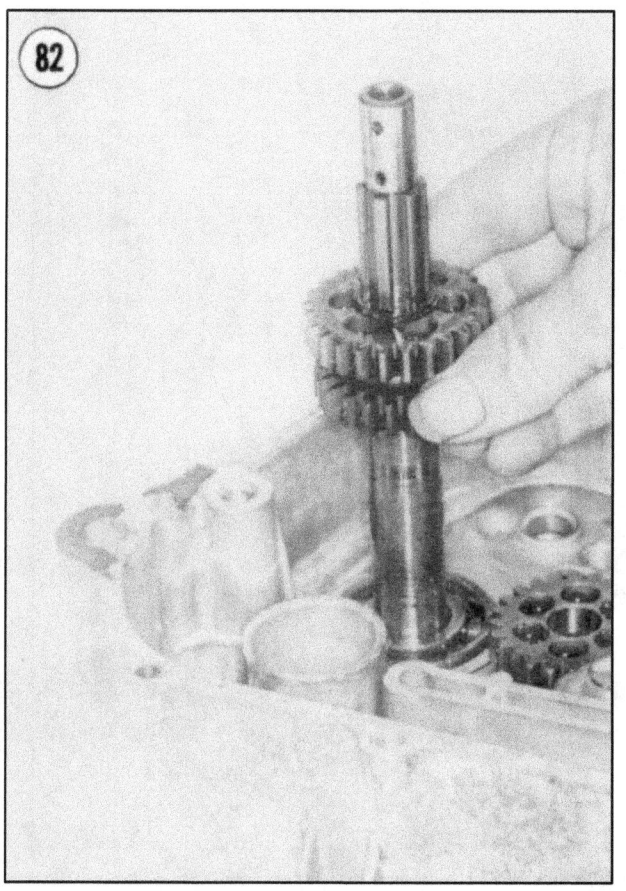

2. Pull out the input shaft (**Figure 79**).

3. Remove 3rd input gear (**Figure 80**).

4. Pull out the shift drum together with 2nd output gear (**Figure 81**).

5. Remove the output shaft (**Figure 82**).

6. Remove 4th input gear (**Figure 83**).

7. Individual gears may be removed from their shafts, if necessary, by removing the snap rings which retain them.

8. Remove shift forks from the shift drum by pulling out each guide pin clip (**Figure 84**). Shift forks are not identical. Be very sure to install them properly upon reassembly.

Inspection

1. Any burrs, pits, or roughness on gear teeth will cause wear on mating gears. Examine all gears carefully, and replace them in pairs if there is any doubt about condition.

2. Measure clearance between each sliding gear and its shaft. If clearance exceeds 0.004 in. (0.10 millimeter), replace the gear and/or its shaft.

3. Measure clearance between shafts and bearings. Replace shafts and/or bearings if clearance exceeds 0.005 inch (0.13 millimeter).

4. Measure clearance between each shift fork and the shift drum. Replace shift forks and/or the shift drum if clearance exceeds 0.006 inch (0.15 millimeter).

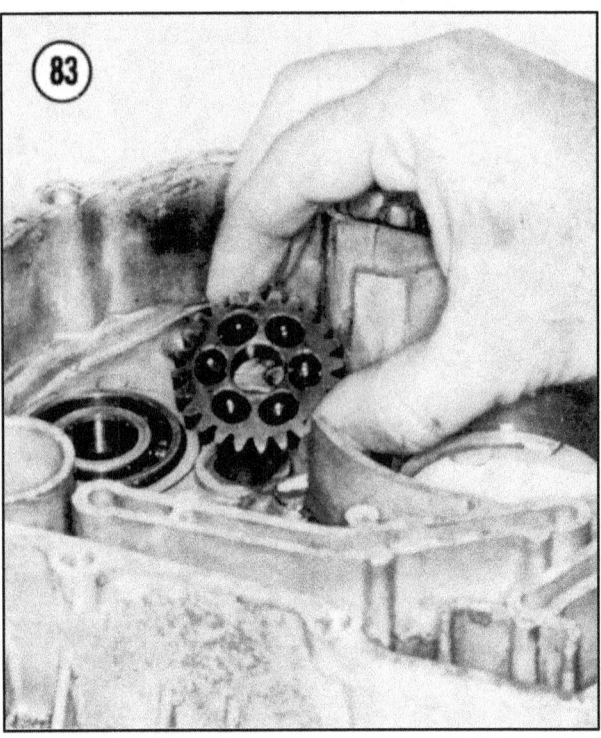

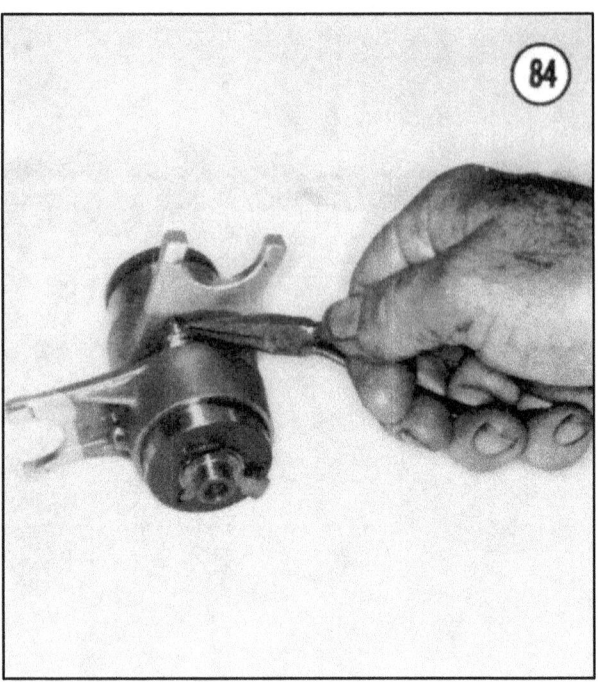

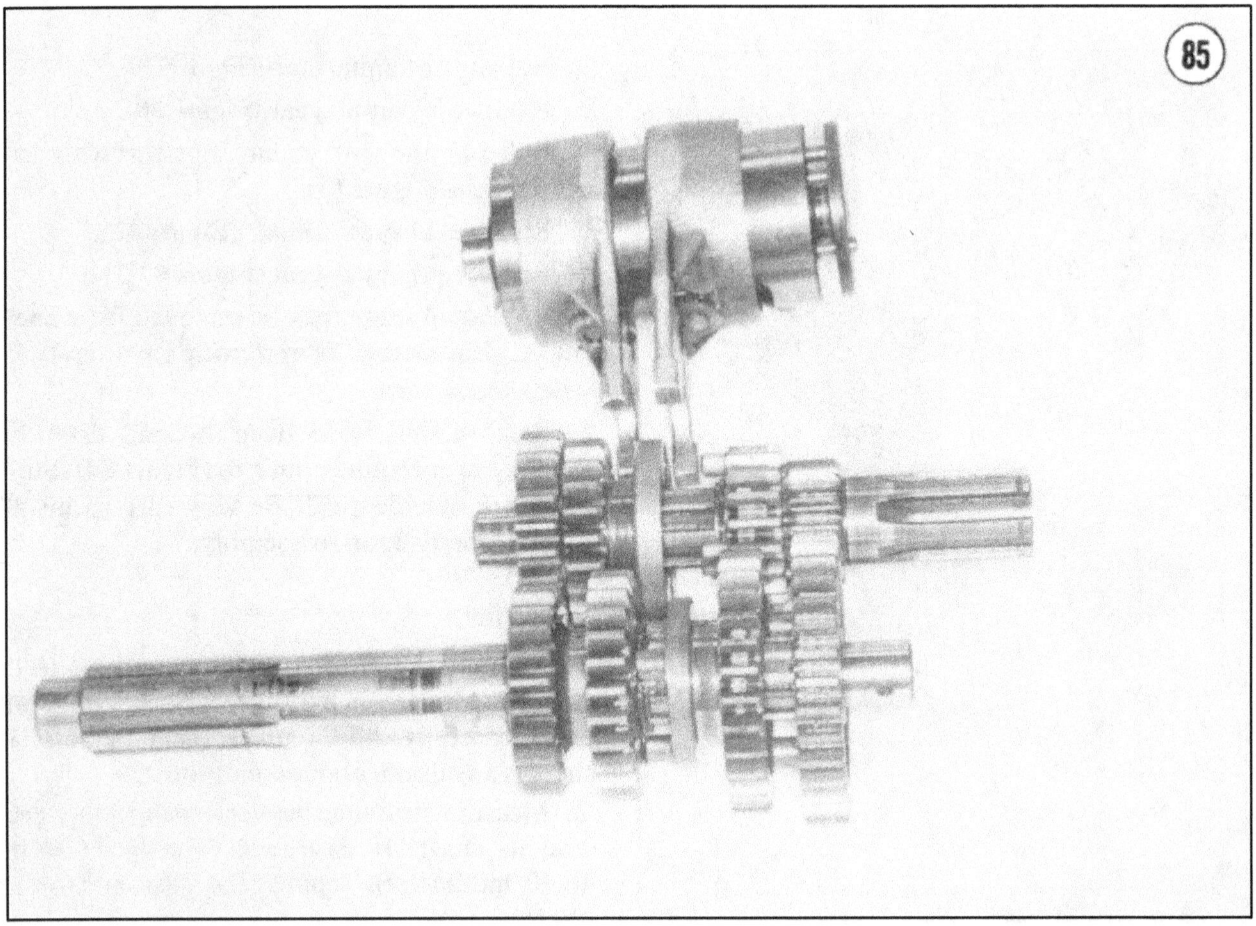

Installation

It is easier to assemble the transmission (**Figure 85**), then install it into the left crankcase as a unit. Be sure that all thrust washers are in place. **Figure 86** illustrates the transmission installed.

BEARINGS

Bearings may be removed by heating crankcase halves in an oven to approximately 300°F (150°C), then rapping them smartly with a wooden hammer handle.

To check bearings, clean them thoroughly with solvent, then oil lightly. Spin each bearing by hand, and check for abnormal noise or roughness as it coasts down. Do not spin dry bearings and never spin them with an air blast.

Be sure that bearing counterbores are absolutely clean before installing bearings. Heat crankcase halves approximately 300°F (150°C) before bearing installation.

CHAPTER FOUR

FUEL SYSTEM

For proper operation, a gasoline engine must be supplied with fuel and air, mixed in proper proportions by weight. A mixture in which there is excess fuel is said to be rich. A lean mixture is one which contains insufficient fuel. It is the function of the carburetor to supply the proper mixture to the engine under all operating conditions.

CARBURETOR OPERATION

Essential functional parts of Keihin carburetors, standard on Honda motorcycles, are a float and float valve mechanism for maintaining a constant fuel level in the float bowl; a pilot system for supplying fuel at low speeds; a main fuel system, which supplies the engine at medium and high speeds; and a choke system, which supplies the very rich mixture needed to start a cold engine. Operation of each system is discussed in the following paragraphs.

Float Mechanism

Figure 1 illustrates a typical float mechanism. Proper carburetor operation is dependent on maintaining a constant fuel level in the carburetor float bowl. As fuel is drawn from the float bowl, the float drops. When the float drops, the float needle valve moves away from its seat and allows fuel to flow past the valve and seat into the float bowl. As this occurs, the float is then raised, pressing the valve against its seat, thereby shutting off fuel flow. It can be seen from this discussion that a small piece of dirt can be trapped between the valve and seat, preventing the valve from closing and allowing fuel to rise beyond its normal level, resulting in flooding. **Figure 2** illustrates this condition.

Pilot System

Under idle or low speed conditions, at less than $\frac{1}{8}$ throttle, the engine doesn't require much fuel or air, and the throttle valve is almost closed. A separate pilot system is required for operation under such conditions.

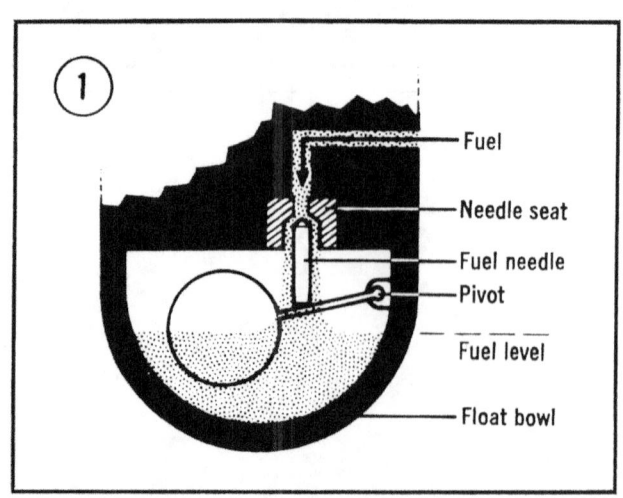

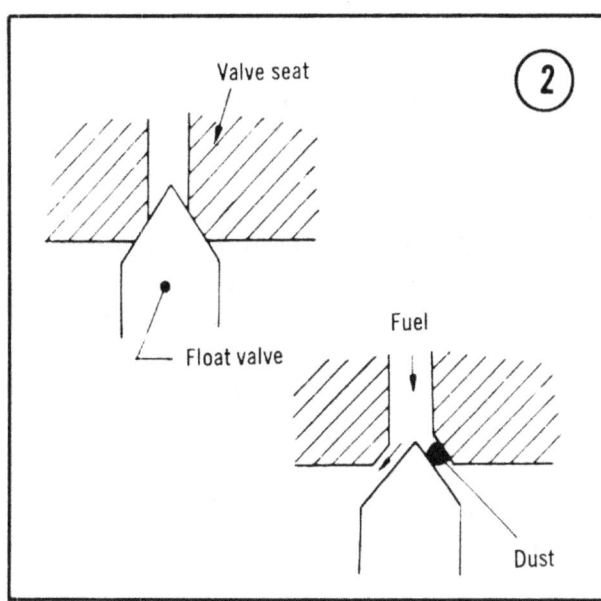

Figure 3 illustrates pilot system operation. Air is drawn through the pilot air inlet and controlled by the pilot air screw. This air is then mixed with fuel drawn through the pilot jet. The air/fuel mixture then travels from the pilot outlet into the main air passage, where it is further mixed with air prior to being drawn into the engine.

A pilot air screw controls idle mixture. Turning the screw counterclockwise allows more air to flow, thereby leaning the mixture at small throttle openings.

If proper idle and low speed mixture cannot be obtained within normal adjustment range of the idle mixture screw, refer to **Table 1** for possible causes.

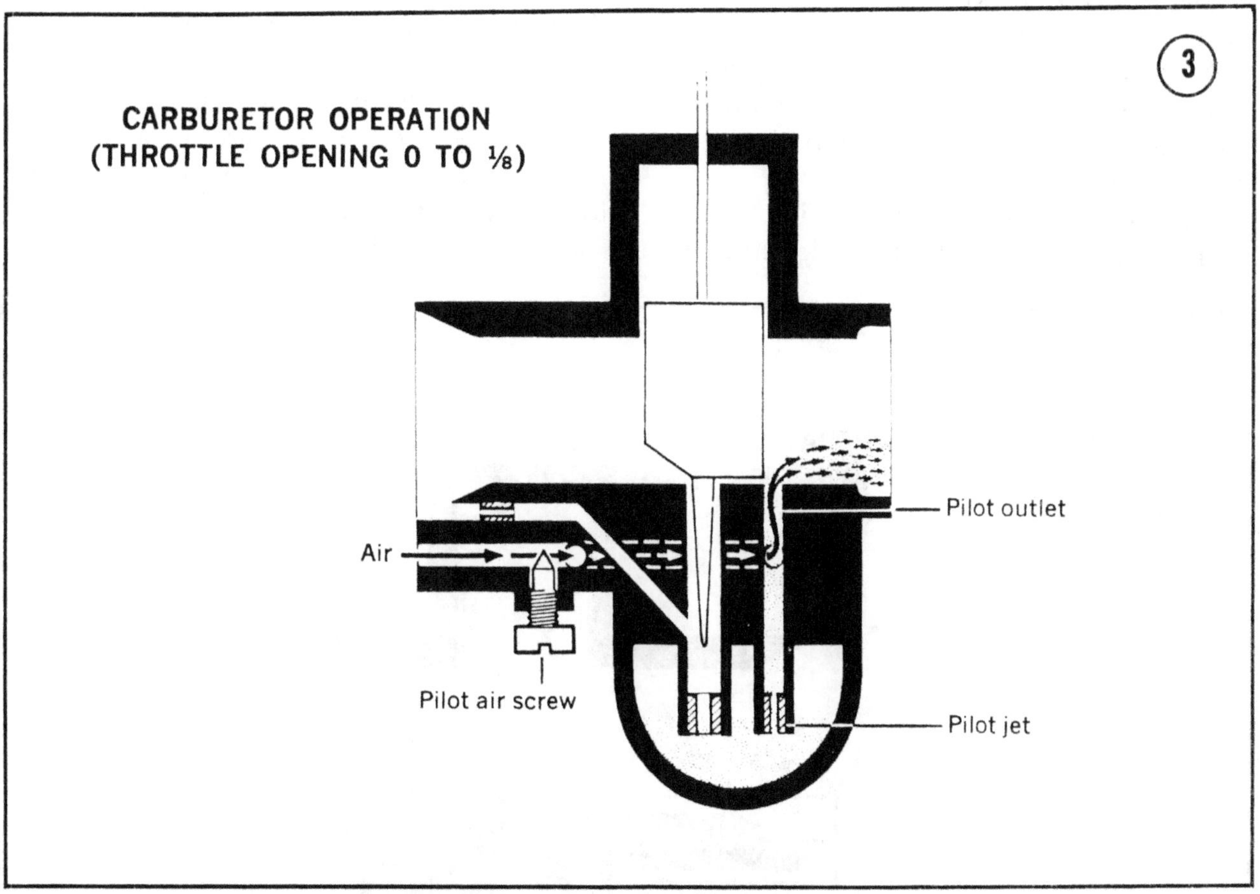

Table 1   LOW SPEED PROBLEMS

Too Rich	Too Lean
Clogged pilot air intake	Obstructed pilot jet
Clogged air passage	Obstructed jet outlet
Clogged air bleed opening	Worn throttle valve
Pilot jet loose	Carburetor mounting loose

Main Fuel System

As the throttle is opened still more, up to about ¼ open, the pilot circuit begins to supply less of the mixture to the engine, as the main fuel system, **Figure 4**, begins to function. The main jet, needle jet, jet needle, and air jet make up the main fuel circuit. As the throttle valve opens more than about ⅛ of its travel, air is drawn through the main port, and passes under the throttle valve in the main bore. Air stream velocity results in reduced pressure around the jet needle. Fuel then passes through the main jet, past the needle jet and jet needle, and into the air stream where it is atomized and sent to the cylinder. As the throttle valve opens, more air flows through the carburetor, and the jet needle, which is attached to the throttle slide, rises to permit more fuel to flow.

A portion of the air bled past the air jet passes through the needle jet bleed air inlet into the needle jet, where the air is mixed with the main air stream and atomized.

Air flow at small throttle openings is controlled primarily by the throttle slide cutaway.

As the throttle is opened wider, up to about ¾ open, the circuit draws air from 2 sources, as shown in **Figure 5**. The first source is air passing through the venturi; the second source is through the air jet. Air passing through the venturi draws fuel through the needle jet. The jet needle is tapered, and therefore allows more fuel to pass as the jet needle emerges from the needle jet. Air passes through the air jet to the needle jet to aid atomization of fuel.

Figure 6 illustrates the circuit at high speeds. The jet needle is withdrawn almost completely from the needle jet. Fuel flow is then controlled by the main jet. Air passing through the air jet continues to aid atomization of the fuel as described in the foregoing paragraphs.

Any dirt which collects in the main jet or in the needle jet obstructs fuel flow and causes a lean mixture. Any clogged air passage, such as the air bleed opening or air jet may result in an overrich mixture. Other causes of a rich mixture are a worn needle jet, loose needle jet, and loose main jet. If the jet needle is worn, it should be replaced, however, it may be possible

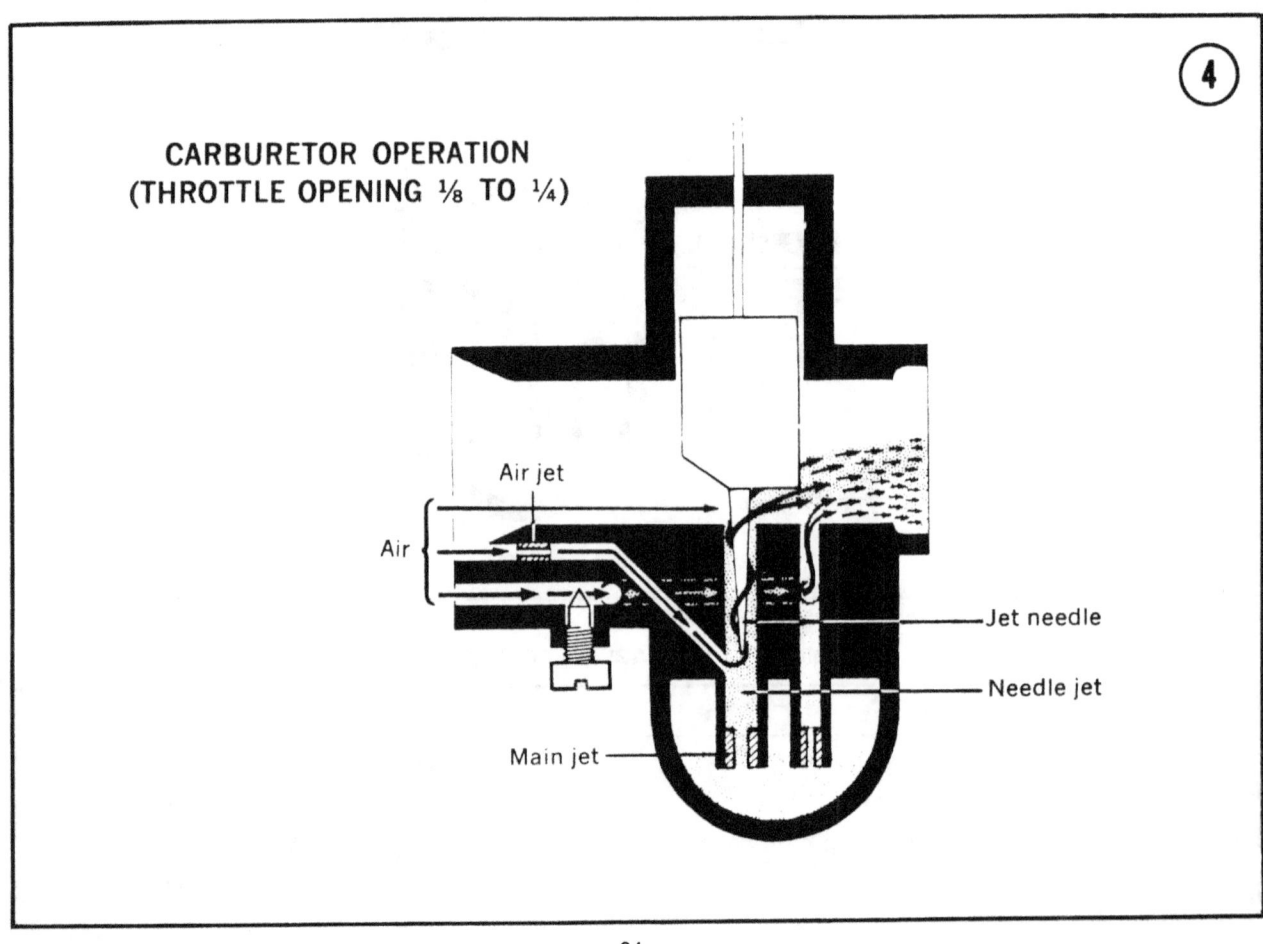

**CARBURETOR OPERATION
(THROTTLE OPENING ¼ TO ¾)**

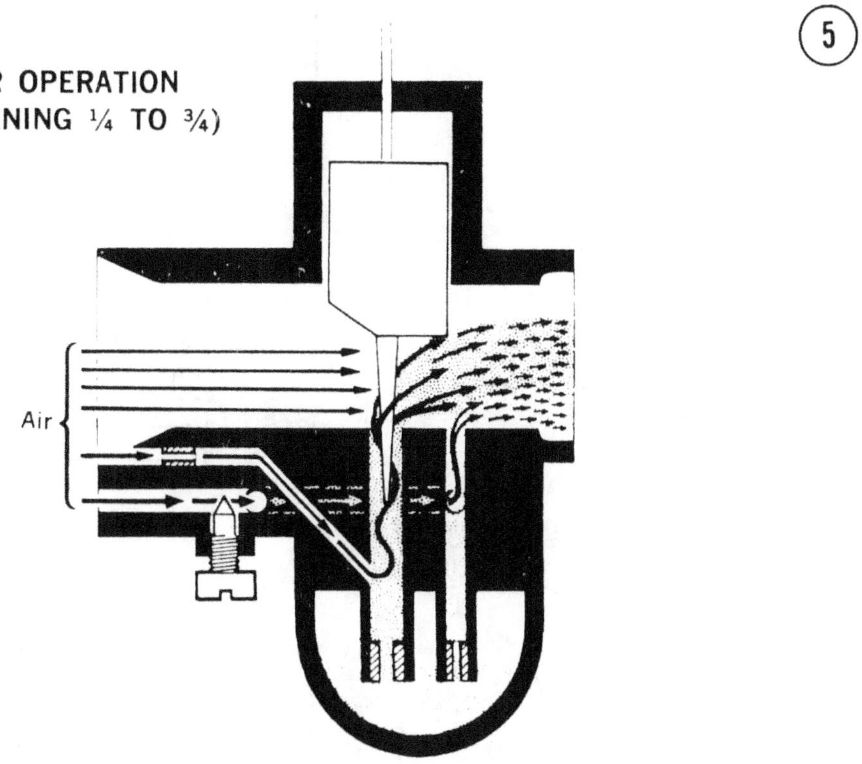

Air

⑤

**CARBURETOR OPERATION
(THROTTLE OPENING ¾ TO FULL)**

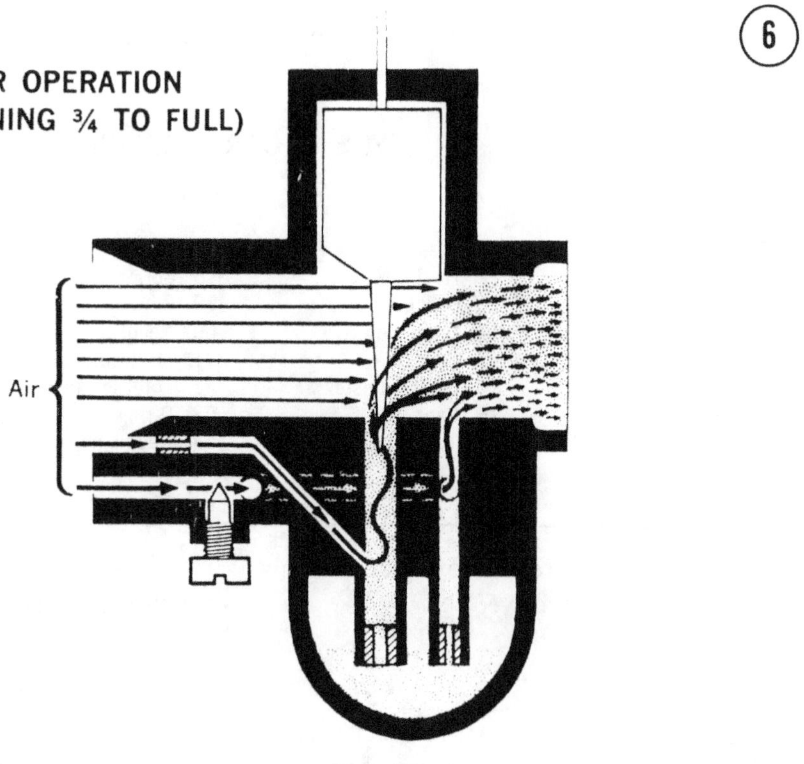

Air

⑥

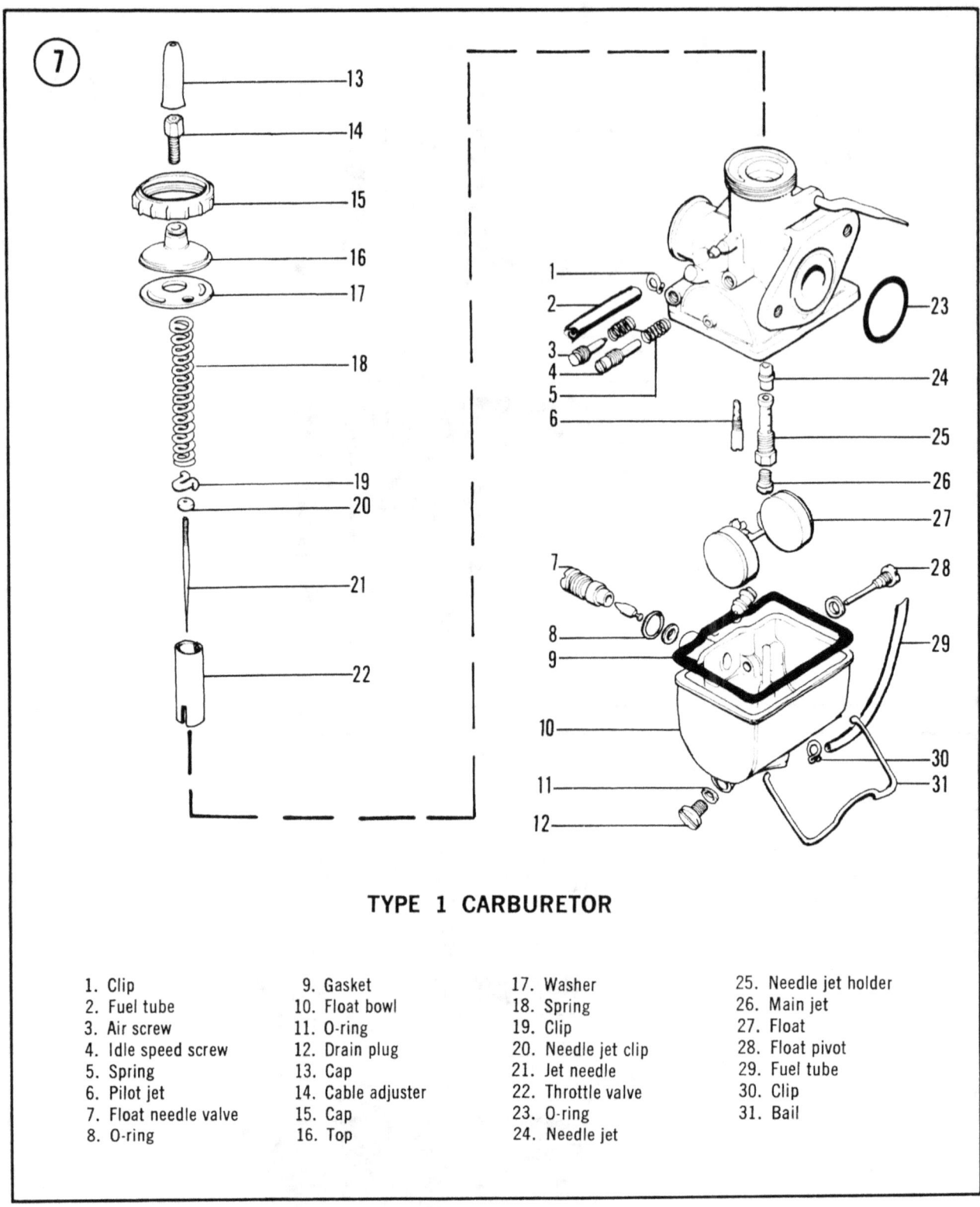

TYPE 1 CARBURETOR

1. Clip
2. Fuel tube
3. Air screw
4. Idle speed screw
5. Spring
6. Pilot jet
7. Float needle valve
8. O-ring
9. Gasket
10. Float bowl
11. O-ring
12. Drain plug
13. Cap
14. Cable adjuster
15. Cap
16. Top
17. Washer
18. Spring
19. Clip
20. Needle jet clip
21. Jet needle
22. Throttle valve
23. O-ring
24. Needle jet
25. Needle jet holder
26. Main jet
27. Float
28. Float pivot
29. Fuel tube
30. Clip
31. Bail

to effect a temporary repair by placing the needle jet clip in a high groove.

Choke Valve

A cold engine requires a mixture much richer than that normally required. Keihin carburetors are equipped with a choke valve which partially restricts air flow at the carburetor inlet, resulting in a richer mixture.

CARBURETOR OVERHAUL

There is no set rule regarding frequency of carburetor overhaul. A carburetor used on a machine used primarily for street riding may go

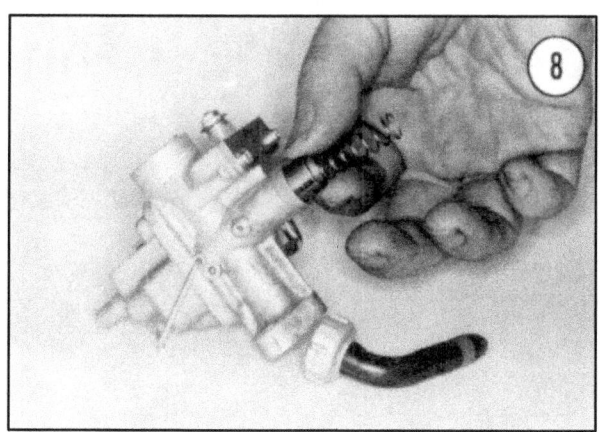

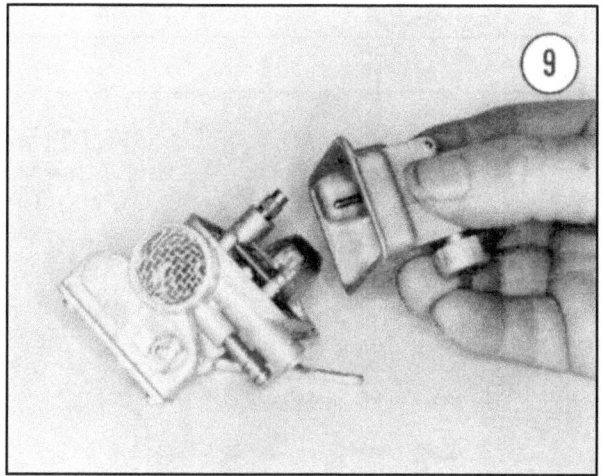

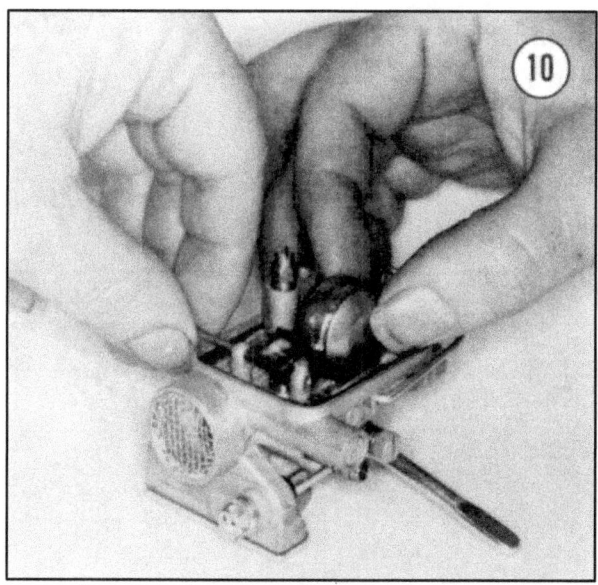

5,000 miles without attention. If the machine is used in dirt, the carburetor might need an overhaul in less than 1,000 miles. Poor engine performance, hesitation, and little or no response to idle mixture adjustment are all symptoms of possible carburetor malfunctions.

Remove the carburetor from the engine and disassemble it. Shake the float to check for gasoline inside. If fuel leaks into the float, the float chamber fuel level will rise, resulting in an overrich mixture. Replace the float if it is deformed or leaking.

Clean all parts in carburetor cleaning solvent. Dry the parts with compressed air. Clean jets and other delicate parts with compressed air after the float bowl has been removed. Use new gaskets upon reassembly.

Never blow compressed air into any assembled carburetor; doing so may result in damage to the float needle valve.

CARBURETOR (1963-1977 MODELS)

For convenience, carburetors used on 1963-1977 models are described as Types 1, 2, and 3. Type 1 carburetors are used on most 50-70cc models. Models C100 and C102 are equipped with Type 2 carburetors. Type 3 carburetors are used on CL90 and similar models.

Type 1 Disassembly/Assembly

Figure 7 is an exploded view of a typical carburetor of this type. Refer to that illustration during disassembly and assembly.

1. Remove the cap, then pull out the throttle valve and spring (**Figure 8**).

2. Pull off the float bowl (**Figure 9**) after pushing its retaining bail out of the way.

3. Pull out the float pivot shaft, then gently remove the float (**Figure 10**). Take care not to bend the float arm during this operation.

4. Remove the float needle (**Figure 11**).

5. Remove the float valve seat (**Figure 12**). A hooked wire may be used to remove its sealing washer.

6. Remove the needle jet holder and main jet together (**Figure 13**).

7. Push out the needle jet, using a plastic or fiber tool (**Figure 14**). Do not use any metal tool for this purpose.

8. Remove the pilot jet (**Figure 15**).

9. Remove the idle speed and idle mixture screws (**Figure 16**). Take care not to lose either spring.

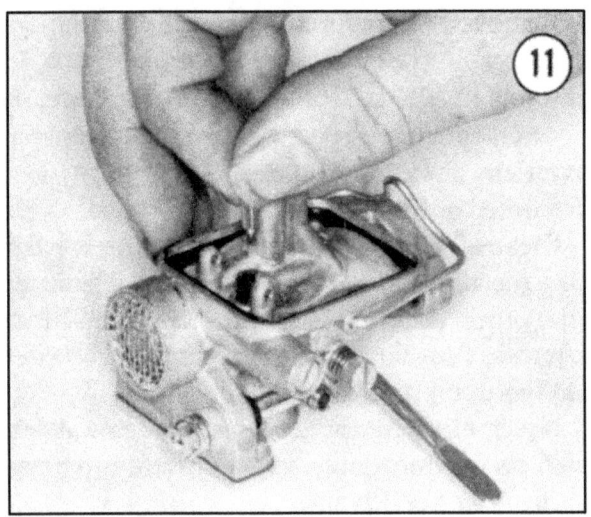
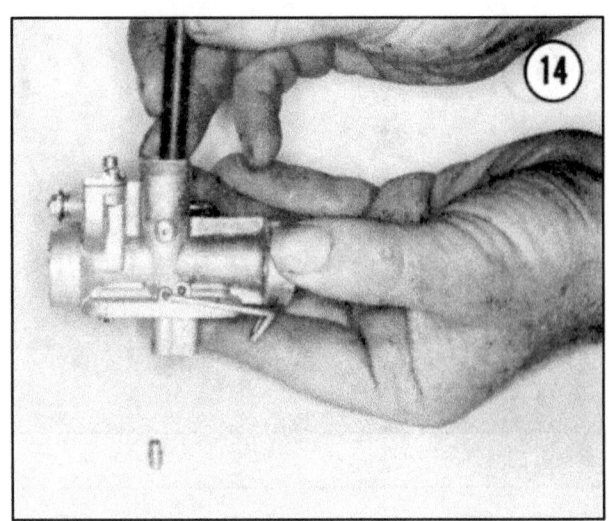
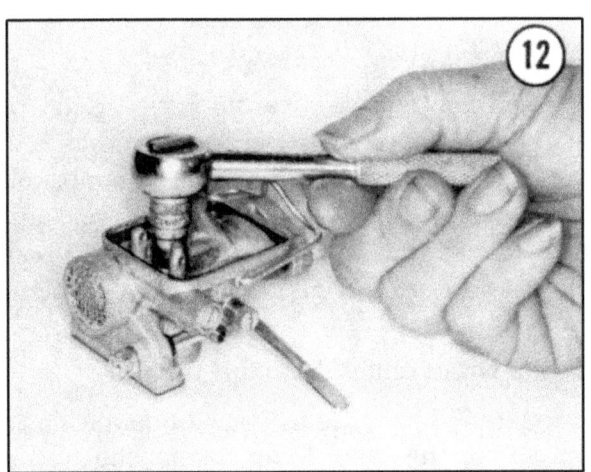
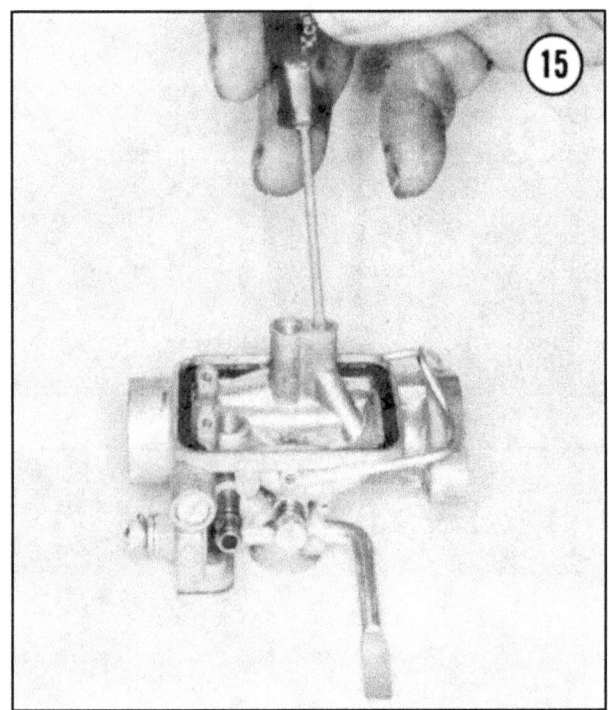
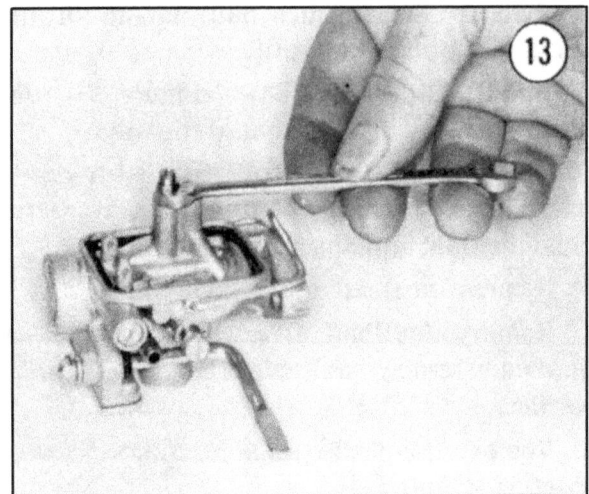
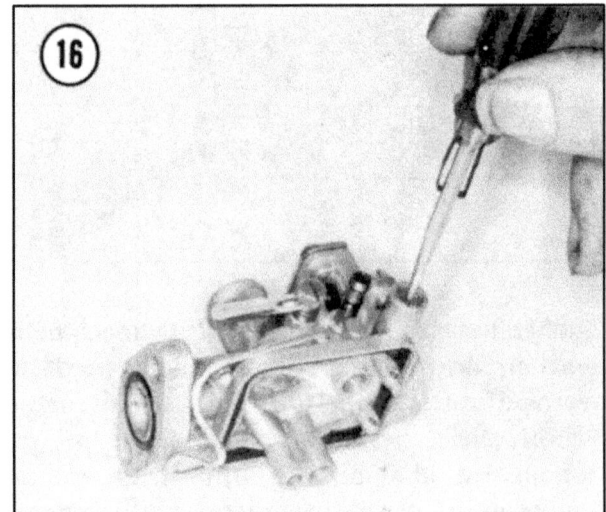

10. Remove 2 retaining screws, then the choke cover and its gasket (**Figure 17**). Disassemble the choke mechanism, if necessary, by removing the nut from the end of the choke lever shaft.

11. Remove the O-ring from mounting flange.

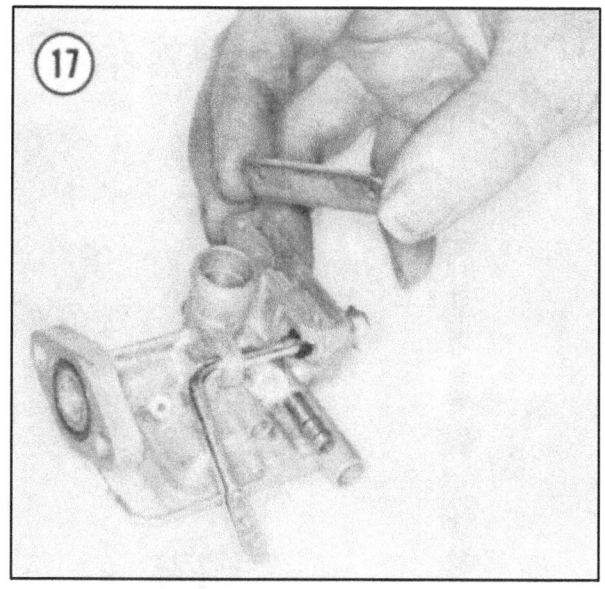

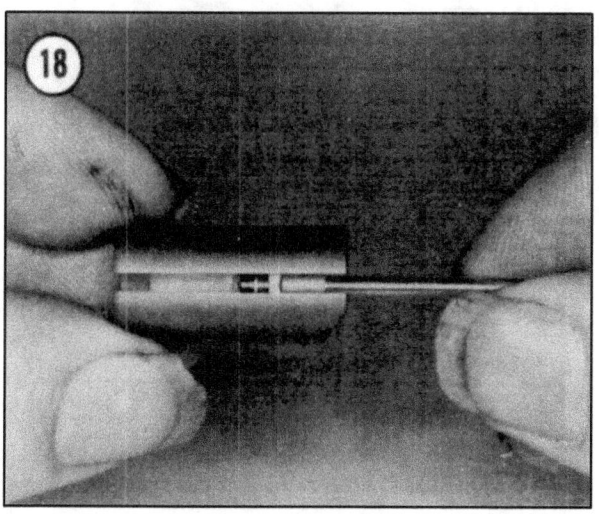

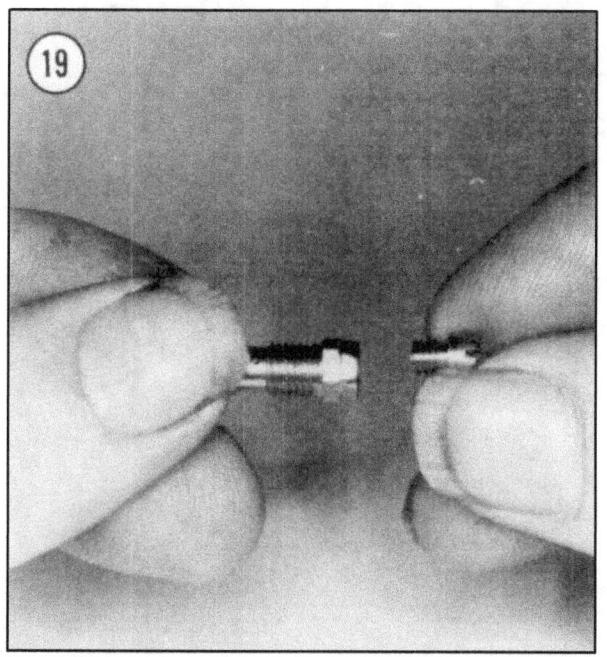

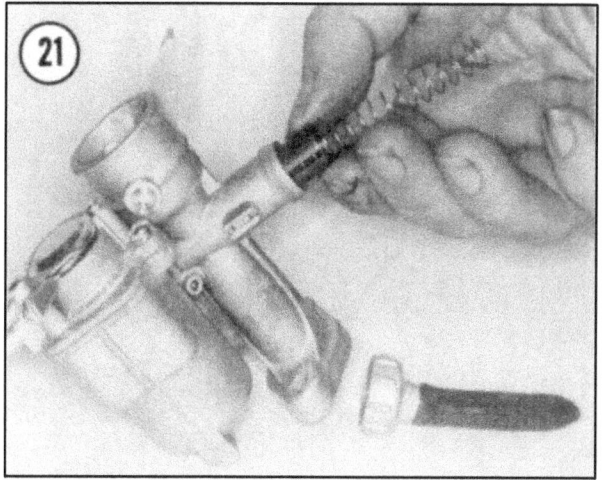

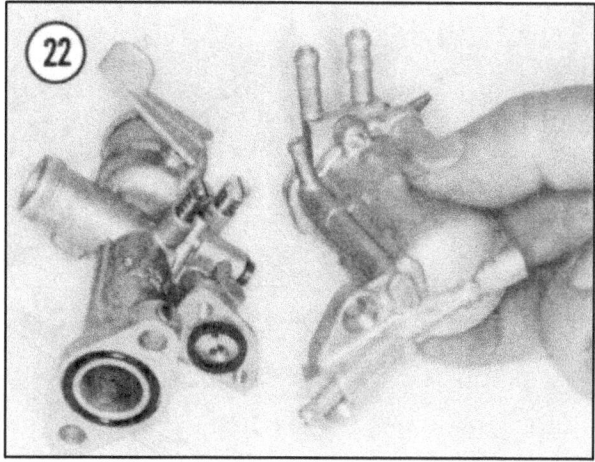

12. Push the jet needle from the throttle slide (**Figure 18**). Do not lose the jet needle retaining clip. Upon reassembly, be sure that the retaining clip does not interfere with the slot in the throttle slide.

13. Separate the main jet from the needle jet holder (**Figure 19**).

14. Remove the drain screw from the float bowl.

15. Reverse procedure to assemble.

Type 2 Disassembly/Assembly

Figure 20 (next page) is an exploded view of this type carburetor. Refer to that illustration during disassembly.

1. Remove the cap, then pull out the throttle valve and its return spring (**Figure 21**).

2. Remove 2 screws, then separate the float chamber from the mixing chamber body (**Figure 22**). Take note of how the sealing washer is installed.

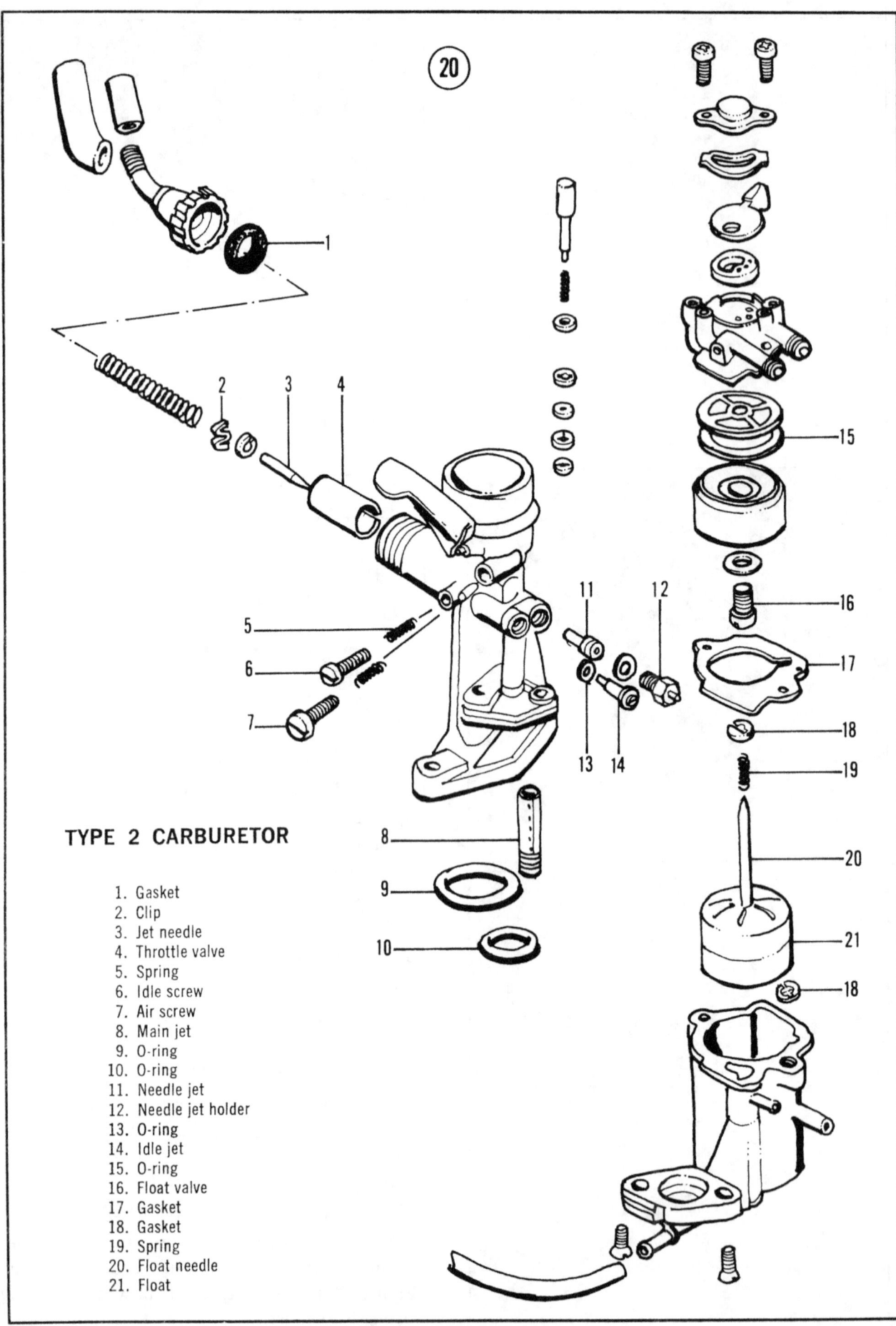

TYPE 2 CARBURETOR

1. Gasket
2. Clip
3. Jet needle
4. Throttle valve
5. Spring
6. Idle screw
7. Air screw
8. Main jet
9. O-ring
10. O-ring
11. Needle jet
12. Needle jet holder
13. O-ring
14. Idle jet
15. O-ring
16. Float valve
17. Gasket
18. Gasket
19. Spring
20. Float needle
21. Float

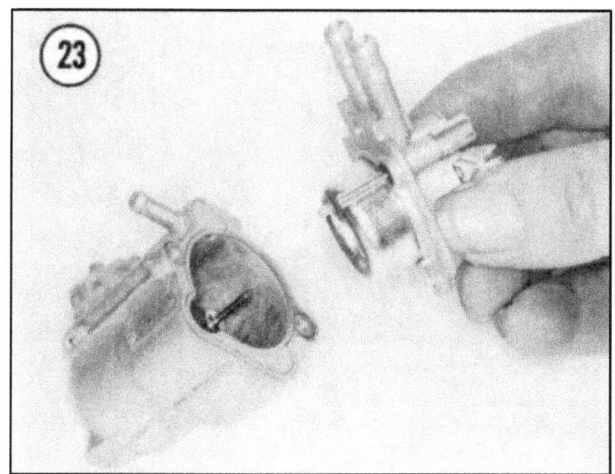
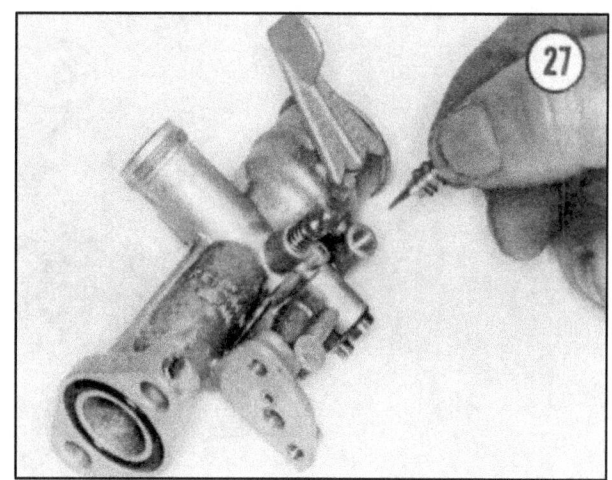
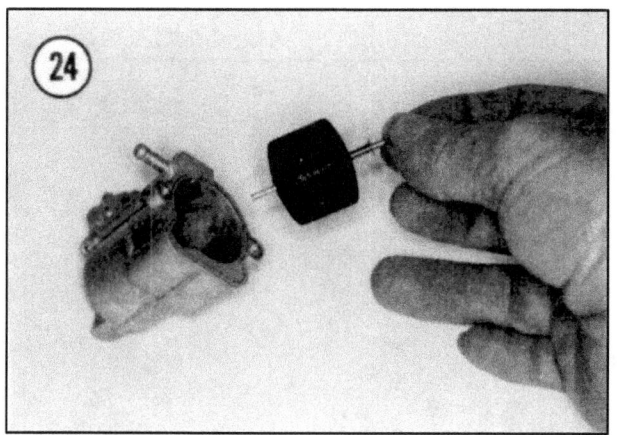
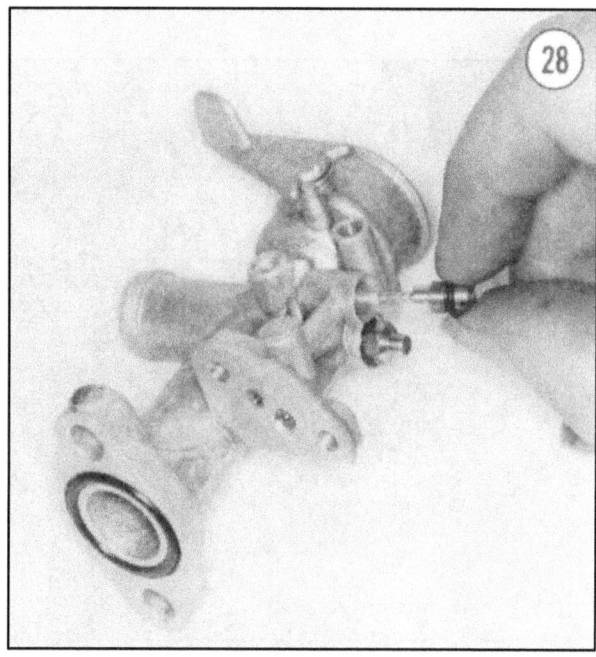
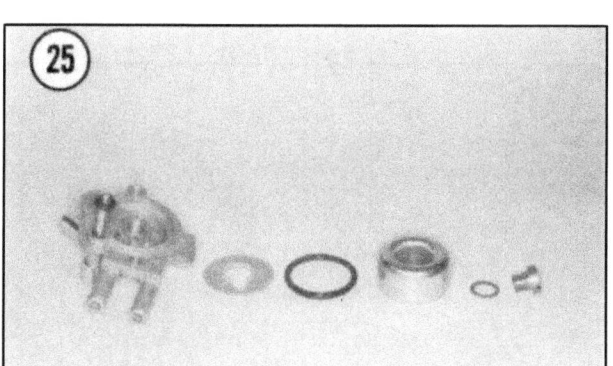
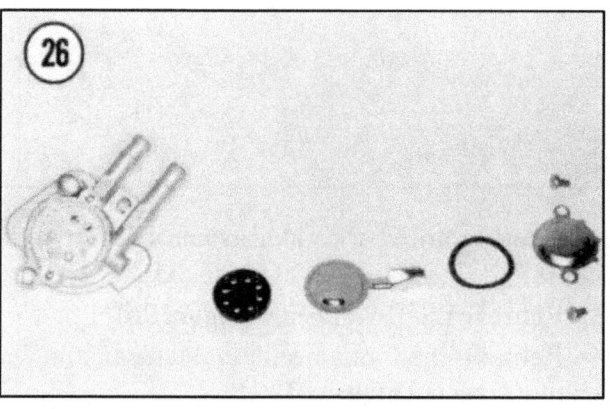

3. Remove 2 retaining screws, then take off the float chamber cover (**Figure 23**).

4. Pull out the float and float needle as an assembly (**Figure 24**).

5. Disassemble the fuel strainer by unscrewing the float valve seat (**Figure 25**).

6. Remove 2 cover retaining screws to disassemble the fuel petcock (**Figure 26**).

7. Remove the idle mixture screw and its spring (**Figure 27**). Also remove the idle speed screw.

8. Remove the idle jet (**Figure 28**).

9. Remove the needle jet holder and its O-ring (**Figure 29**).

10. Using a plastic or fiber tool, push out the needle jet (**Figure 30**).

11. Remove the main jet (**Figure 31**).

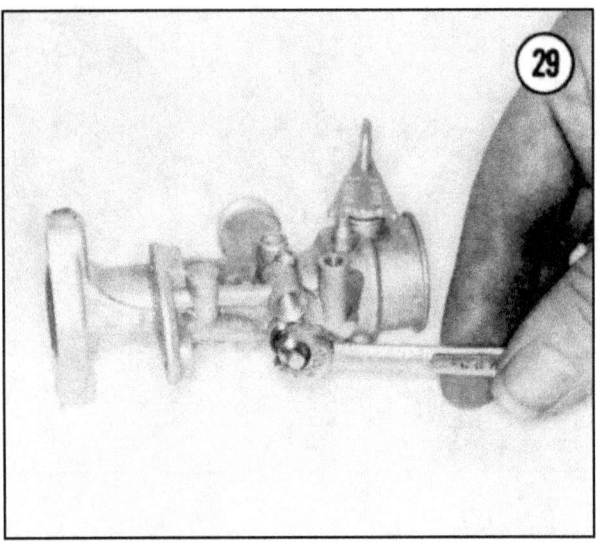

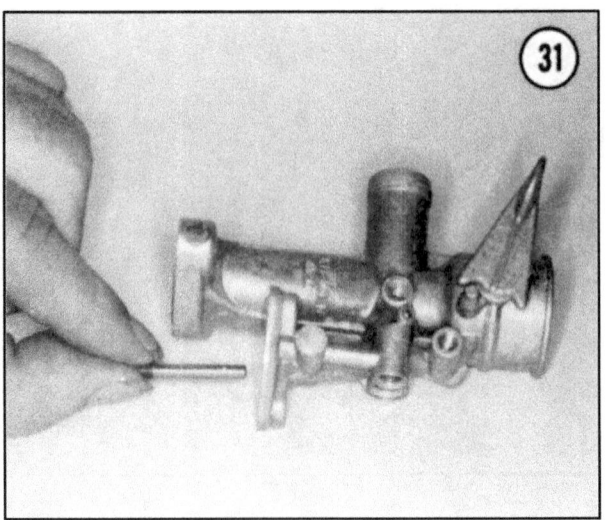

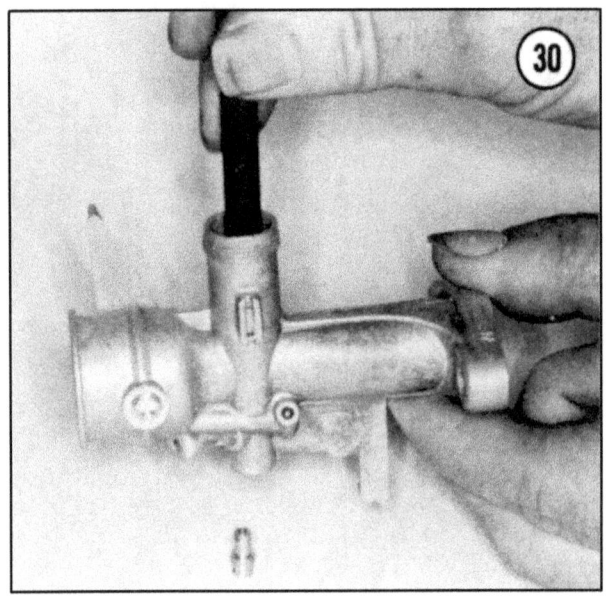

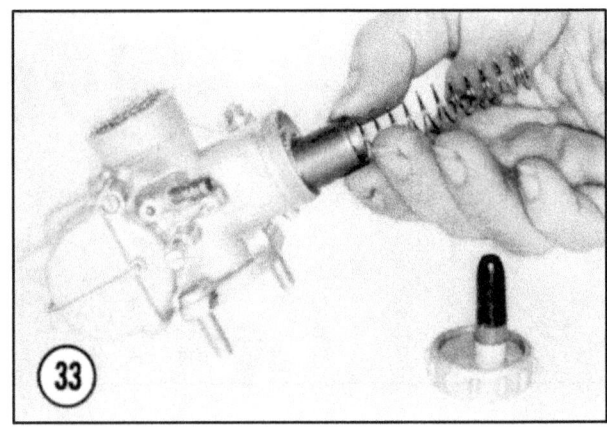

12. Separate needle jet from throttle slide.
13. Remove the O-ring from mounting flange.
14. Reverse Steps 2-14 to reassemble the carburetor.

Type 3 Disassembly/Assembly

Figure 32 is an exploded view of a carburetor typical of this type. Refer to that illustration during disassembly and assembly.

1. Remove both hoses.
2. Remove the mixing chamber top, then pull out the throttle slide valve and its return spring (**Figure 33**).
3. Remove the float bowl (**Figure 34**) after pushing its retaining bail toward the mounting flange.

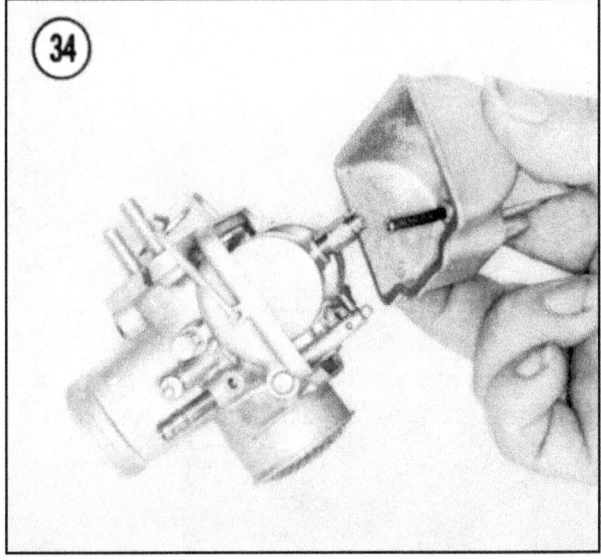

4. Gently remove the float assembly after first pulling out its pivot shaft (**Figure 35**).
5. Remove the float needle (**Figure 36**).
6. Remove the float needle valve seat and its sealing washer (**Figure 37**).

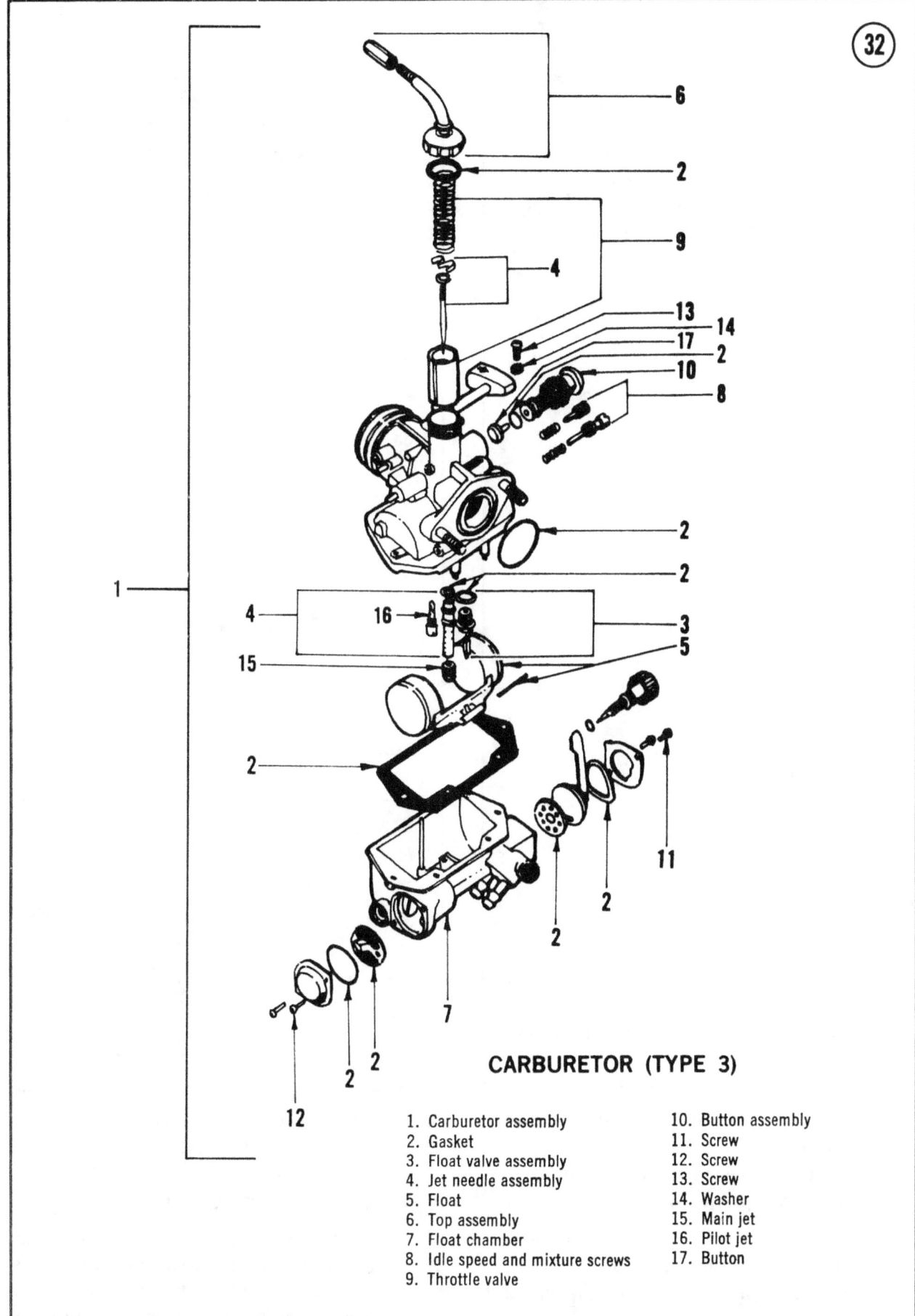

CARBURETOR (TYPE 3)

1. Carburetor assembly
2. Gasket
3. Float valve assembly
4. Jet needle assembly
5. Float
6. Top assembly
7. Float chamber
8. Idle speed and mixture screws
9. Throttle valve
10. Button assembly
11. Screw
12. Screw
13. Screw
14. Washer
15. Main jet
16. Pilot jet
17. Button

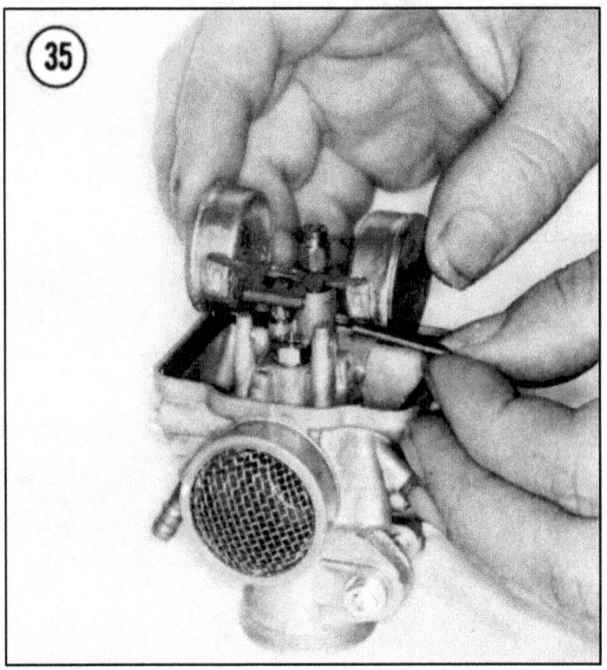

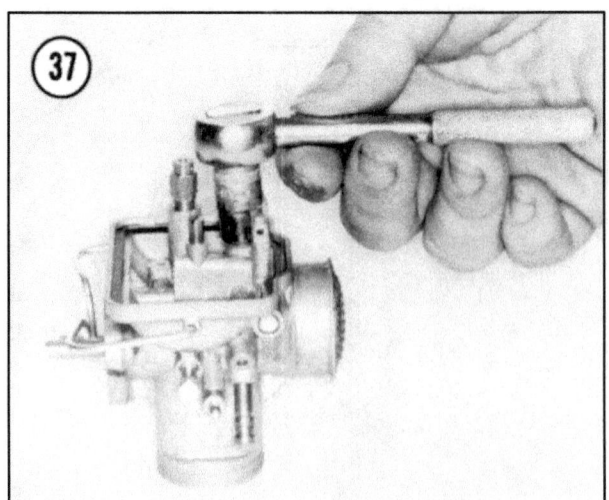

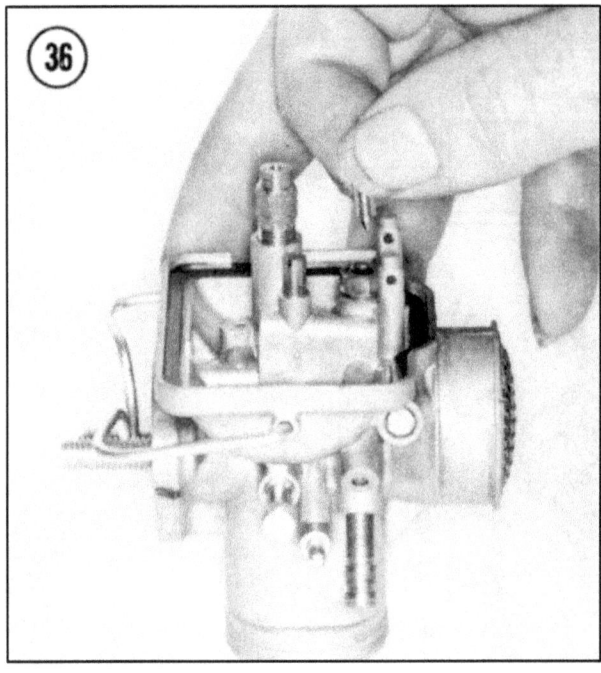

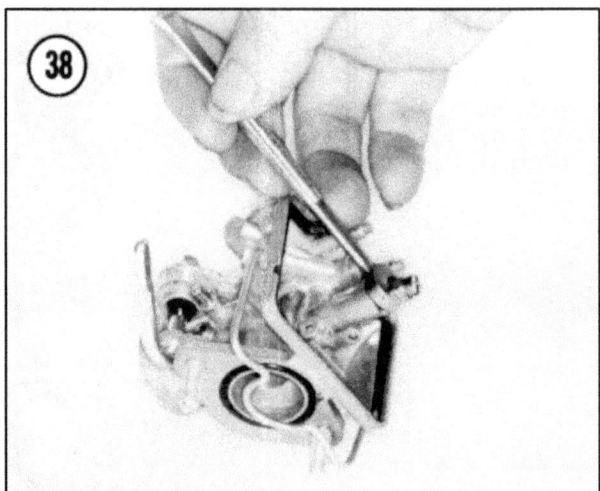

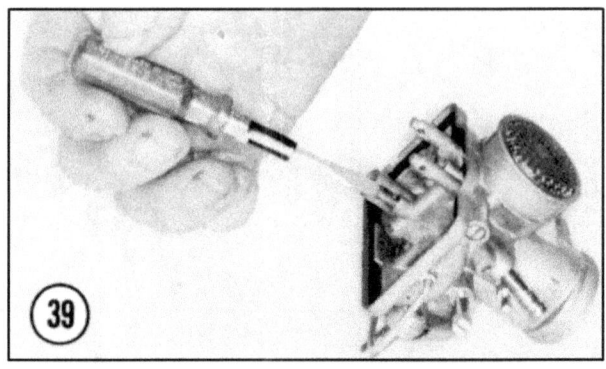

7. Remove the main jet and needle jet holder as a unit (**Figure 38**).

8. Remove the pilot jet (**Figure 39**).

9. Remove idle speed and idle mixture screws.

10. Disassemble the choke mechanism, if necessary, by removing its retaining nut.

11. Remove O-ring from mounting flange.

12. Separate main jet from needle jet holder.

13. Push the jet needle inward to remove it from the throttle slide. Do not lose its retaining clip.

14. Reverse Steps 1 through 13 to reassemble the carburetor. Be sure to check float level before returning the carburetor to service.

Adjustment (1963-1977 Models)

The carburetor was designed to provide the proper mixture under all operating conditions. Little or no benefit will result from experimenting. However, unusual operating conditions

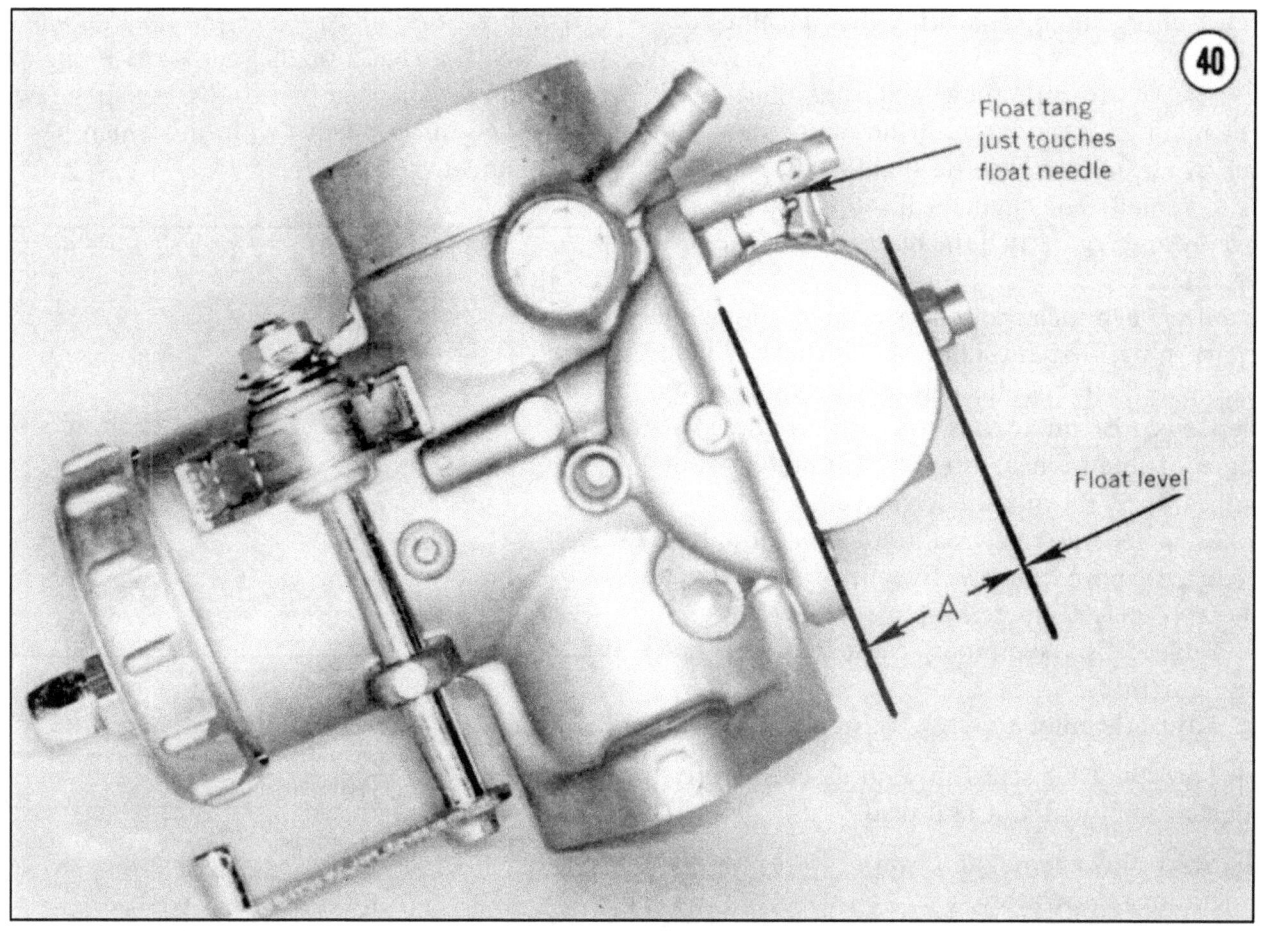

Table 2 FLOAT LEVEL

Model	Float Level Inches	(Millimeters)
Z50A	0.71	(18.0)
C50, C50M	0.61	(15.5)
S50	0.77	(19.5)
C65, C65M	0.69	(17.5)
S65	0.77	(19.5)
CL70, SL70	0.28	(7.0)
C70	0.53	(13.5)
C70M	0.61	(15.5)
CT70	0.78	(20.0)
S90	0.65	(16.5)
CL90, CL90L	0.77	(19.5)
C90, CD90	0.77	(19.5)
CT90 (early)	0.77	(19.5)
CT90 (from 000001A)	1.06	(27.0)
ST90	0.83	(21.0)

such as sustained operation at high altitudes or unusually high or low temperatures may make modifications to the standard specifications desirable. The adjustments described in the following paragraphs should only be undertaken if the rider has definite reason to believe they are required. Make the tests and adjustments in the order specified. Float level should be checked each time the carburetor is disassembled, and adjusted if necessary.

Float Level

To check carburetor float level, refer to **Figure 40**. Tilt the carburetor slowly, until the tang on the float just barely touches the float needle. Measure distance (A) between the bottom of the float and the bottom surface of the carburetor body. Distance (A) must be as specified in **Table 2**, and equal for both floats on carburetors with twin floats. Bend the tang on the float arm (**Figure 41**) as necessary if an adjustment is required.

Idle Mixture

Make a road test at full throttle for final determination of main jet size. To make such a test, operate the motorcycle at full throttle for at least two minutes, then shut the engine off, release the clutch, and bring the machine to a stop.

If at full throttle the engine runs "heavily," the main jet is too large. If the engine runs better by closing the throttle slightly, the main jet is too small. The engine will run at full throttle evenly and regularly if the main jet is of the correct size.

After each such test, remove and examine the spark plug. The insulator should have a light tan color. If the insulator has black sooty deposits, the mixture is too rich. If there are signs of intense heat, such as a blistered white appearance, the mixture is too lean.

As a general rule, main jet size should be reduced approximately five percent for each 3,000 feet (1,000 meters) above sea level.

Table 3 lists symptoms caused by rich and lean mixtures.

Adjust the pilot air screw as follows:

1. Turn pilot air screw in until it seats lightly, then back it out about 1½ turns.

2. Start the engine and warm it to normal operating temperature.

3. Turn the idle speed screw out until the engine runs slower and begins to falter.

4. Adjust the pilot air screw as required to make the engine run smoothly.

5. Repeat Steps 3 and 4 to achieve the lowest stable idle speed.

6. Determine the proper throttle valve cutaway size. With the engine running at idle, open the throttle. If the engine does not accelerate smoothly from idle, turn the pilot air screw in (clockwise) slightly to richen the mixture. If the condition still exists, return the air screw to its original position and replace the throttle valve with one which has a smaller cutaway. If engine operation is worsened by turning the air screw, replace the throttle valve with one which has a larger cutaway.

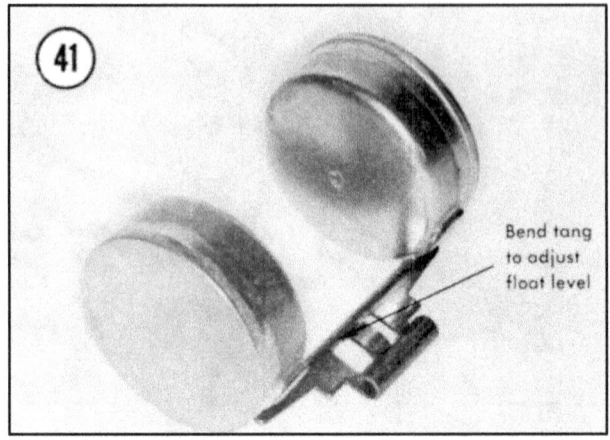

Bend tang to adjust float level

Table 3   IMPROPER FUEL/AIR MIXTURE

Condition	Symptom
Rich mixture	Rough idle Black exhaust smoke Hard starting, especially when hot Black deposits in exhaust pipe Gas-fouled spark plugs Poor gas mileage Engine performs worse as it warms up
Lean mixture	Backfiring Rough idle Overheating Hesitation upon acceleration Engine speed varies at fixed throttle Loss of power White color on spark plug insulators Poor acceleration

Table 4   ADJUSTMENT SUMMARY

Throttle Opening	Adjustment	If Too Rich	If Too Lean
0-⅛	Air screw	Turn out	Turn in
⅛-¼	Throttle valve cutaway	Use larger cutaway	Use smaller cutaway
¼-¾	Jet needle	Raise clip	Lower clip
¾-full	Main jet	Use smaller number	Use larger number

For operation at ¼ to ¾ throttle opening, adjustment is made with the jet needle. Operate the engine at half throttle in a manner similar to that for full throttle tests described earlier. To richen the mixture, place the jet needle clip in a lower groove. Conversely, placing the clip in a higher groove leans the mixture.

A summary of carburetor adjustments is given in **Table 4**.

KEIHIN CARBURETOR (1978 MODELS)

Disassembly/Assembly

Figure 42 shows an exploded view of a typical carburetor fitted to the 1978 (K9) models. Service procedures are identical on all 1978 models as only minor differences exist between carburetors.

1. Remove and plug both hoses (A, **Figure 43**). Unscrew the throttle valve assembly (B), then loosen and remove the air filter assembly (C).

2. Remove the 2 nuts securing the carburetor to the intake manifold (D, **Figure 43**) and remove the carburetor (**Figure 44**).

3. Remove the throttle valve assembly from the throttle cable by pushing the cable down and releasing it.

4. Remove the needle from the throttle valve by pushing the needle up and through the valve. See **Figure 45**.

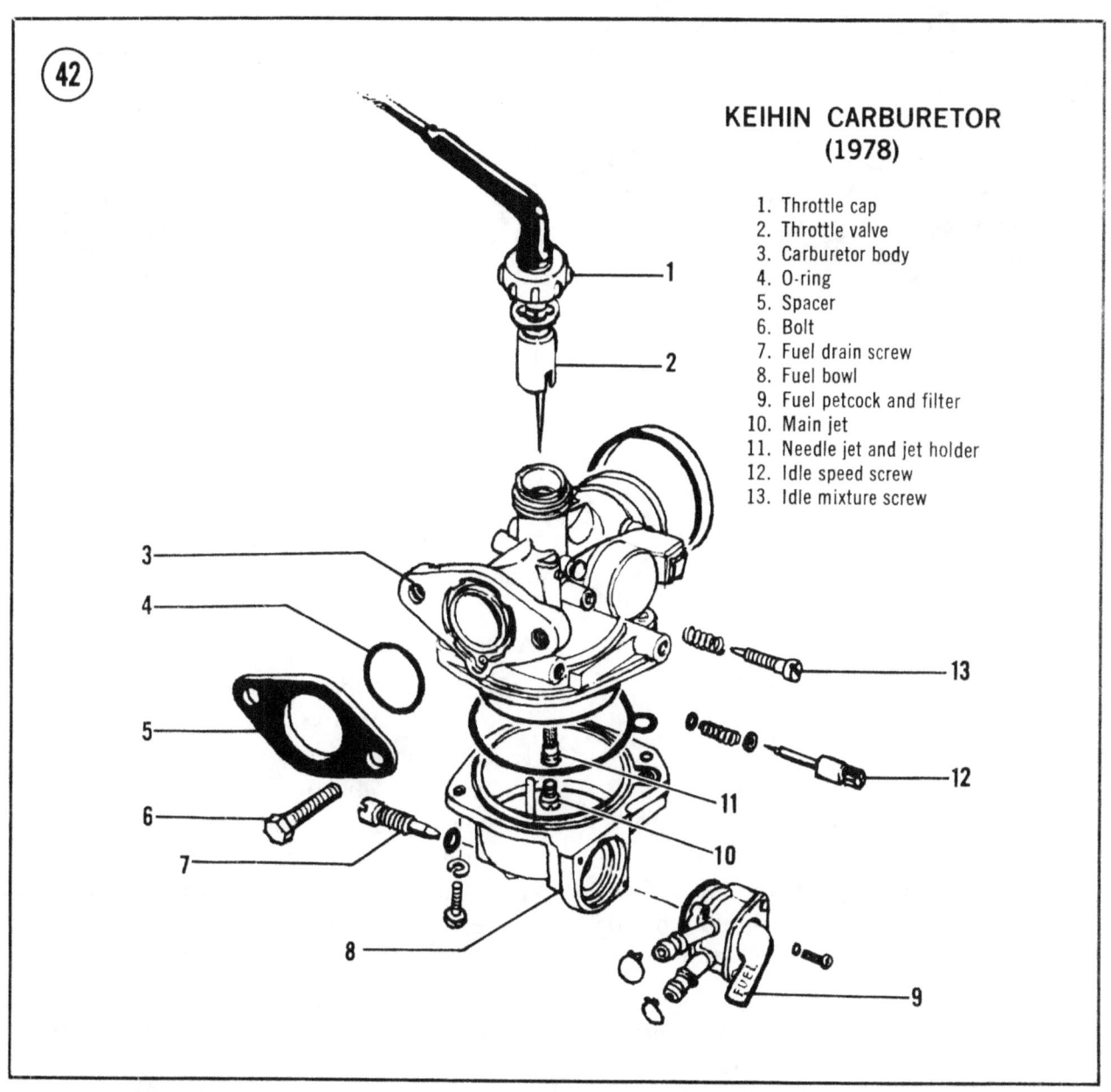

KEIHIN CARBURETOR (1978)

1. Throttle cap
2. Throttle valve
3. Carburetor body
4. O-ring
5. Spacer
6. Bolt
7. Fuel drain screw
8. Fuel bowl
9. Fuel petcock and filter
10. Main jet
11. Needle jet and jet holder
12. Idle speed screw
13. Idle mixture screw

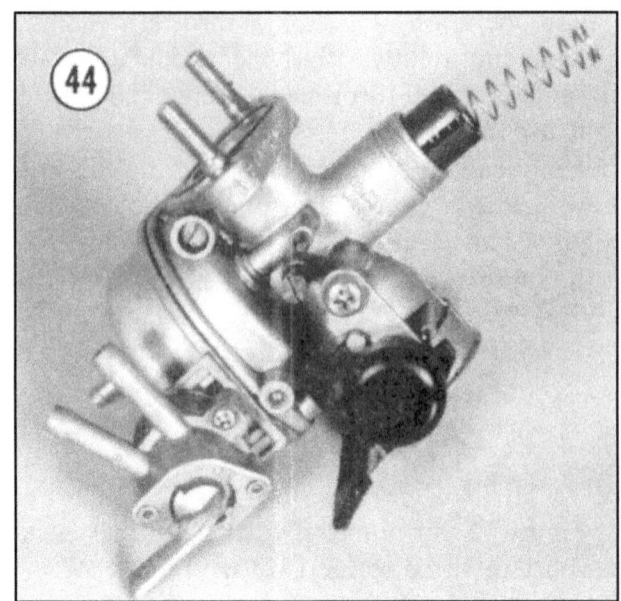

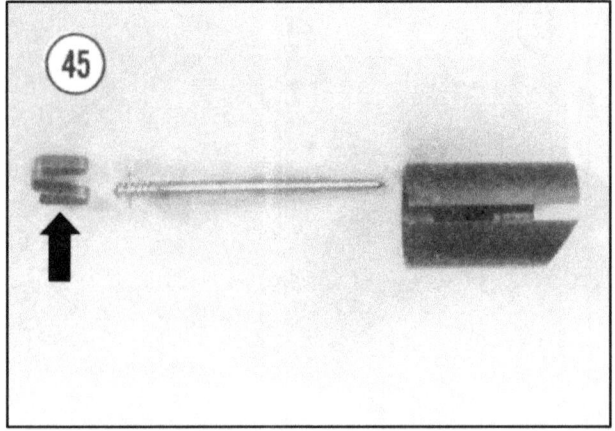

NOTE: *Do not lose the spring plate; this will come out with the needle (arrow, Figure 45). Make sure on assembly that this spring plate does not interfere with the throttle cable.*

5. Invert the carburetor and remove the 2 screws securing the float chamber (**Figure 46**), and remove the float chamber.

6. Remove the float pin (**Figure 47**), then carefully lift out the float (**Figure 48**).

NOTE: *The fuel valve is attached to the float, and will come off at the same time. Take care not to damage or lose the fuel valve.*

7. Remove the main jet (**Figure 49**) with a screwdriver.

8. Remove the needle jet (**Figure 50**).

9. Remove the 2 screws securing the petcock valve. Remove the valve, O-ring and fuel filter (**Figure 51**).

NOTE: *The choke assembly does not normally need to be removed.*

10. Remove both the idle screw (B, **Figure 52**) and air screw (A).

11. Assemble by reversing the removal procedure.

Adjustment

To adjust the carburetor, perform the following procedures.

1. Turn the air screw in until it seats, then screw it out 1¼ turns.

2. Start the engine and warm to the normal operating temperature.

3. Turn the idle screw out until the engine runs slower and begins to falter.

4. Adjust the air screw as required to make the engine run smoothly.

5. Adjust the idle screw to obtain the correct idle speed.

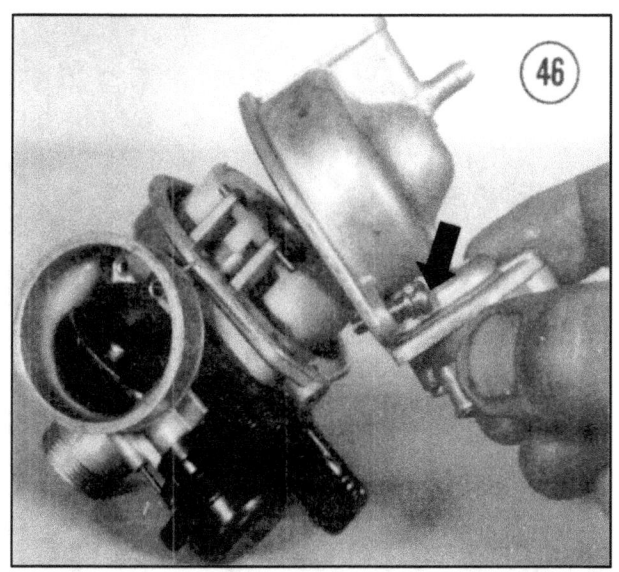
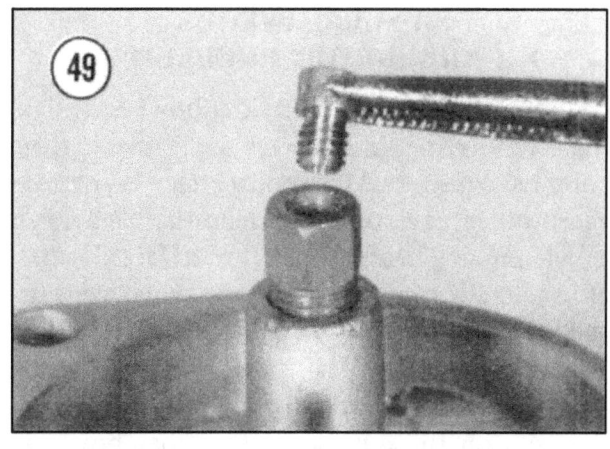
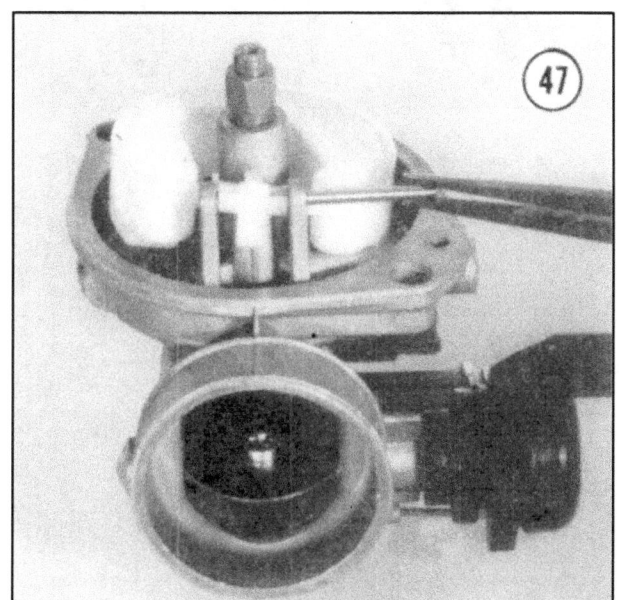
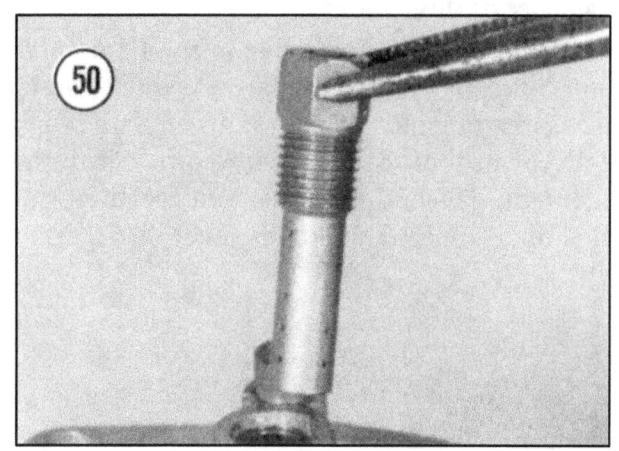
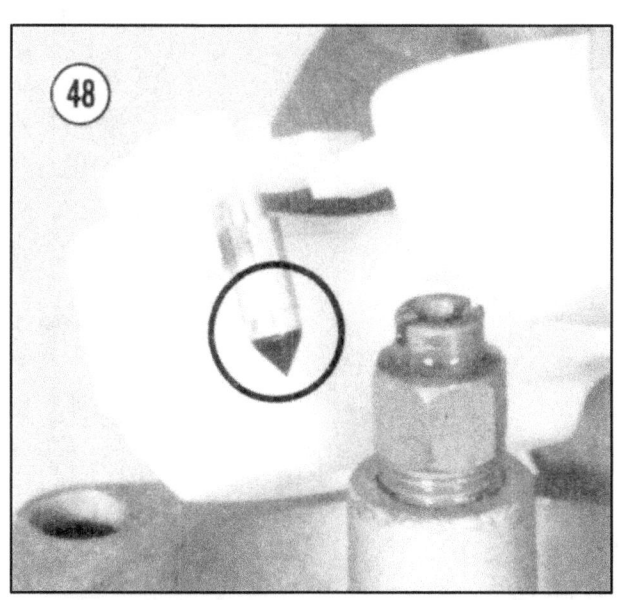
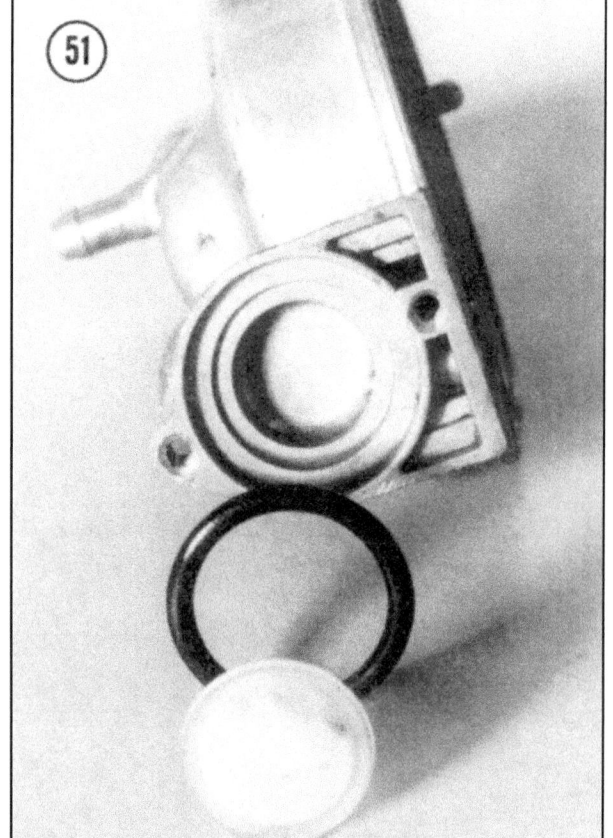

MISCELLANEOUS CARBURETOR PROBLEMS

Water in the carburetor float bowl and sticking carburetor slide valves can result from careless washing of the motorcycle. To remedy the problem, remove and clean the carburetor bowl, main jet, and any other affected parts. Be sure to cover the air intake when washing the machine.

If gasoline leaks past the float bowl gasket, high speed fuel starvation may occur. Varnish deposits on the outside of the float bowl are evidence of this condition.

Dirt in the fuel may lodge in the float valve and cause an overrich mixture. As a temporary measure, tap the carburetor lightly with any convenient tool to dislodge the dirt. Clean the fuel tank, petcock, fuel line, and carburetor at first opportunity, should this situation occur.

CHAPTER FIVE

ELECTRICAL SYSTEM

This chapter discusses operating principles and troubleshooting procedures for Honda ignition and electrical systems. Refer to Chapter Two for tune-up procedures.

BATTERY IGNITION

Honda models equipped with a battery and coil ignition system are similar in many ways to a conventional automobile.

Operation

Figure 1 illustrates a typical battery ignition system as used on a single cylinder motorcycle. Refer to that illustration during the following discussion.

When the breaker points are closed, current flows from the battery through the primary winding of the ignition coil, thereby building a magnetic field around the coil. The breaker cam rotates at ½ crankshaft speed and is so adjusted that the breaker points open as the piston reaches firing position.

As the points open, that magnetic field collapses. When the magnetic field collapses, a very high voltage is induced (up to about 15,000 volts) in the secondary winding of the ignition coil. This high voltage is sufficient to jump the gap at the spark plug.

The condenser assists the coil in developing high voltage, and also protects the points. Inductance of the ignition coil primary winding tends to keep a surge of current flowing through the circuit even after the points have started to open. The condenser stores this surge and thus prevents arcing at the points.

Troubleshooting

Ignition system problems can be classified as no spark, weak spark, or improperly timed spark. **Table 1** lists common causes and remedies for ignition system malfunctions.

Ignition failures are easy to isolate.

1. Rotate the engine until the points are closed.

2. Disconnect the high voltage lead from the spark plug and hold it ¼ in. away from the cylinder head. Turn on the ignition. With an insulated tool, such as a piece of wood, open the points. A fat, blue-white spark should jump fron the spark plug to the cylinder head. If the spark is good, clean or replace the spark plug. If there is no spark, or if it is thin, yellowish, or weak, continue with Step 3.

3. Connect the leads of a voltmeter to the wire on the points and to a good ground. Turn on the ignition switch. If the meter indicates more than ⅛ volt, the problem is defective points. Replace them.

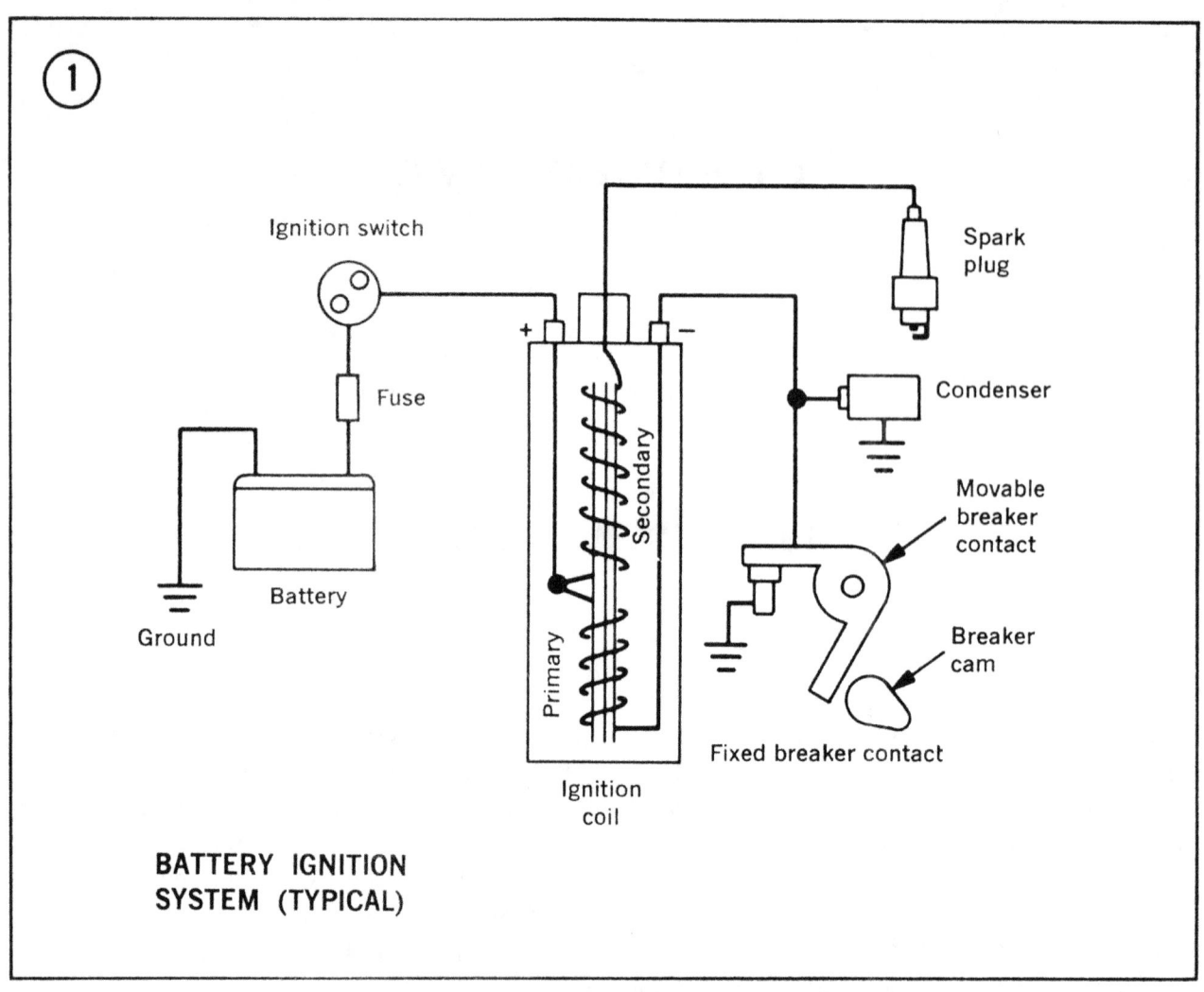

Table 1   IGNITION TROUBLESHOOTING

Symptom	Probable Cause	Remedy
No spark or weak spark	Discharged battery	Charge battery
	Defective fuse	Replace
	Defective main switch	Replace
	Loose or corroded connections	Clean and tighten
	Broken wire	Repair
	Incorrect point gap	Reset points. Be sure to readjust ignition timing
	Dirty or oily points	Clean points
	Spark plug lead damaged	Replace wire
	Broken primary wire	Repair wire
	Open winding in coil	Replace coil
	Shorted winding in coil	Replace coil
	Defective condenser	Replace condenser
Misfires	Dirty spark plug	Clean or replace plug
	Spark plug is too hot	Replace with colder plug
	Spark plug is too cold	Replace with hotter plug
	Spring on ignition points is weak	Replace points, reset timing
	Incorrect timing	Adjust timing

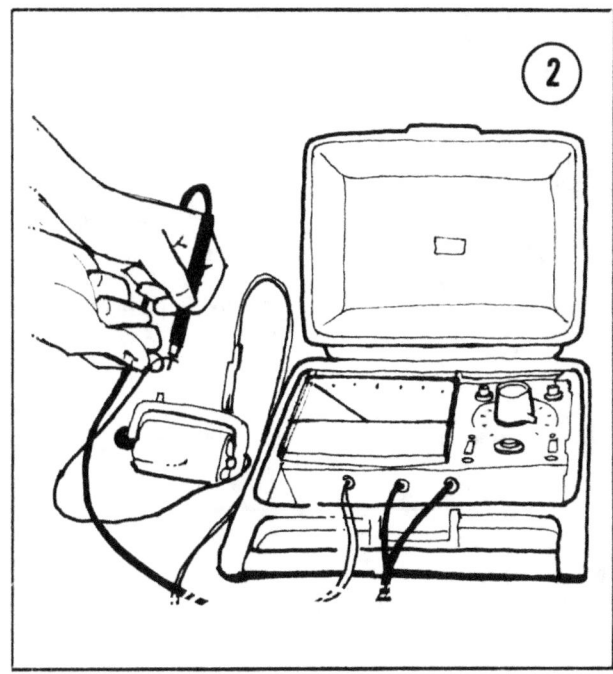

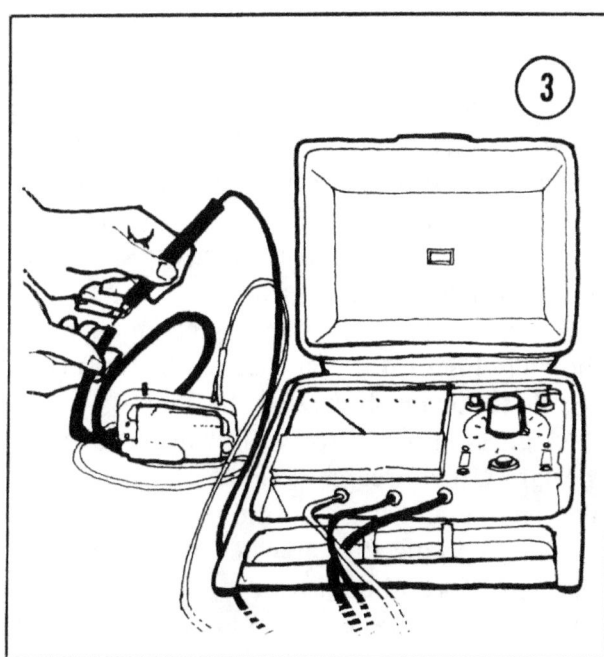

4. Open points with an insulated tool, such as a piece of wood. The voltmeter should indicate battery voltage. If not, there are 3 possibilities:

 a. Shorted points
 b. Shorted condenser
 c. Open coil primary circuit

5. Disconnect the condenser and the wire from the points. Connect the ungrounded voltmeter lead to the wire which was connected to the points. If the voltmeter does not indicate battery voltage, the problem is an open coil primary circuit. Replace the suspected coil with a known good one. If that coil does not work, the problem is in the primary wiring.

6. If the voltmeter indicates battery voltage in Step 5, the coil primary circuit is OK. Connect the positive voltmeter lead to the wire which goes from the coil to the points. Block the points open with a business card or similar piece of cardboard. Connect the negative voltmeter lead to the movable point. If the voltmeter indicates any voltage, the points are shorted. Replace them.

7. If the foregoing checks are satisfactory, the problem is in the coil or condenser. Substitute each of these separately with known good ones to determine which is defective.

Ignition Coil

The ignition coil is a form of transformer which develops the high voltage required to jump the spark plug gap. The only maintenance required is that of keeping the electrical connections clean and tight, and occasionally checking to see that the coil is mounted securely.

If coil condition is doubtful, there are several checks which may be made.

1. Measure coil primary resistance, using an ohmmeter, between both coil primary terminals (**Figure 2**). Resistance should measure approximately 5 ohms. Some coils, however, have a primary resistance of less than one ohm. Compare the measurement obtained with that of a known good coil.

2. Measure resistance between either primary terminal and the high voltage terminal (**Figure 3**). Resistance should be in range of 5,000 to 15,000 ohms.

3. If the coil has a metal housing, scrape the paint from the coil housing down to bare metal. Set the ohmmeter to its highest range, then measure insulation resistance between this bare spot and the high voltage terminal (**Figure 4**). Insulation resistance must be at least 3 megohms (3 million ohms).

4. If these checks do not reveal any defects, but coil condition is still doubtful, substitute a known good one.

Be sure to connect all wires to their proper terminals when replacing the coil.

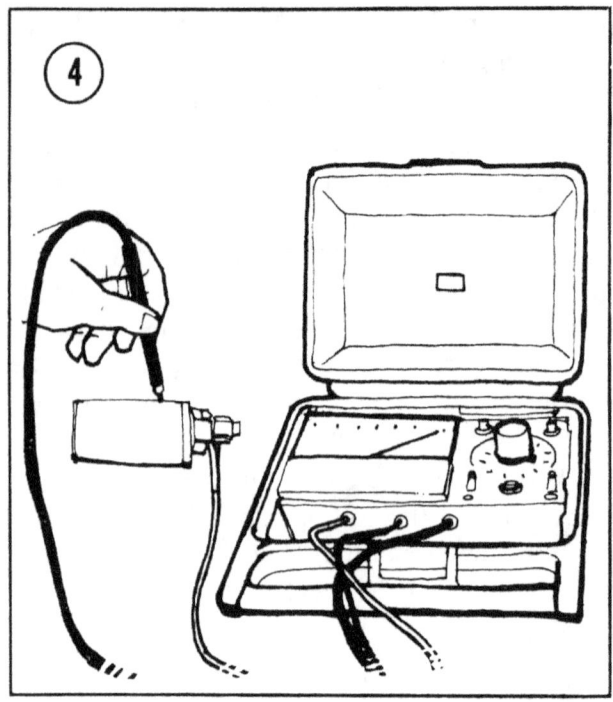

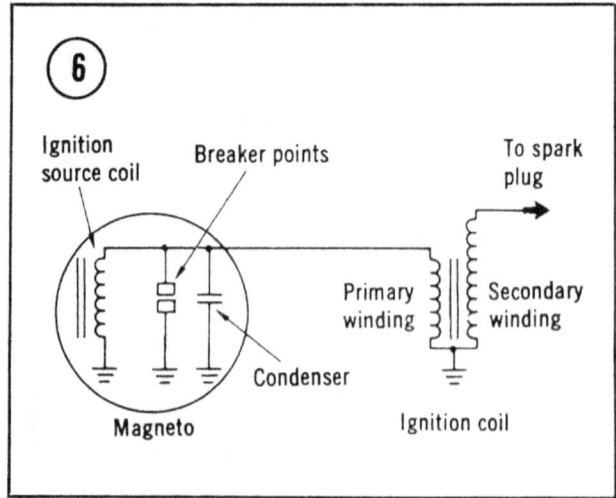

Condenser

The condenser is a sealed unit that requires no maintenance. Be sure that both connections are clean and tight.

Two tests can be made on the condenser. Measure condenser capacity with a condenser tester. Capacity should be 0.23 to 0.26 microfarad. The other test is insulation resistance, which should not be less than 5 megohms, measured between the condenser pigtail and case.

In the event that no test equipment is available, a quick test of the condenser may be made by connecting the condenser case to the negative terminal of a 6-volt battery, and the positive lead to the positive battery terminal. Allow the condenser to charge for a few seconds, then quickly disconnect the battery and touch the condenser pigtail to the condenser case. If you observe a spark as the pigtail touches the case, you may assume that the condenser is OK.

Arcing between the breaker points is a common symptom of condenser failure.

Service

Two major service items are required on battery ignition models: breaker point service and ignition timing. Both are vitally important to proper engine operation and reliability.

Refer to Chapter Two for breaker point service and ignition timing procedures.

MAGNETO IGNITION OPERATION

Most models smaller than 90cc are equipped with flywheel magnetos to furnish ignition power. Magnetos are simple, rugged devices which require little service. On many models, the magneto also furnishes power for lights and battery charging. **Figure 5** is an exploded view of a typical flywheel magneto.

A circuit diagram of a typical magneto is shown in **Figure 6**. Refer to this illustration during the following discussion.

Magnets attached to the flywheel move past the ignition source coil as the flywheel turns. The source coil is so positioned that a strong current is induced in it when the crankshaft, and therefore the piston, approaches firing position. The breaker points are closed, causing current in the ignition source coil to be shorted to ground.

When the piston reaches firing position, the breaker cam, attached to the crankshaft, opens the breaker points. Current in the ignition source coil is then no longer grounded, and must flow into the primary winding of the ignition coil. The ignition coil is a form of transformer, which steps up voltage of ignition source coil to a very high value, sufficient to fire the spark plug.

The condenser assists in generating the required high voltage, and also serves to protect the ignition points from burning and pitting.

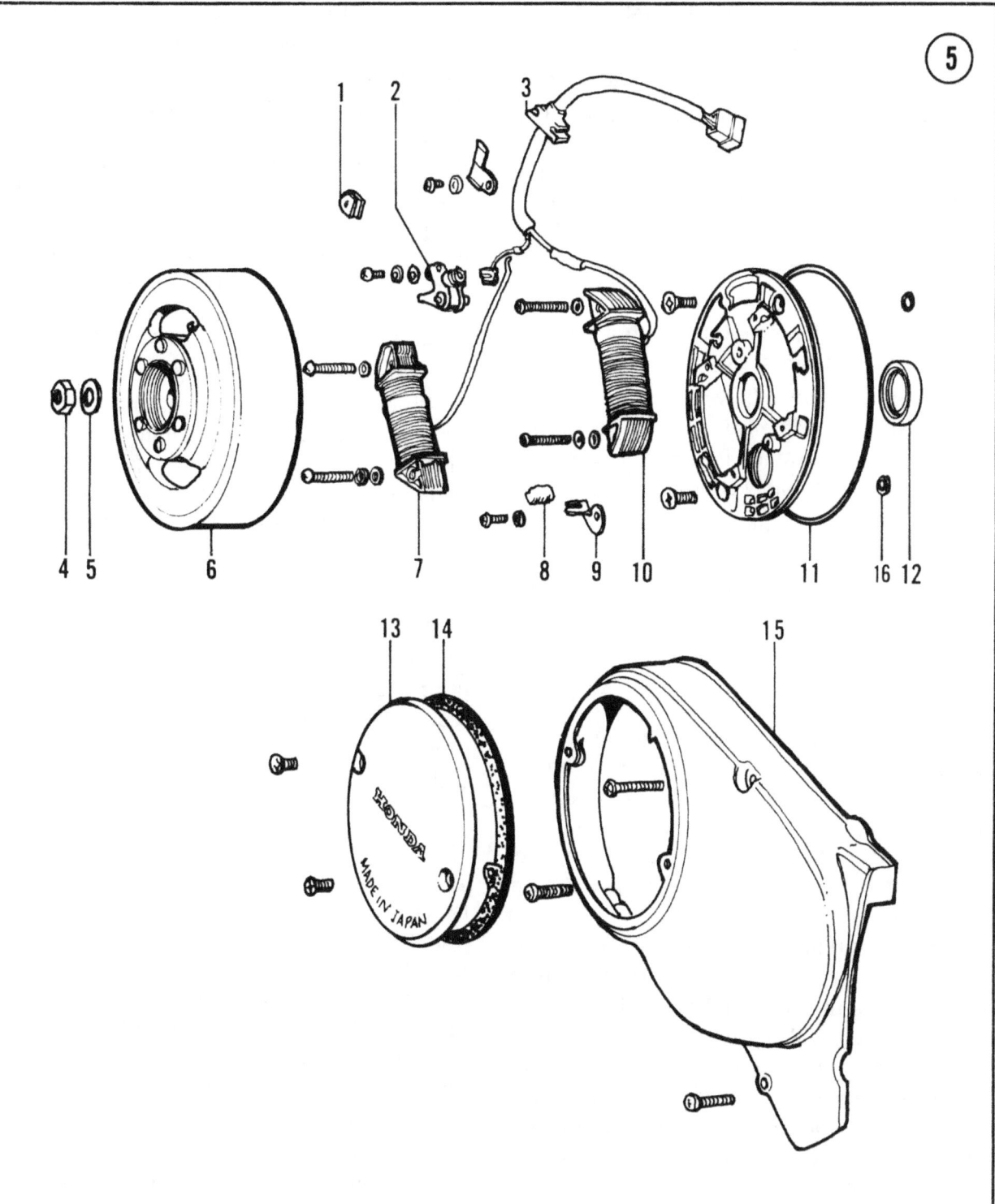

FLYWHEEL MAGNETO

1. Grommet
2. Breaker assembly
3. Grommet
4. Nut
5. Washer
6. Flywheel
7. Ignition primary coil
8. Cam lubricator
9. Lubricator holder
10. Lighting coil
11. O-ring
12. Oil seal
13. Cover
14. Gasket
15. Cover
16. O-ring

MAGNETO IGNITION TROUBLESHOOTING

A magneto is a simple, rugged device which rarely gives trouble. In the event that an ignition, lighting, or charging malfunction is believed to be caused by a defective magneto, the following checks should isolate the trouble.

Ignition Source Coil

1. With the magneto wiring disconnected, block the breaker points open with a piece of paper such as a business card.
2. Measure resistance between ignition source coil output wire and ground with a low-range ohmmeter. If resistance is approximately 0.5 ohm, the coil is probably good.
3. If possible, disconnect the ground wire between the ignition coil and the magneto base. Measure insulation resistance between the iron core and the coil. Insulation resistance should be at least 5 megohms.

Condenser

Measure condenser capacity, using a condenser tester. The value should be in the range of 0.18 to 0.25 microfarad. With the condenser ground wire disconnected, measure insulation resistance between the outer case and the positive terminal. Insulation resistance should be over 5 megohms.

In the event that test equipment is not available, a quick test of the condenser may be made by connecting the negative lead to the negative terminal of a 6-volt battery, and the positive lead to the positive terminal. Allow the condenser to charge for a few seconds, then quickly disconnect the battery and touch the condenser leads together. If you observe a spark as the leads touch, the condenser is good.

Arcing between the breaker points is a common symptom of a defective condenser.

Breaker Points

Check that the insulation between the breaker contacts and the contact breaker base is not defective. A short circuit will prevent the machine from running. To test for this condition, disconnect the wiring at the points, and with the points still blocked open, measure insulation resistance between the movable point and a good ground, using the highest range on an ohmmeter. If there is any indication at all on the ohmmeter, the points are shorted.

Contact surfaces may become pitted or worn from normal use. If they are not too damaged, they can be dressed with a few strokes of a clean point file. Do not use sandpaper, as particles may remain on the points and cause arcing and burning. If a few strokes of the file do not smooth the points completely, replace them.

Oil or dirt may get on the points, resulting in premature failure. Common causes for this condition are defective crankshaft seals, improper lubrication of the rubbing block, or lack of care when crankcase cover is removed and replaced.

If point spring is weak or broken, points will bounce, causing misfiring at high speeds.

Ignition Coil

The ignition coil is a form of transformer which develops the high voltage required to jump the spark plug gap. The only maintenance required is that of keeping the electrical connections clean and tight, and making sure that the coil is mounted securely.

If the condition of the coil is doubtful, there are several checks which should be made.

1. Measure resistance with an ohmmeter between the positive and negative primary terminals. Resistance should indicate approximately 5 ohms for most coils on these machines. Some coils, however, have a primary resistance less than one ohm. Some coils have only one primary terminal. In this case, measure between that terminal and ground to measure primary resistance.
2. Measure resistance between either primary terminal and the secondary high voltage terminal. Resistance should be in the range of 5,000 to 15,000 ohms.
3. On coils with 2 primary terminals and metal housings, scrape the paint from the coil housing down to bare metal. Measure resistance between this bare spot and the high voltage terminal. Insulation resistance must be at least 3 megohms (3 million ohms). This test is not possible on coils with only one primary terminal.

4. If these checks do not reveal any defects, but coil condition is still doubtful, replace the coil with a known good one.

Be sure to connect primary wires correctly.

Some coils have permanently attached high voltage leads. If so, it is worth a try to cut off ¼ in. from the end of the lead, then reattach the spark plug connector. It sometimes happens that a poor connection at this point exhibits symptoms of a defective coil.

CHARGING SYSTEM (MAGNETO IGNITION)

Additional coils within the flywheel magneto generate alternating current, which is then rectified and used for battery charging. Before checking for possible charging system malfunctions, be sure that the battery is in good condition and is at least half charged. To check the charging coil in the magneto, proceed as follows.

1. Disconnect the wire which runs from the magneto to the rectifier. This wire is green on most models. If there is any doubt, disconnect the wire at the *magneto* side of the rectifier. Connect a small 6-volt lamp between the wire from the magneto and a good ground.

2. Crank the engine briskly with the kickstarter. The bulb should light briefly each time the engine turns over. If not, replace the charging/lighting coil in the magneto.

If the magneto proves to be OK, check the rectifier. To do so, proceed as follows.

1. Disconnect the 2 wires to the rectifier.

2. Using an ohmmeter, check for continuity through the rectifier, then reverse the ohmmeter leads, and check again. The ohmmeter should indicate very high resistance in one direction and very low resistance in the other. If resistance was very high or very low in both directions, replace the rectifier.

CHARGING SYSTEM (BATTERY IGNITION)

Charging systems on these models consist of an alternator (**Figure 7**), full-wave bridge rectifier, battery, and interconnecting wiring. If charging system problems are suspected, first check the alternator, then the rectifier.

To test the alternator, proceed as follows.

1. At the battery, disconnect the red/white charging wire coming from the alternator. Connect a short length of wire to the charging wire.

2. With the engine running at about 2,000 rpm, quickly brush free end of test wire against a good ground. There should be a small spark.

3. Turn on lights. Again brush test wire against a good ground. There should be a larger spark.

If there was no spark in either Steps 2 or 3, connect a 6-volt test lamp to the pink and yellow wires coming from the alternator. Crank the engine briskly. The lamp should light briefly each time the engine turns over. Then connect the lamp between the pink and white wires, and again crank the engine. The bulb should light again. If the bulb does not light in each test, replace the alternator stator assembly.

With the alternator disconnected, measure resistance between the pink and yellow wires coming from the alternator. Resistance should be approximately 1.1 ohms. Then measure resistance between the pink and white wires. Resistance should be approximately 0.5 ohm. Finally, be sure that there is no continuity between ground and pink, yellow, or white wires.

To test the rectifier, measure continuity, using an ohmmeter, between each pair of wires listed. Then repeat each measurement with the ohmmeter leads reversed.

a. Green and pink
b. Pink and red/white
c. Green and yellow
d. Red/white and yellow

For each pair of measurements, the ohmmeter should indicate continuity in one direction and no continuity in the other. Replace rectifier if any pair of measurements showed continuity in both directions, or no continuity in both directions.

ELECTRIC STARTER

Some models are equipped with electric starters. Service procedures for all starters are similar.

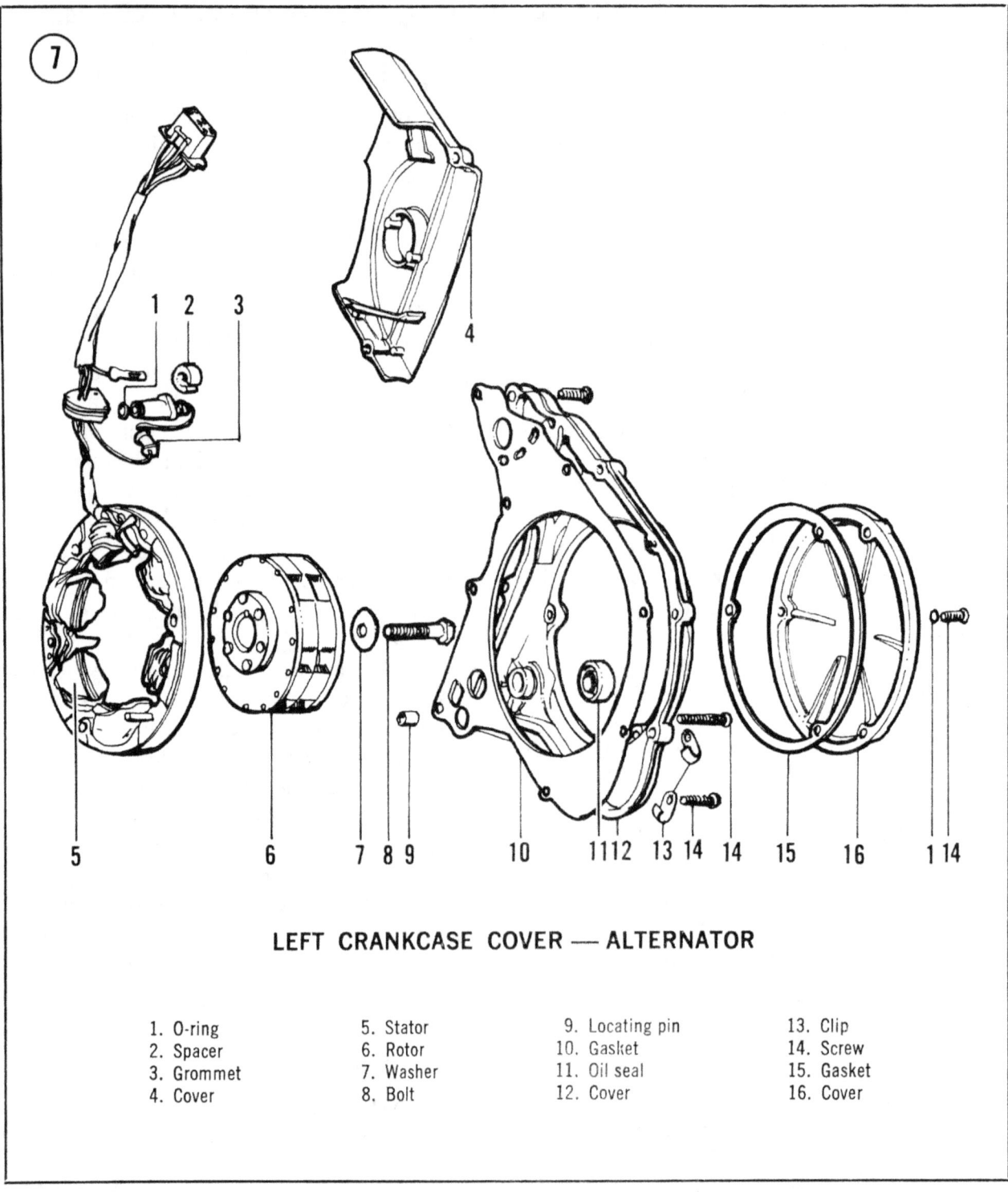

LEFT CRANKCASE COVER — ALTERNATOR

1. O-ring
2. Spacer
3. Grommet
4. Cover
5. Stator
6. Rotor
7. Washer
8. Bolt
9. Locating pin
10. Gasket
11. Oil seal
12. Cover
13. Clip
14. Screw
15. Gasket
16. Cover

Operation

Figure 8 illustrates a typical starter circuit. When the rider presses the starter button, current flows from the battery through the starter relay coil.

Troubleshooting

Table 2 lists symptoms, probable causes, and remedies for starter malfunctions.

Overhaul

Figure 9 is an exploded view of a typical starter motor. Refer to that illustration during disassembly.

1. Examine commutator for rough, burned, or scored segments, and for possible signs of overheating or thrown solder.

2. Mount the armature in a lathe, V-blocks, or other suitable centering device and measure the

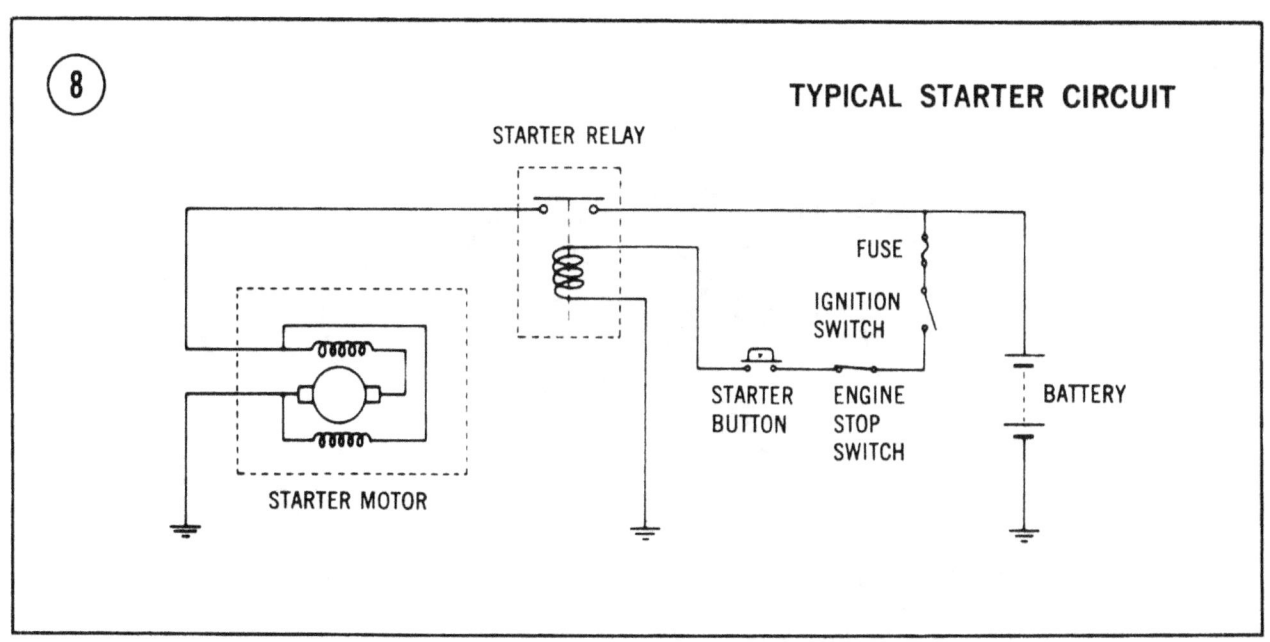

Table 2 STARTER TROUBLESHOOTING

Symptom	Probable Cause	Remedy
Starter does not work	Low battery	Recharge battery
	Worn brushes	Replace brushes
	Internal short	Repair or replace defective component
	Relay inoperative	Replace relay
	Defective wiring or connections	Repair wire or clean and tighten connections
	Defective switch	Replace switch
Starter action is weak	Low battery	Recharge battery
	Pitted relay contacts	Clean contacts or replace relay
	Brushes worn	Replace brushes
	Defective wiring or connections	Repair wire or clean and tighten connections
	Short in commutator	Replace armature
Starter runs continuously	Stuck relay	Dress contacts or replace relay

commutator for runout. If runout exceeds 0.012 in. (0.3mm), turn it down. This is a job best left to a small-motor specialist.

3. After turning, undercut the mica insulators between commutator segments to 0.020-0.030 in. (0.5-0.8mm). If commutator turning was not required, be sure that the mica insulators are undercut at least 0.012 in. (0.3mm), as shown in **Figure 10**. A broken hacksaw blade is a suitable tool for undercutting mica. Be sure to clean each slot thoroughly.

4. Using an ohmmeter or armature growler, test each commutator segment to be sure that it is not shorted to ground. Replace the armature if any short exists. Do not connect either test prod to the bearing surfaces of the shaft.

5. Using an armature growler, test for armature coil shorts. Follow the manufacturer's instructions on the test equipment.

6. Using an ohmmeter or armature tester, check for open windings in the armature.

7. With the starter disassembled, be sure that

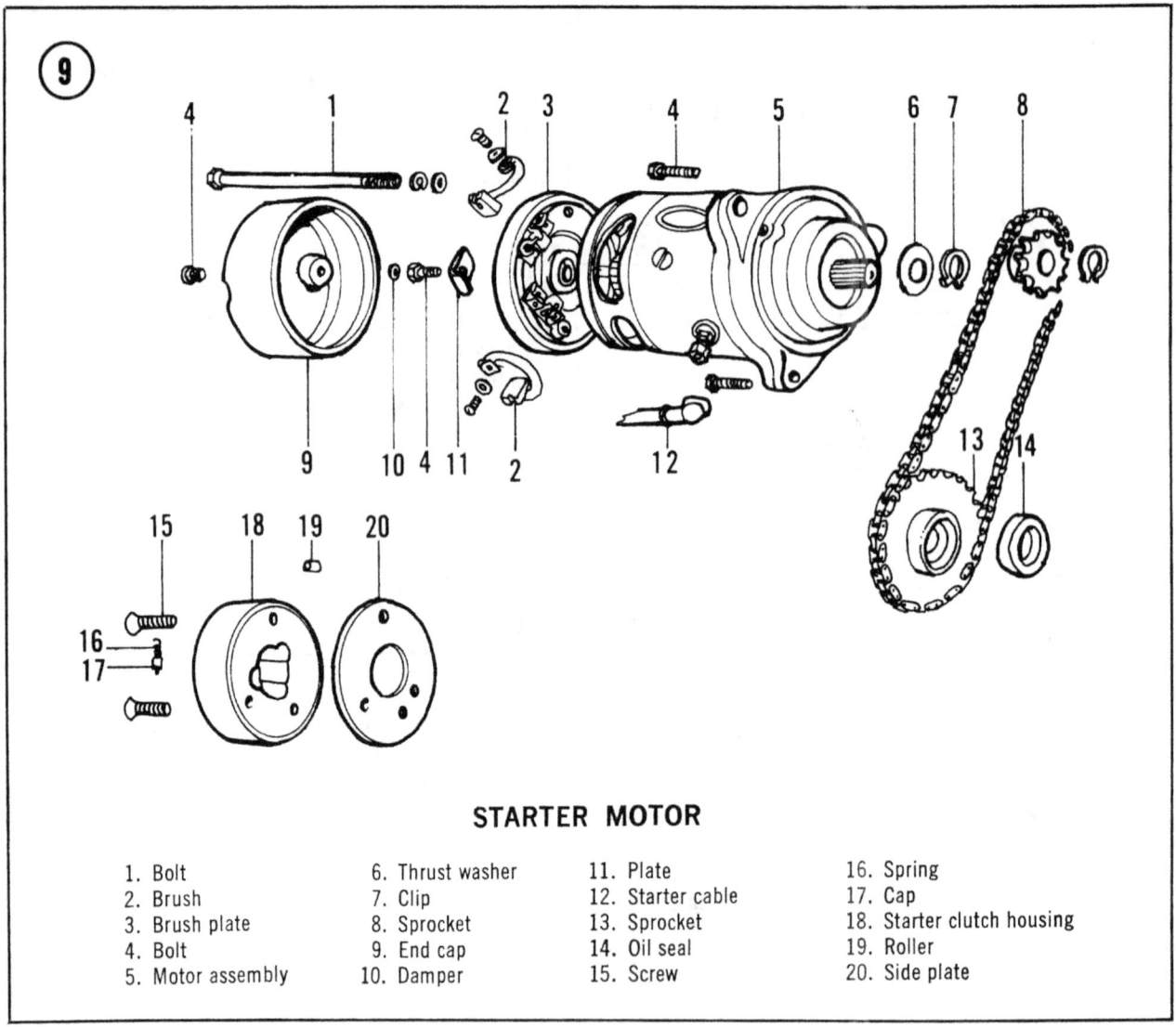

STARTER MOTOR

1. Bolt
2. Brush
3. Brush plate
4. Bolt
5. Motor assembly
6. Thrust washer
7. Clip
8. Sprocket
9. End cap
10. Damper
11. Plate
12. Starter cable
13. Sprocket
14. Oil seal
15. Screw
16. Spring
17. Cap
18. Starter clutch housing
19. Roller
20. Side plate

continuity exists between the cable thermal and the ungrounded brush holder.

8. With the starter disassembled, be sure that there is no continuity between the ungrounded brush holder and the starter housing.

9. Upon reassembly, observe the following notes:

   a. Apply a small amount of multipurpose grease to both armature bushings.
   b. Install armature brushes into the brush holders after the armature is installed.
   c. Be sure that all shims and thrust washers are positioned correctly.
   d. Be sure that the shaft turns freely.

BATTERY

Most Honda motorcycles are equipped with lead-acid storage batteries, smaller in size but similar in construction to batteries used in automobiles.

WARNING
Read and thoroughly understand the Safety Precautions section before doing any battery service.

Safety Precautions

When working with batteries, use extreme care to avoid spilling or splashing electrolyte. This electrolyte is sulfuric acid, which can destroy clothing and cause serious chemical burns. If any electrolyte is spilled or splashed on clothing or body, it should immediately be neutralized with a solution of baking soda and water, then flushed with plenty of clean water.

Electrolyte splashed into the eyes is extremely dangerous. Safety glasses should always be worn when working with batteries. If elec-

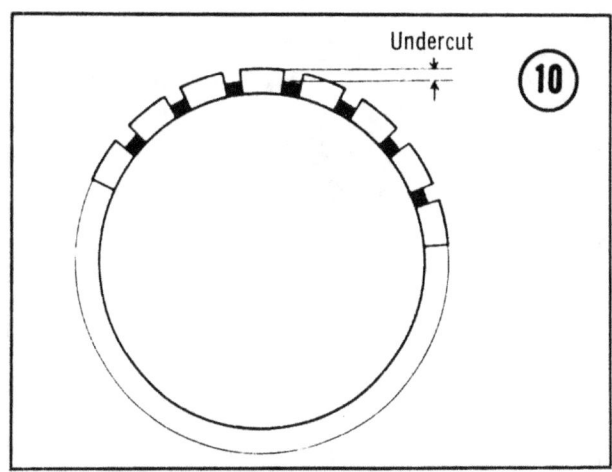

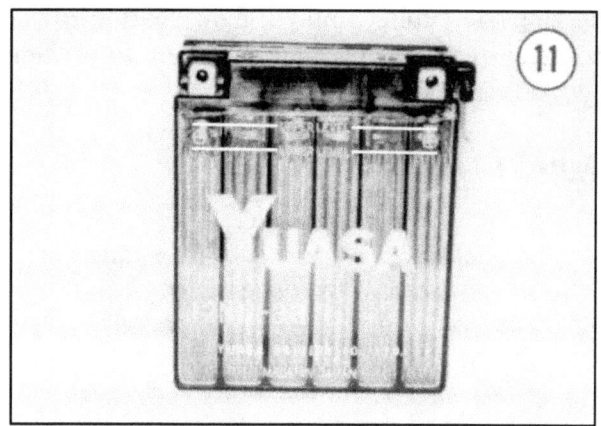

trolyte is splashed into the eye, force the eye open, flood with cool clean water for about 5 minutes, and *call a physician immediately*.

If electrolyte is spilled or splashed onto painted or unpainted surfaces, it should be neutralized immediately with baking soda solution and then rinsed with clean water.

When batteries are being charged, highly explosive hydrogen gas forms in each cell. Some of this gas escapes through the filler openings and may form an explosive atmosphere around the battery. *This explosive atmosphere may exist for several hours.* Sparks, open flame, or a lighted cigarette can ignite this gas, causing an internal explosion and possible serious personal injury. The following precautions should be taken to prevent an explosion.

1. Do not smoke or permit any open flame near any battery being charged or which has been recently charged.

2. Do not disconnect live circuits at battery terminals, because a spark usually occurs where a live circuit is broken. Care must always be taken when connecting or disconnecting any battery charger; be sure its power switch is off before making or breaking connections. Poor connections are a common cause of electrical arcs which cause explosions.

Electrolyte Level

Battery electrolyte level shoul be checked regularly, particularly during hot weather. Most batteries are marked with electrolyte level limit lines (**Figure 11**). Always maintain the fluid level between the 2 lines, using distilled water as required for replenishment. Distilled water is available at almost every supermarket. It is sold for use in steam irons and is quite inexpensive.

Overfilling leads to loss of electrolyte, resulting in poor battery performance, short life, and excessive corrosion. Never allow the electrolyte level to drop below the top of the plates. That portion of the plates exposed to air may be permanently damaged, resulting in loss of battery performance and shortened life.

Excessive use of water is an indication that battery is being overcharged. The 2 most common causes of overcharging are high battery temperature or high voltage regulator setting.

Cleaning

Check the battery occasionally for presence of dirt or corrosion. The top of the battery, in particular, should be kept clean. Acid film and dirt permit current to flow between terminals, which will slowly discharge the battery.

For best results when cleaning, wash first with diluted ammonia or baking soda solution, then flush with plenty of clean water. Take care to keep filler plugs tight so that no cleaning solution enters the cells.

Battery Cables

To ensure good electrical contact, cables must be clean and tight on battery terminals. If the battery or cable terminals are corroded, the cables should be disconnected and cleaned separately with a wire brush and baking soda solution. After cleaning, apply a very thin coating of petroleum jelly to the battery terminals before installing the cables. After connecting the cables, apply a light coating to the connection. This procedure will help to prevent future corrosion.

Battery Charging

> WARNING
> *Do not smoke or permit any open flame in any area where batteries are being charged, or immediately after charging. Highly explosive hydrogen gas is formed during the charging process. Be sure to re-read **Safety Precautions** in the beginning of this section.*

Motorcycle batteries are not designed for high charge or discharge rates. For this reason, it is recommended that a motorcycle battery be charged at a rate not exceeding 10 percent of its ampere-hour capacity. That is, do not exceed 0.5 ampere charging rate for a 5 ampere-hour battery, or 1.5 amperes for a 15 ampere-hour battery. This charge rate should continue for 10 hours if the battery is completely discharged, or until specific gravity of each cell is up to 1.260-1.280, corrected for temperature. If after prolonged charging, specific gravity of one or more cells does not come up to at least 1.230, the battery will not perform as well as it should, but it may continue to provide satisfactory service for a time.

Some temperature rise is normal as a battery is being charged. Do not allow the electrolyte temperature to exceed 110°F. Should temperature reach that figure, discontinue charging until the battery cools, then resume charging at a lower rate.

Testing

Although sophisticated battery testing devices are on the market, they are not available to the average motorcycle owner, and their use is beyond the scope of this book. A hydrometer, however, is an inexpensive tool, and will tell much about battery condition.

To use a hydrometer, place the suction tube into the filler opening and draw in just enough electrolyte to lift the float **(Figure 12)**. Hold the instrument in a vertical position and read specific gravity on the scale, where the float stem emerges from the electrolyte **(Figure 13)**.

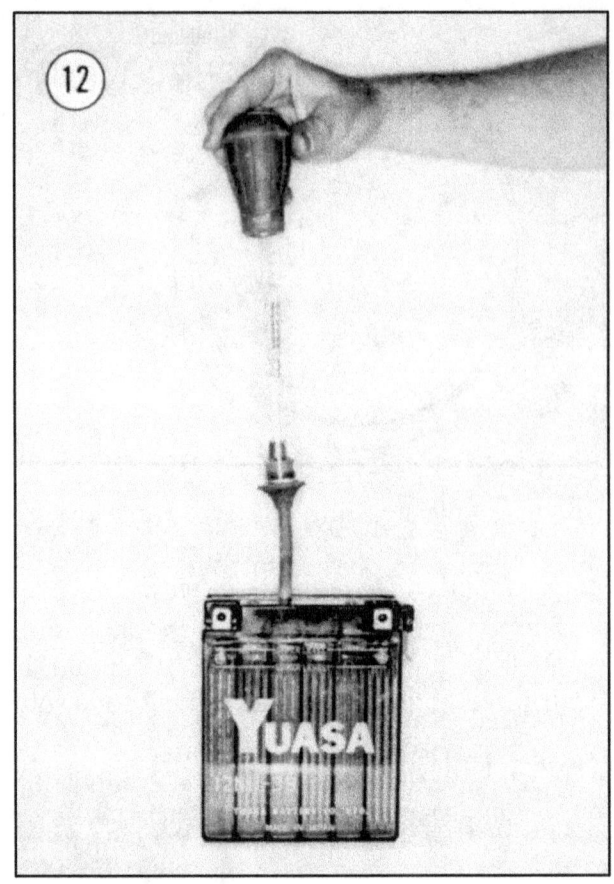

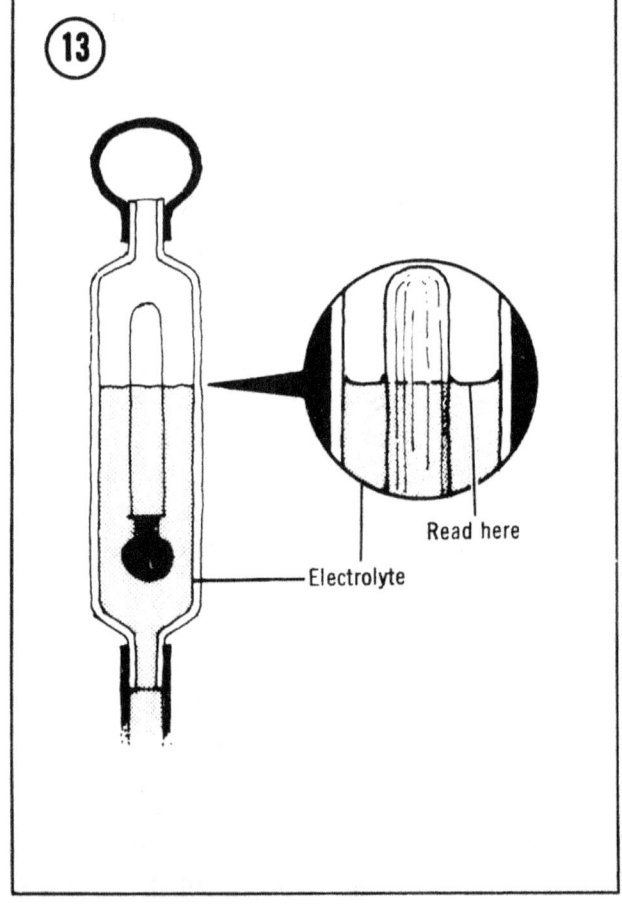

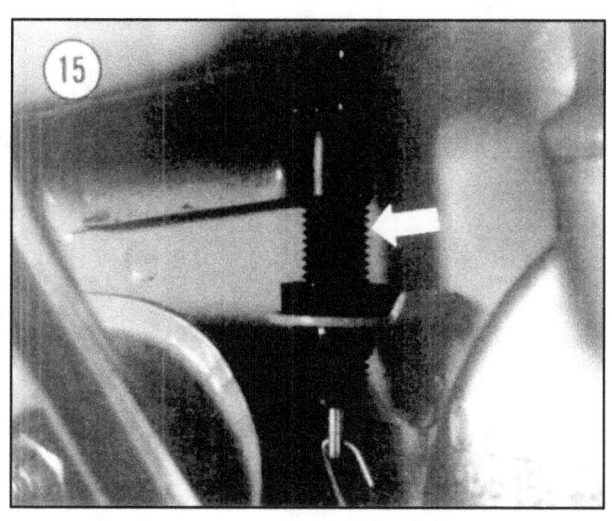

Table 3 STATE OF CHARGE

Specific Gravity	State of Charge
1.110-1.130	Discharged
1.140-1.160	Almost discharged
1.170-1.190	One-quarter charged
1.200-1.220	One-half charged
1.230-1.250	Three-quarters charged
1.260-1.280	Fully charged

Table 4 SPECIFIC GRAVITY

Specific Gravity	(Degrees F) Freezing Temperature
1.100	18
1.120	13
1.140	8
1.160	1
1.180	−6
1.200	−17
1.220	−31
1.240	−50
1.260	−75
1.280	−92

Specific gravity of the electrolyte varies with temperature, so it is necessary to apply a temperature correction to the reading so obtained. For each 10° that battery temperature exceeds 80°F, add 0.004 to the indicated specific gravity. Likewise, subtract 0.004 from the indicated value for each 10° that battery temperature is below 80°F.

Repeat this measurement for each battery cell. If there is more than 0.050 difference (50 points) between cells, battery condition is questionable.

State of charge may be determined from **Table 3**.

Do not measure specific gravity immediately after adding water. Ride the machine a few miles to ensure thorough mixing of the electrolyte.

It is most important to maintain batteries fully charged during cold weather. A fully charged battery freezes at a much lower temperature than does one which is partially discharged. Freezing temperature depends on specific gravity. See **Table 4**.

LIGHTS AND SIGNALS

Motorcycles that are intended for street use are equipped with lights and horns. These devices should be checked periodically for proper operation, and any necessary adjustment or repair made at once.

Lights

Figure 14 (next page) is an exploded view of a typical headlight assembly. It consists primarily of a headlight lens and reflector unit, rim, and related hardware.

In the event of lighting troubles, first check the affected bulb. Poor ground connections are another cause for lamp malfunctions.

Headlights and taillights on many magneto-equipped motorcycles operate from alternating current supplied by the magneto. If one lamp burns out or has a loose or poor connection to it, excess current will be diverted to remaining lamps in the circuit, causing rapid failure.

Turn signals usually operate from direct current supplied by the battery. When replacing the signal bulbs, always be sure to use the proper type. Erratic operation or even failure to flash may result from use of wrong bulbs.

Stoplights usually operate from direct current also. Stoplight switches should be adjusted so that the lamp comes on just before braking action begins. **Figure 15** illustrates a typical stoplight switch. Front brake stoplight switches are frequently built into the front brake cable, and are not adjustable.

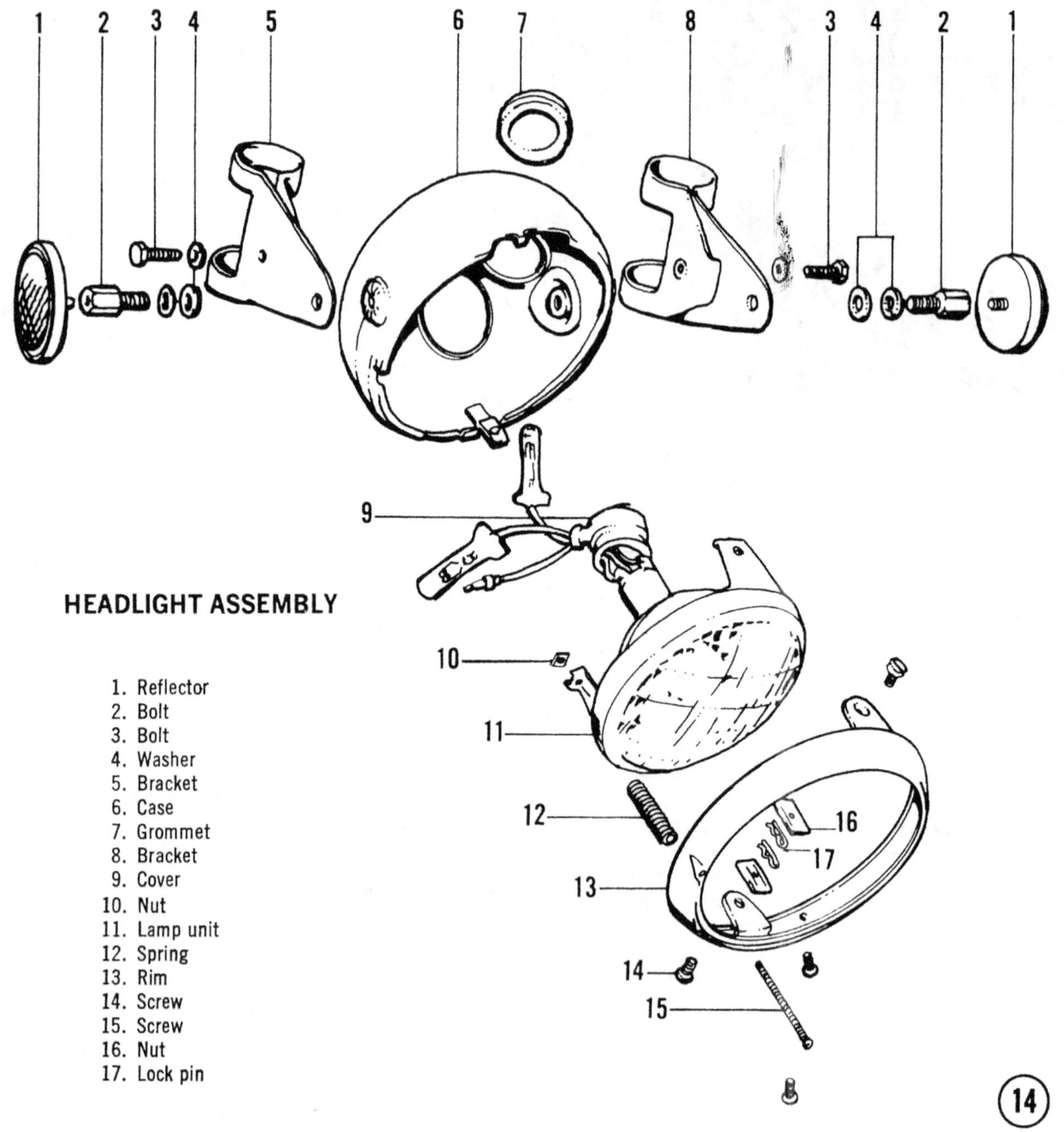

1
2
3
4
5
6
7
8
9
10
11
12
13
14
15
16
17
HEADLIGHT ASSEMBLY
1. Reflector
2. Bolt
3. Bolt
4. Washer
5. Bracket
6. Case
7. Grommet
8. Bracket
9. Cover
10. Nut
11. Lamp unit
12. Spring
13. Rim
14. Screw
15. Screw
16. Nut
17. Lock pin

14

HORN

Figure 16 is a typical horn circuit. Current for the horn is supplied by the battery. One terminal is connected to the battery through the main switch. The other terminal is grounded when the horn button is pressed.

When the rider presses the horn button, current flows through the coil; the core then becomes magnetized and attracts the moving plate, or armature. As the armature moves toward the coil, it opens the contact points, cutting off current to the coil. The diaphragm

16

Diaphragm
Contact point
Moving plate
Anti-arc
resistor
Battery
Coil
Horn button
Iron core

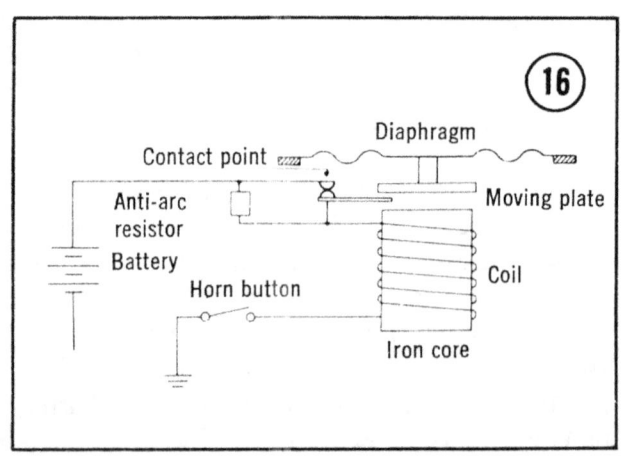

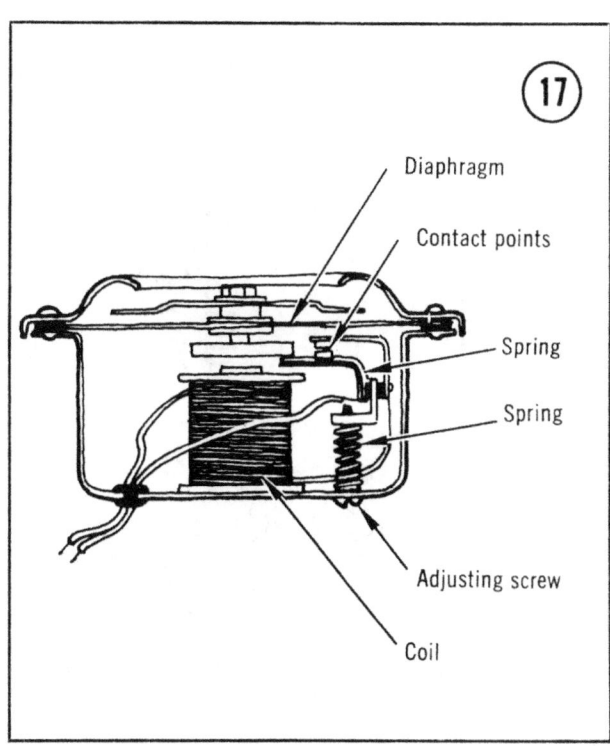

spring then returns the armature to its original position. This process repeats rapidly until the horn button is released. The action of the armature striking the end of the core produces sound, which is amplified by the resonator diaphragm **(Figure 17)**.

Horn tone may be adjusted by turning the adjuster screw. Loosen the locknut before adjustment, and be sure to tighten it after adjustment is complete.

The horn will not sound if its contact points are burned. Dress them if necessary, using a small point file or flex-stone. Adjust horn tone after dressing its contact points.

WIRING DIAGRAMS

Wiring diagrams are shown on the following pages. Reference to these diagrams will make electrical system troubleshooting easier.

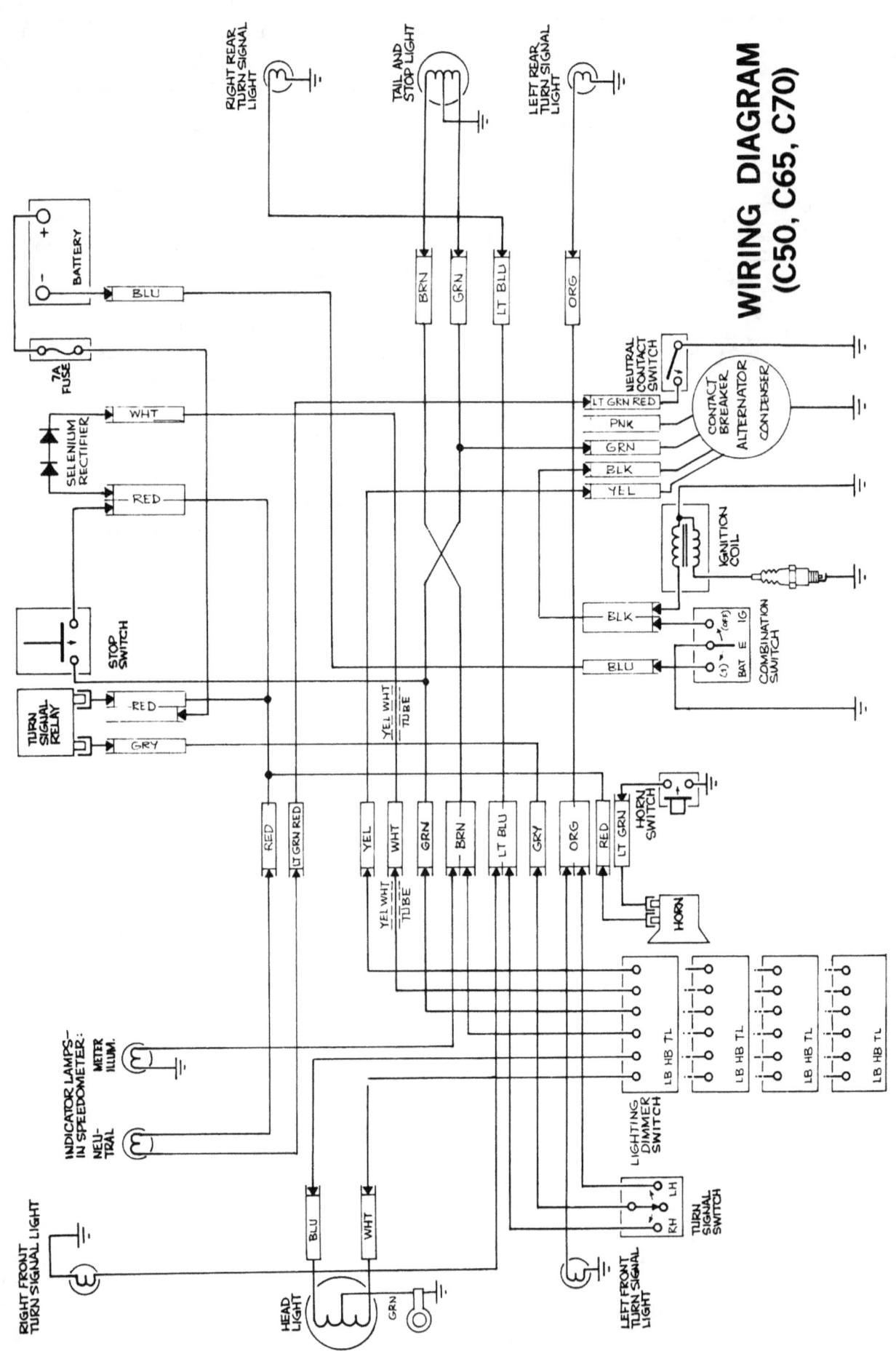

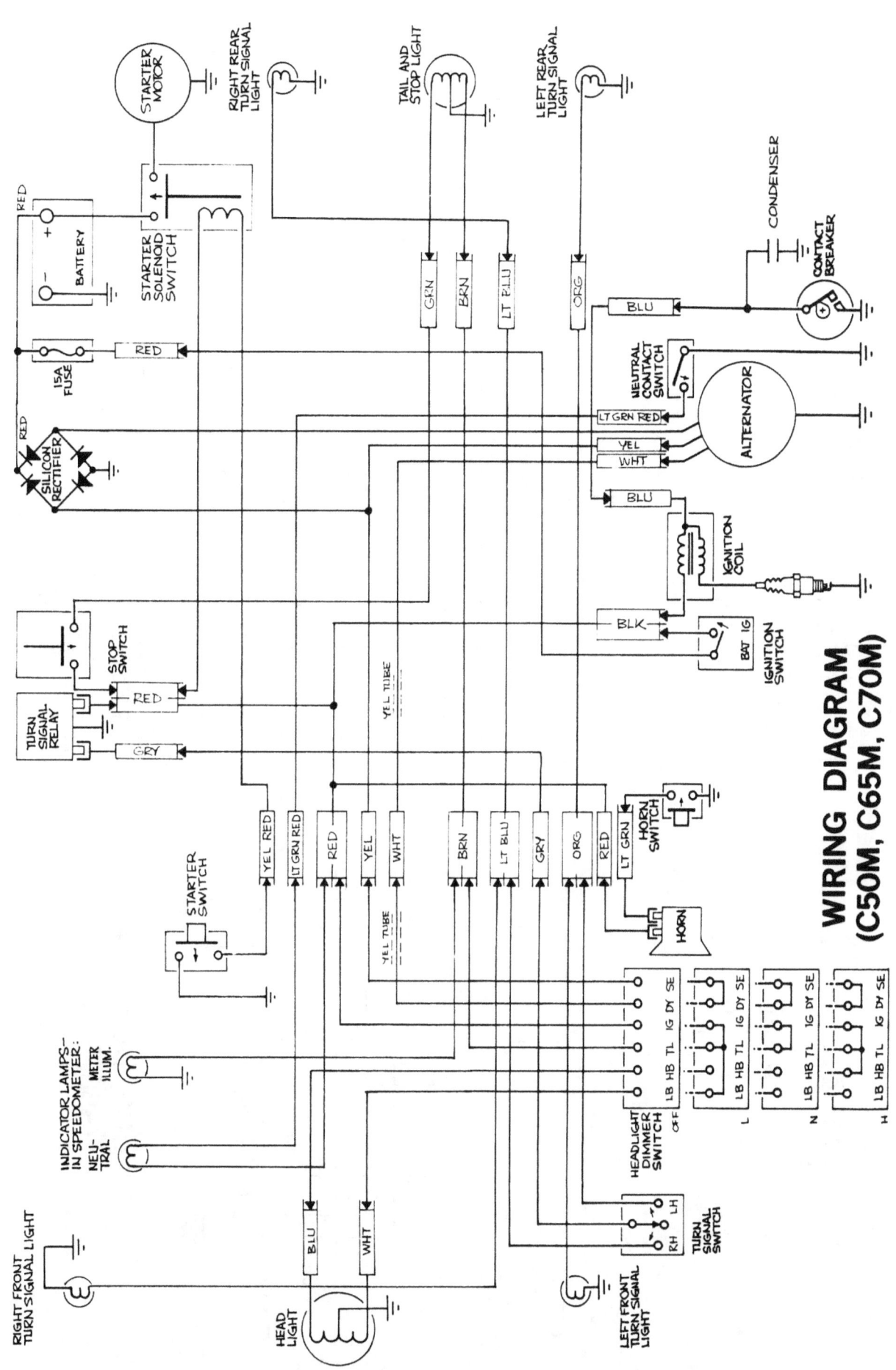

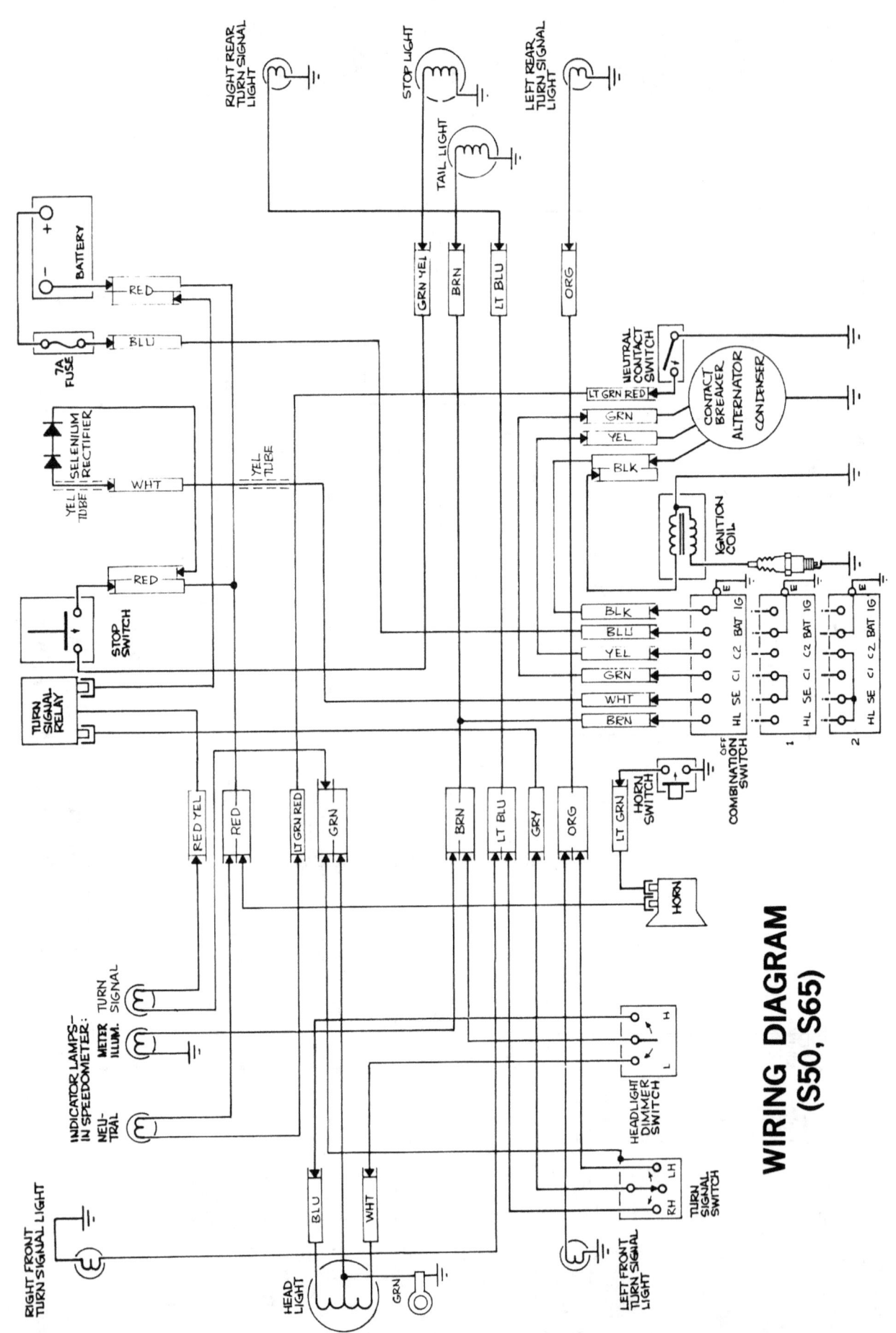

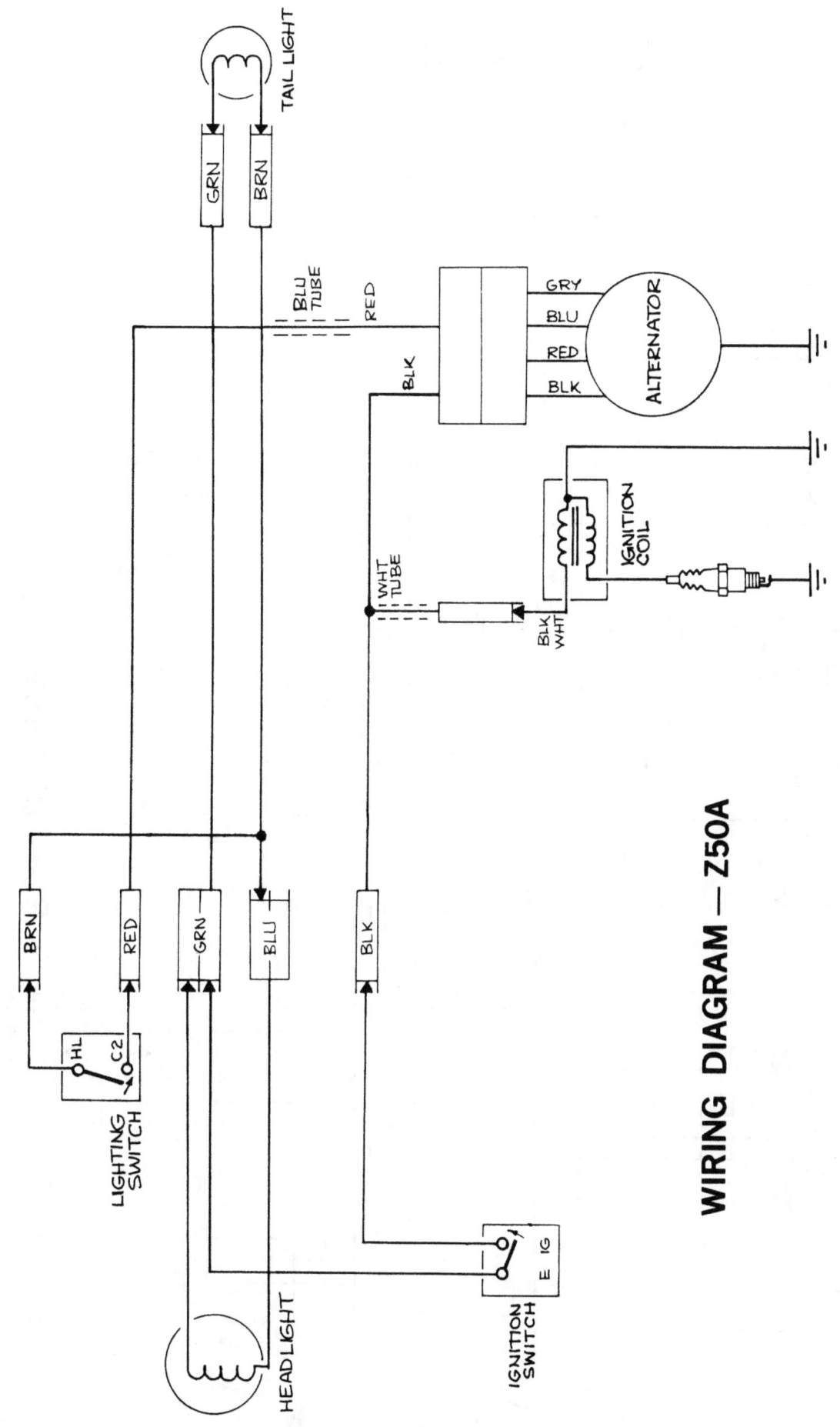

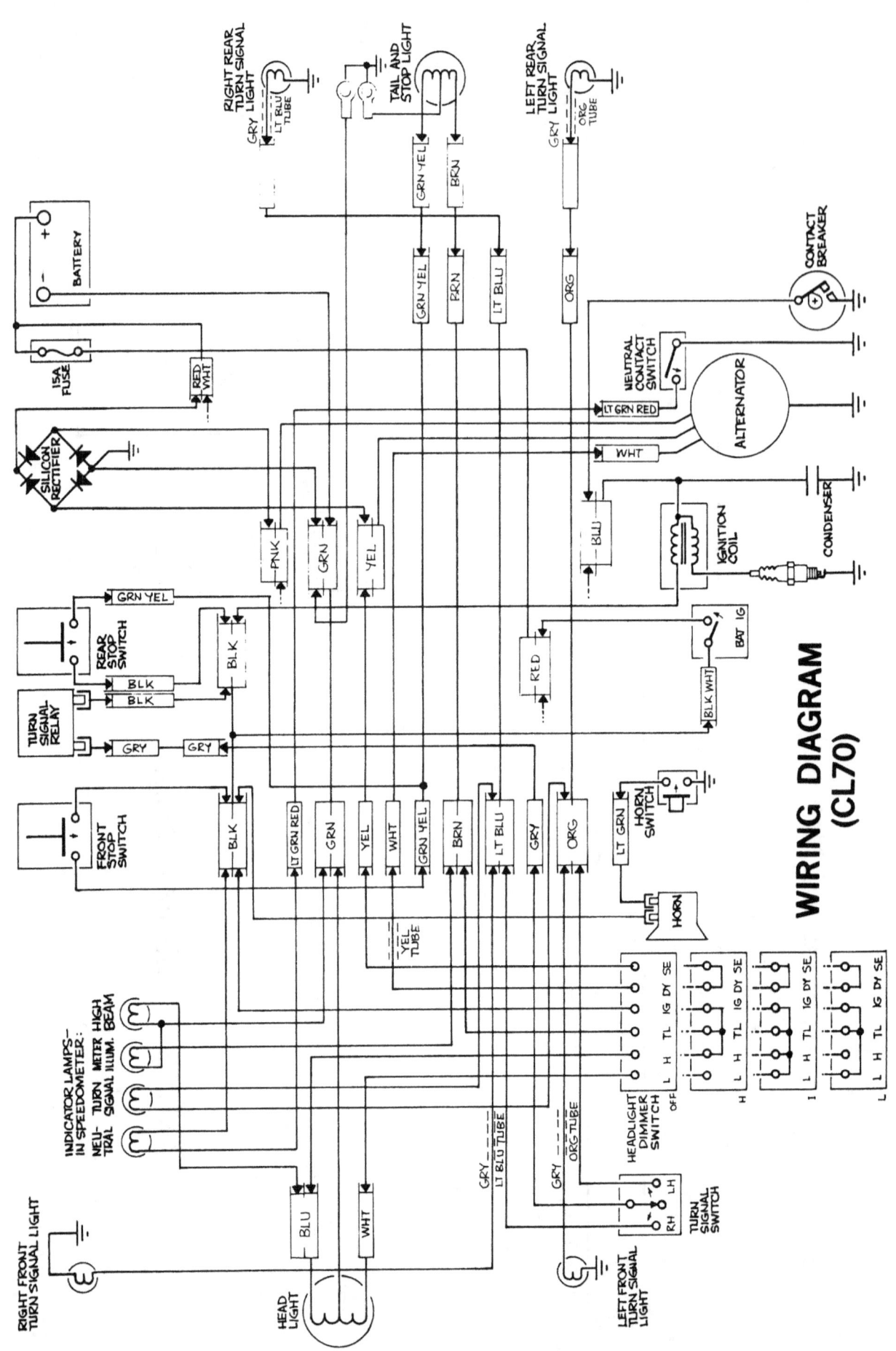

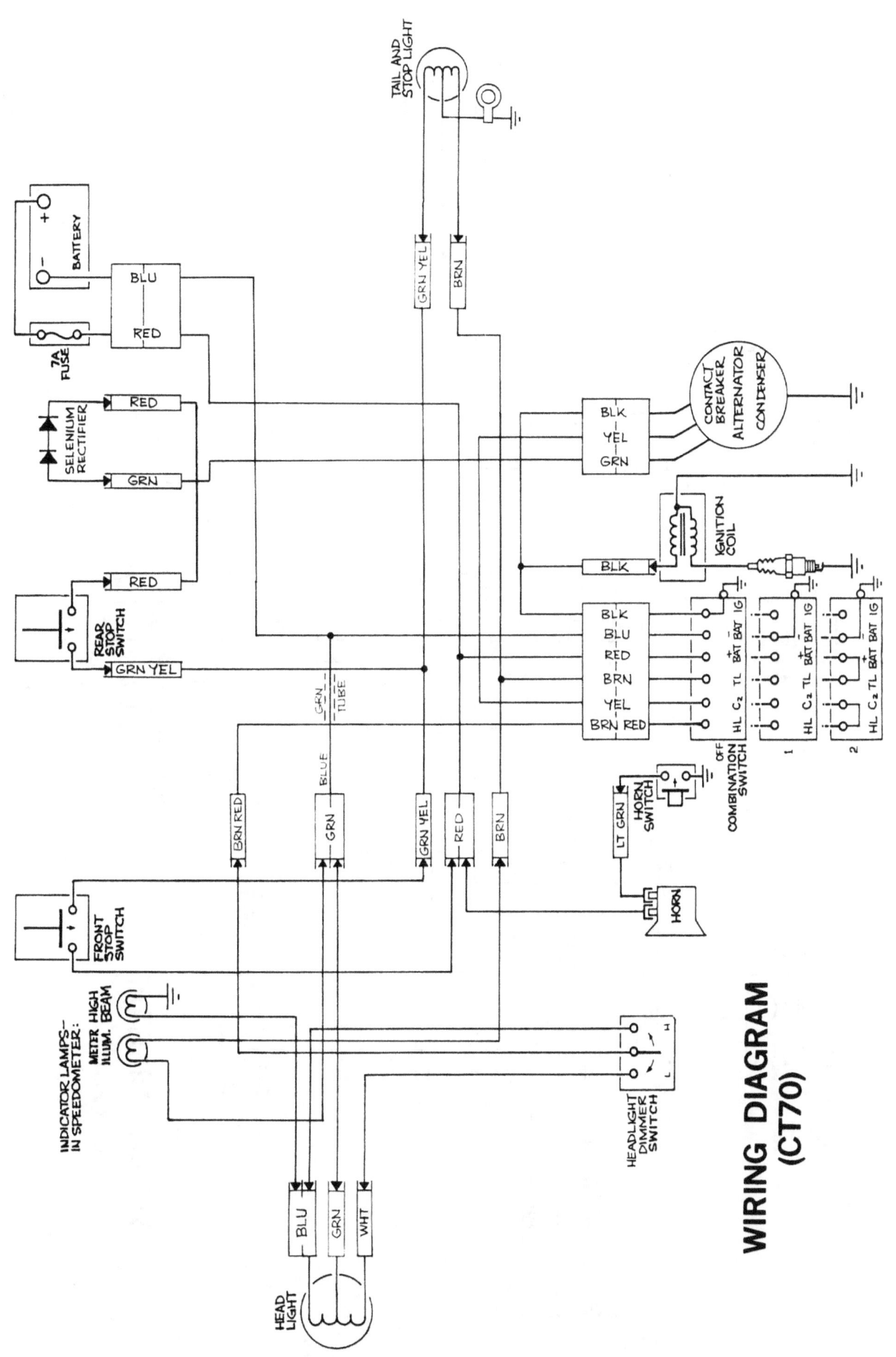

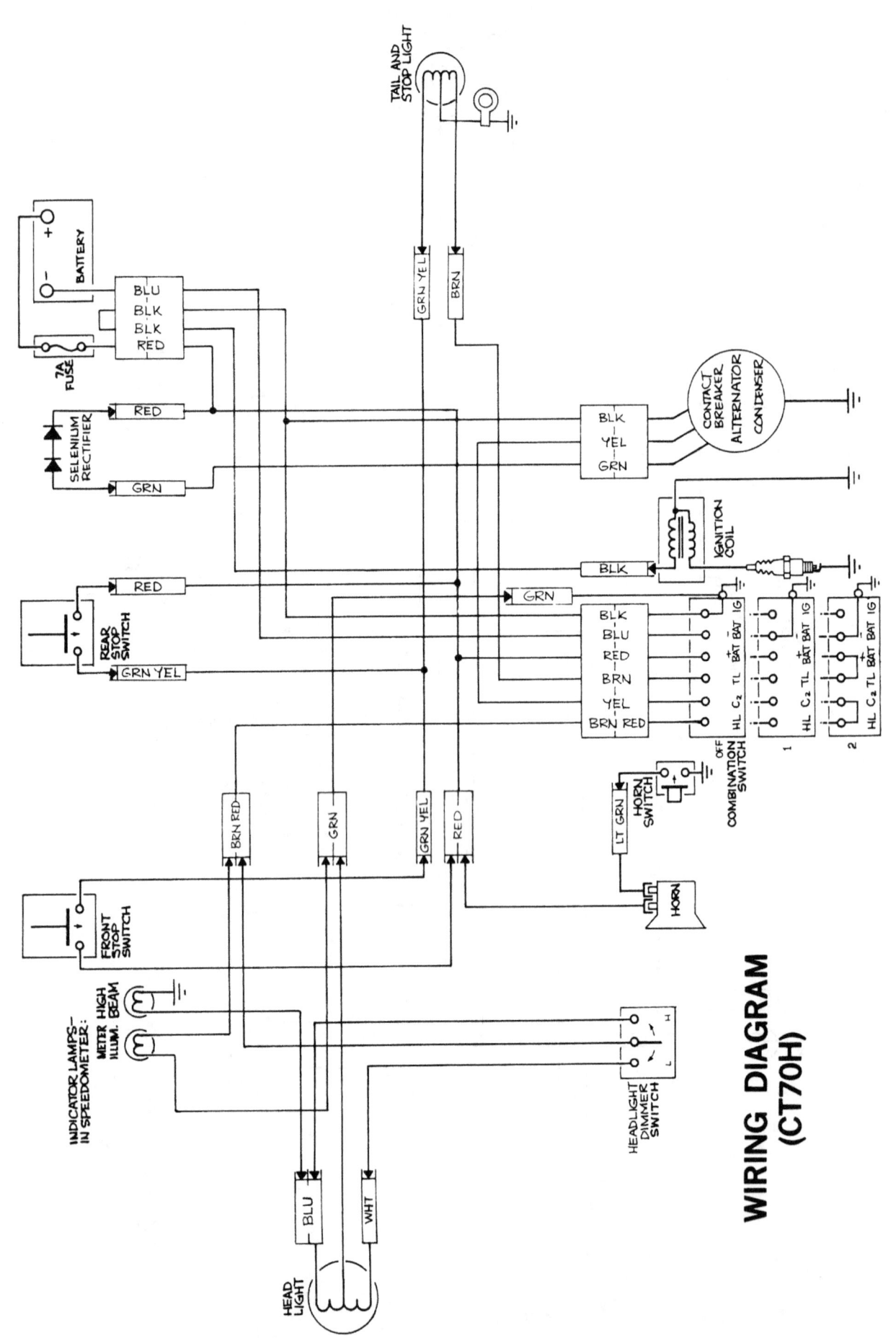

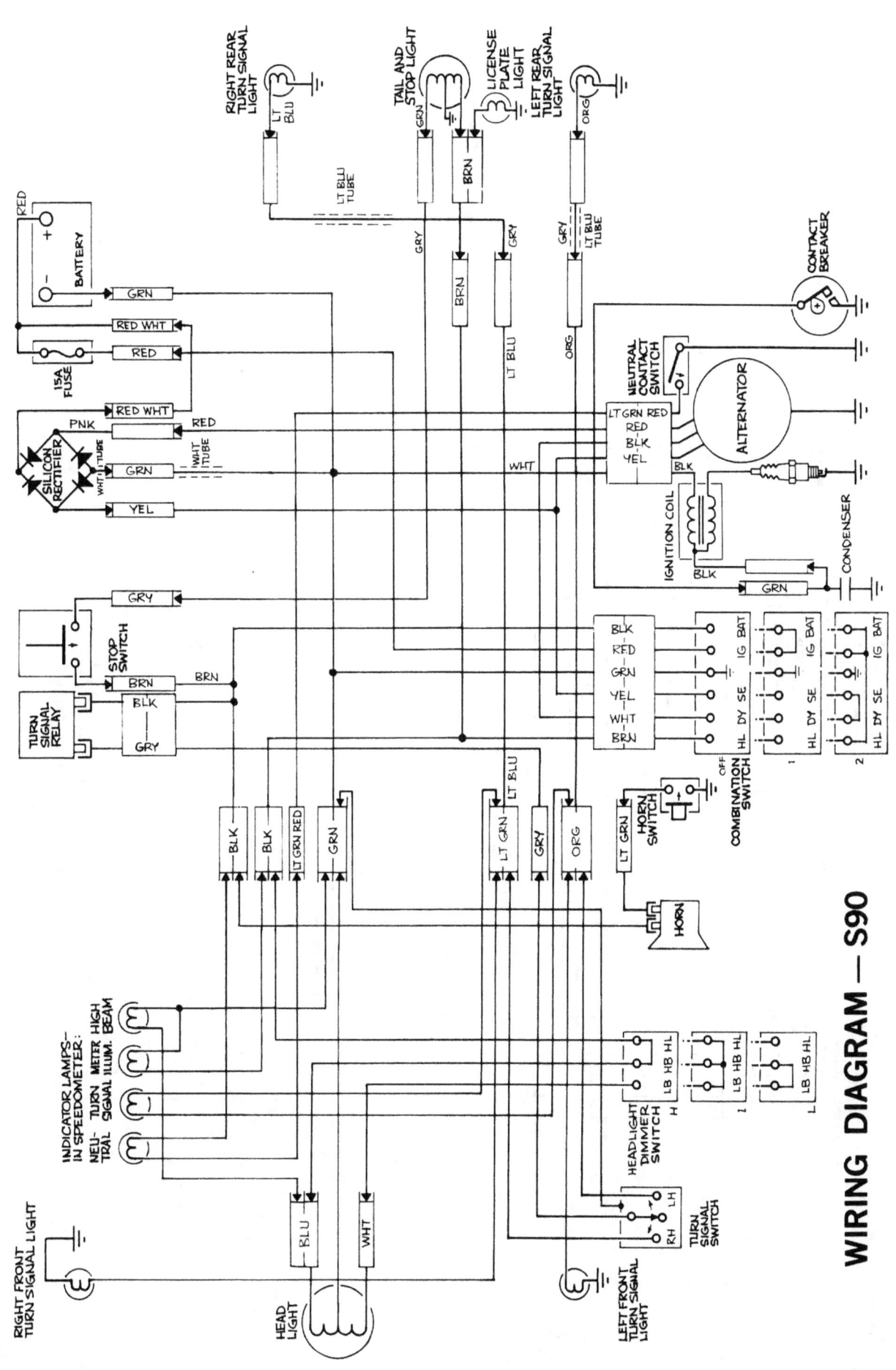

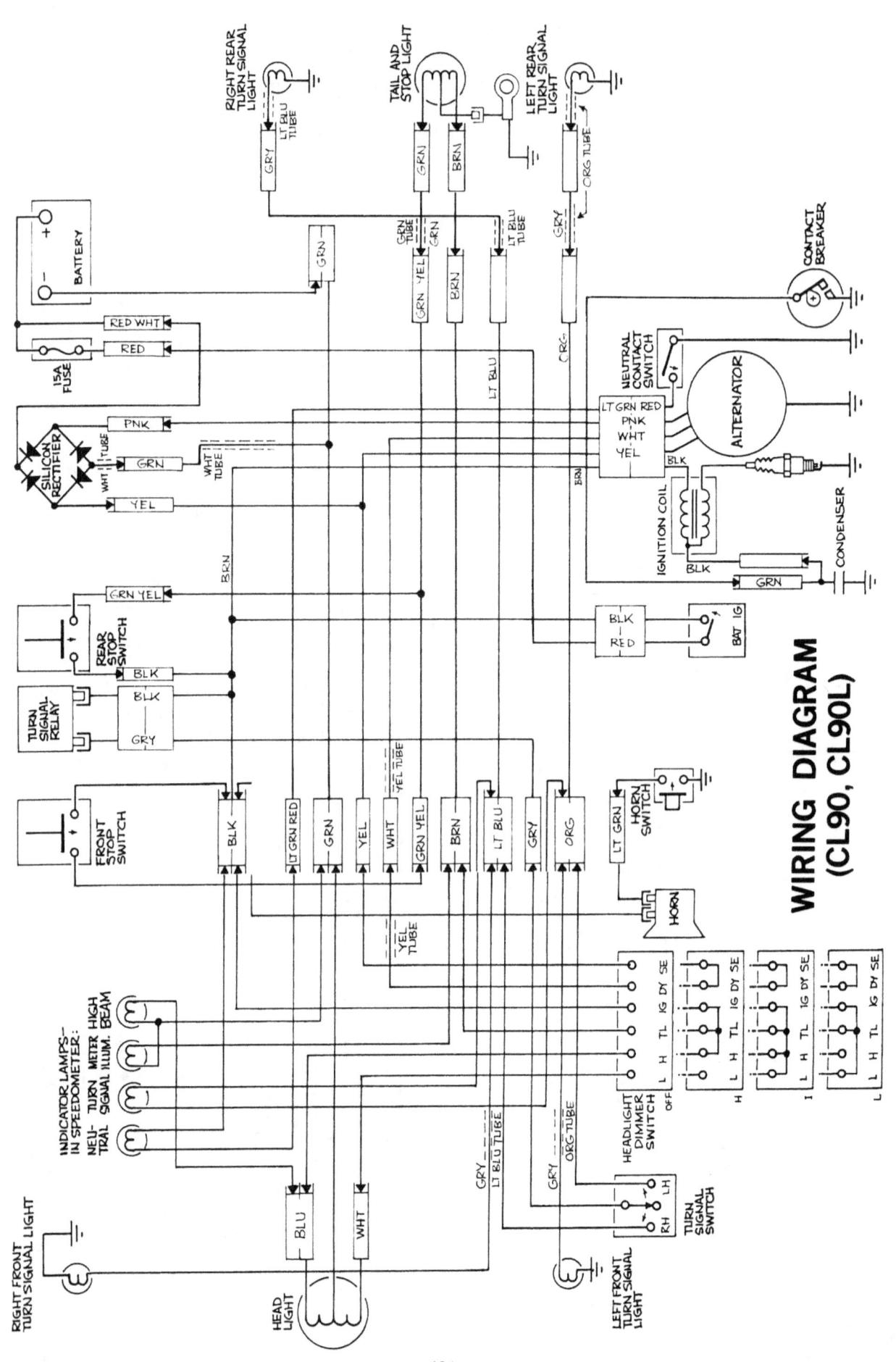

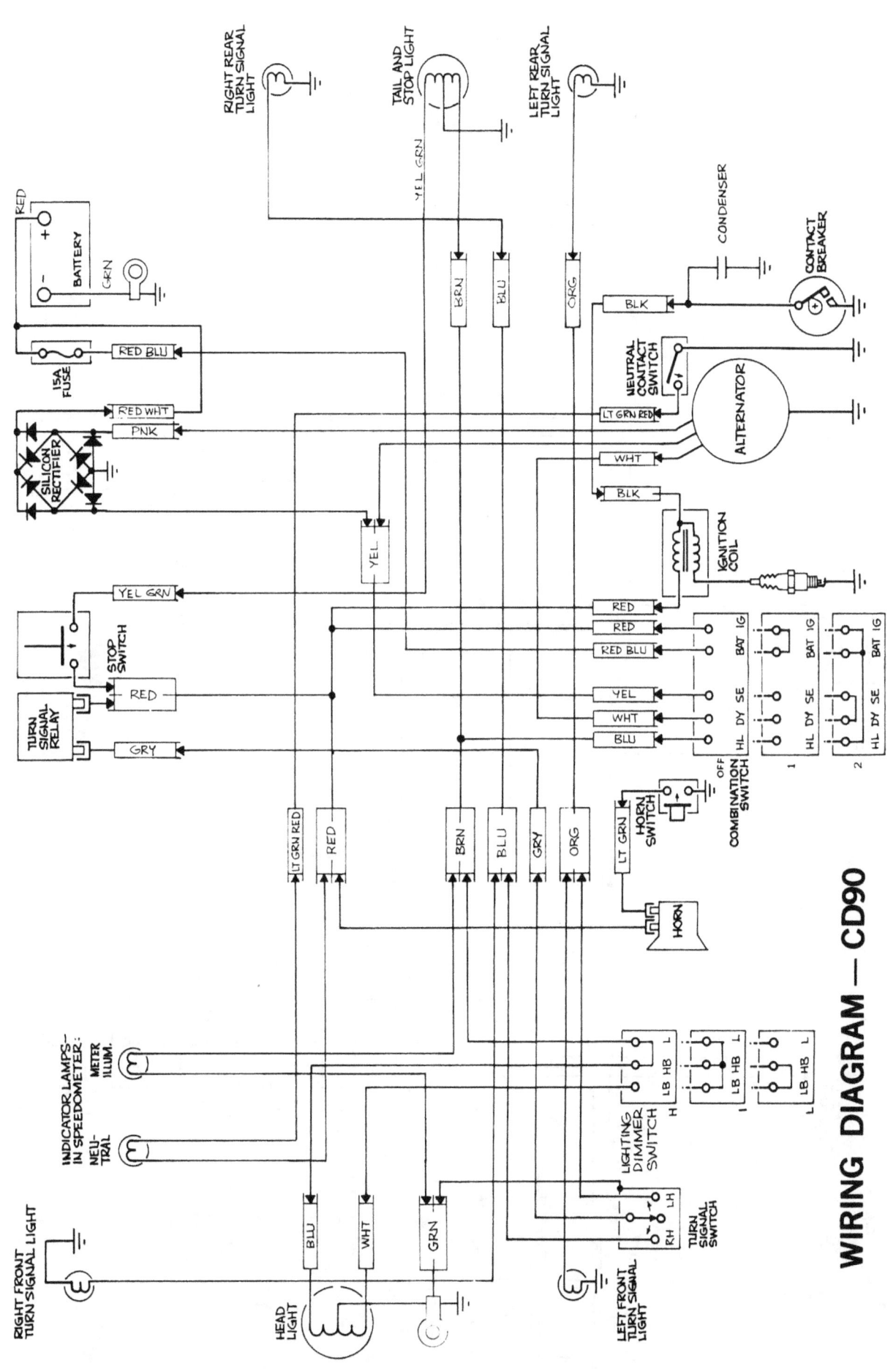

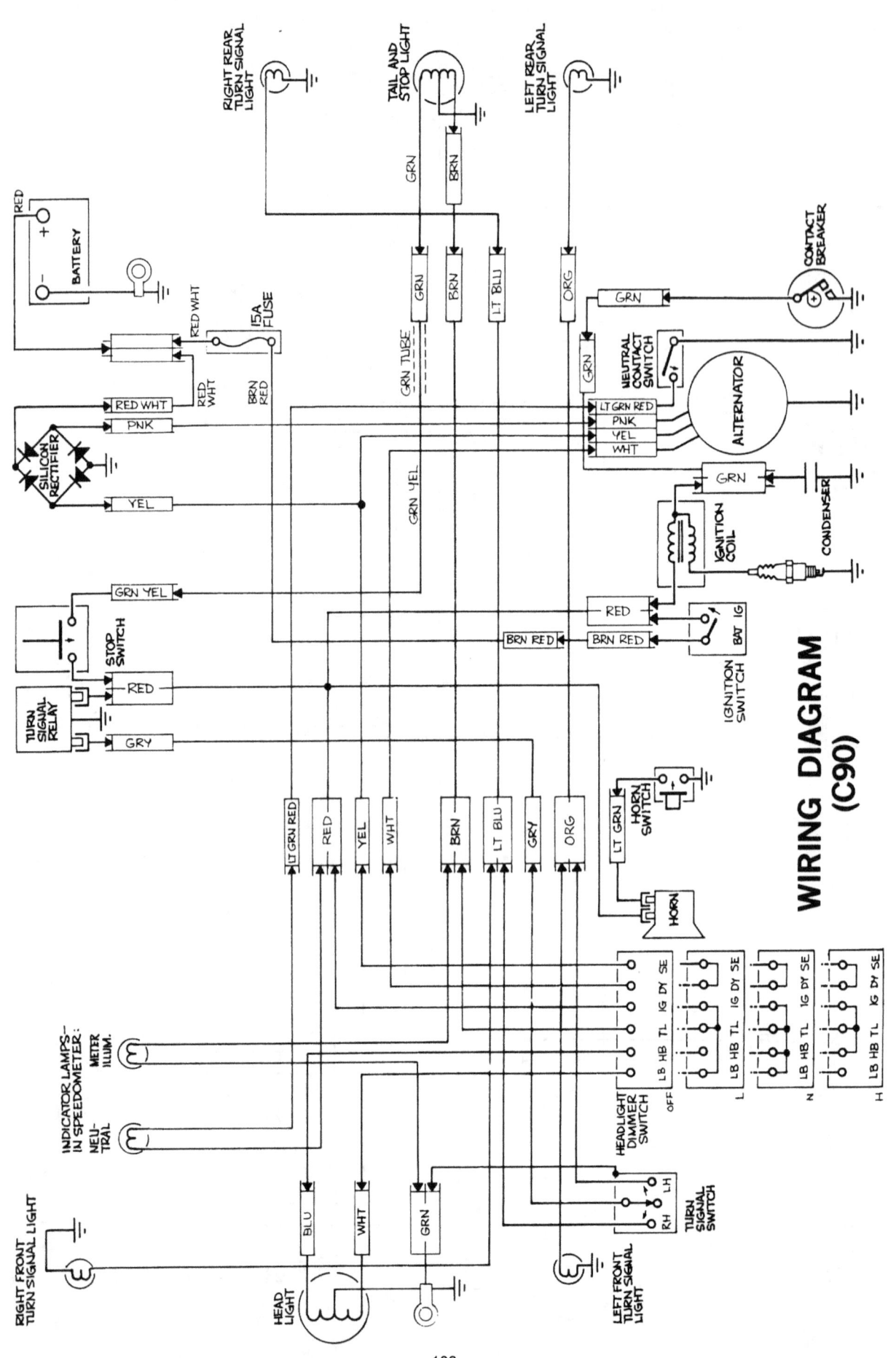

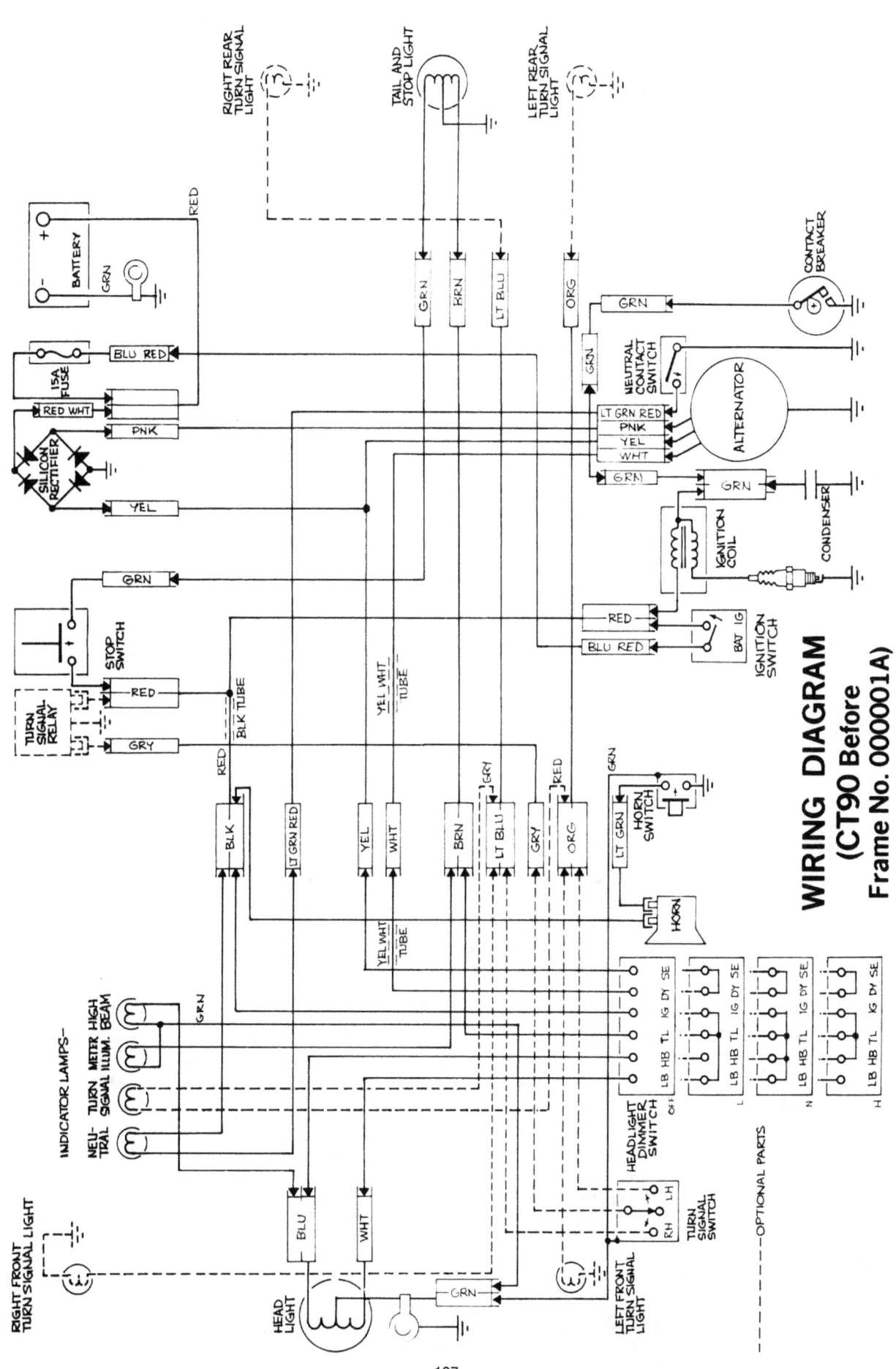

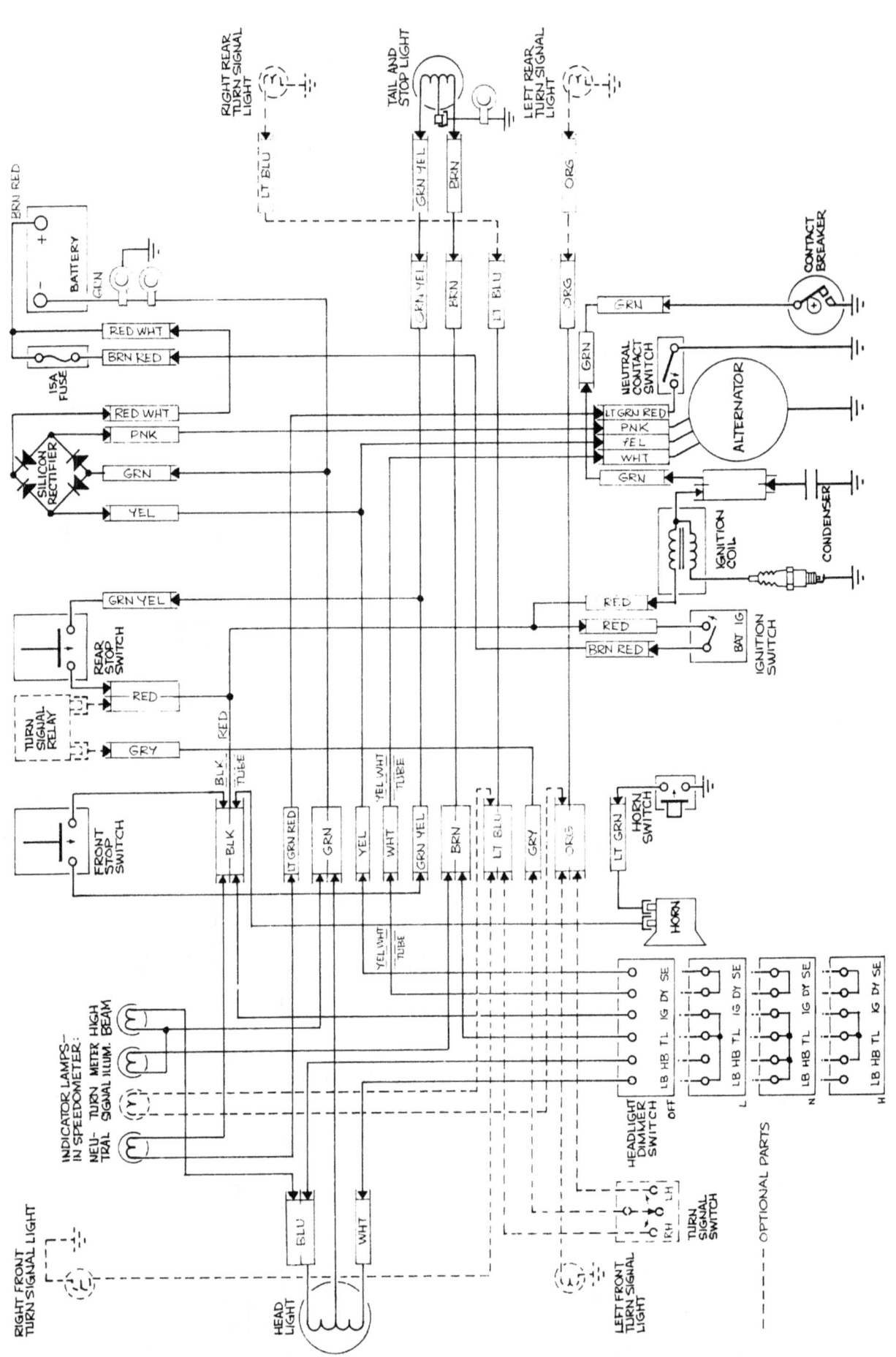

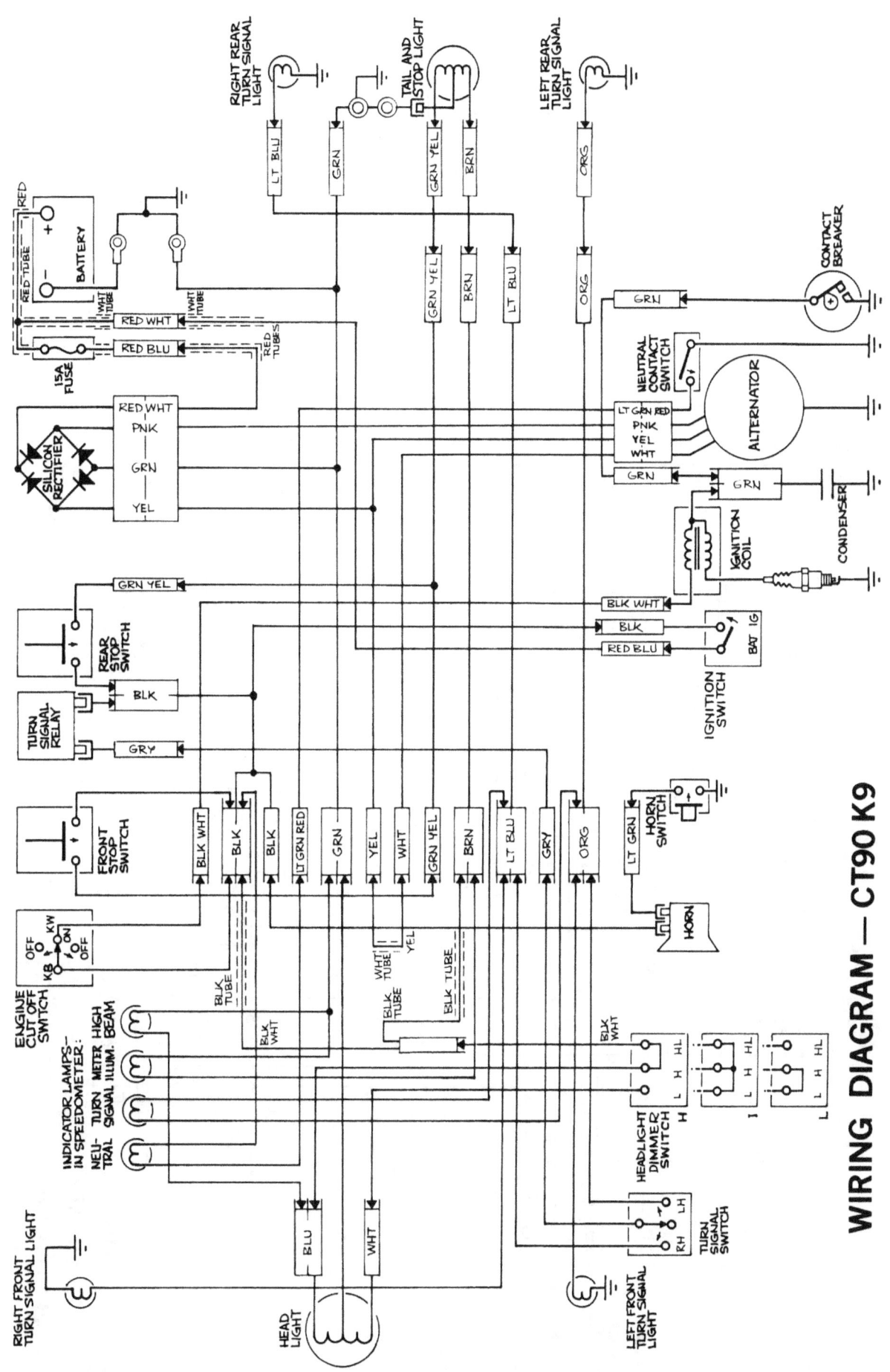

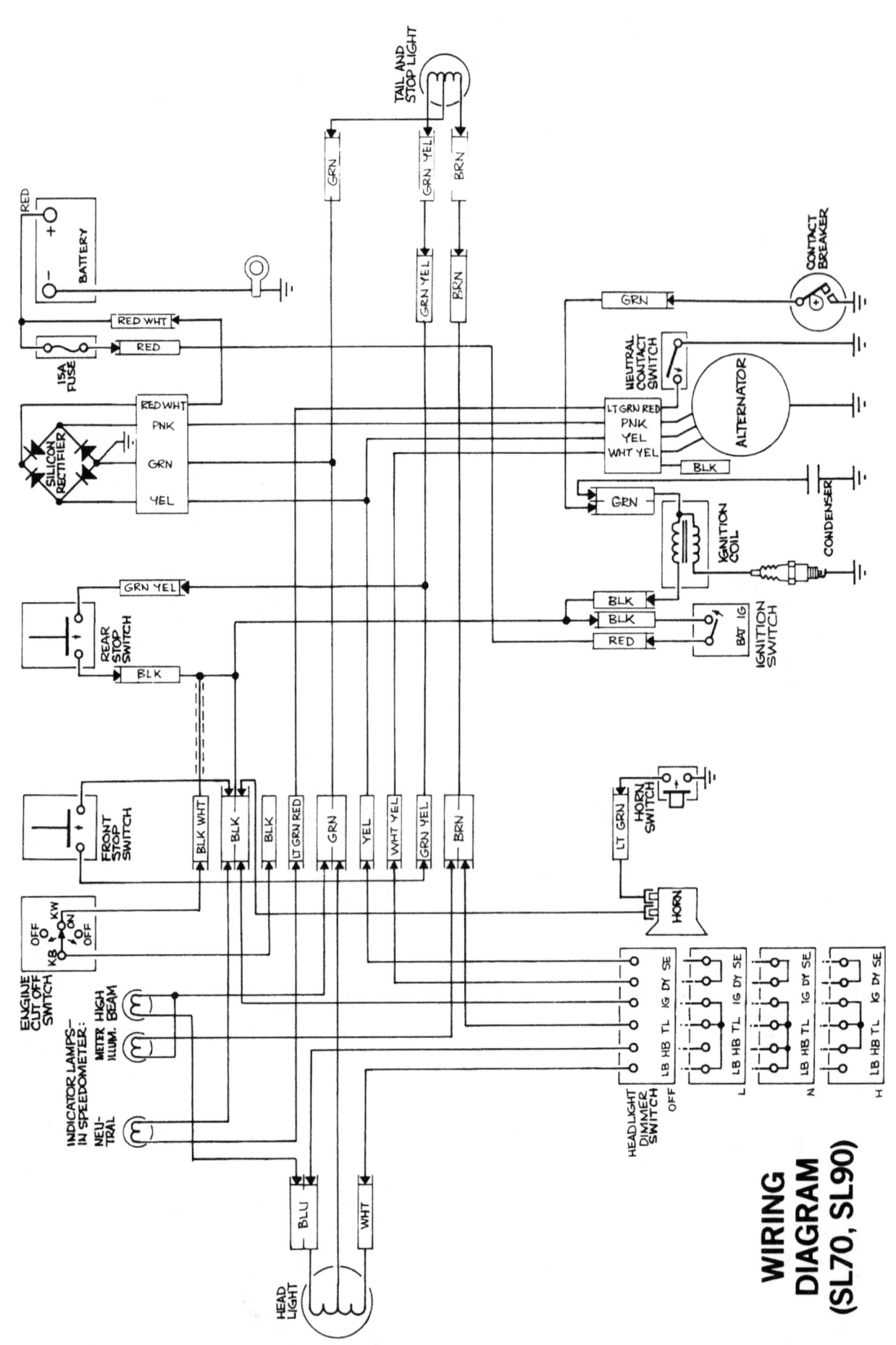

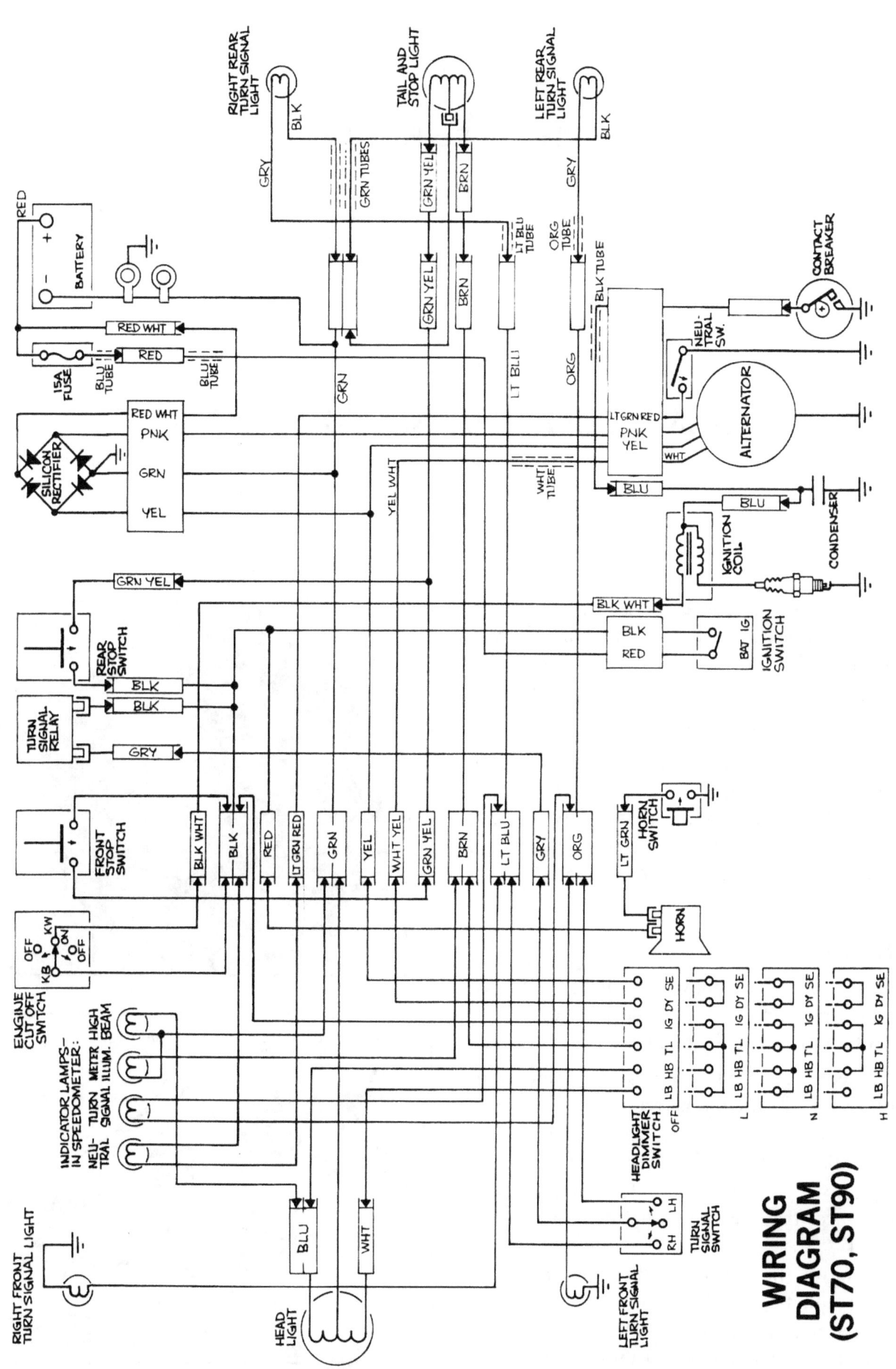

CHAPTER SIX

FRAME, SUSPENSION, AND STEERING

This chapter discusses service operations on chassis, wheels, brakes, and related components.

HANDLEBAR

The handlebar is made from solid drawn steel tubing. Most manual controls (**Figure 1**) are mounted on the handlebar assembly. Wiring from switches is routed to the headlight, where it is connected to the main wiring harness.

Removal

Although details may vary slightly between various models, the following procedure may be followed as a guide to removal.

1. Disconnect speedometer cable (1) and front brake cable (2) at front wheel (**Figure 2**).

2. On automatic clutch models, disconnect the rear brake cable at the left-hand lever.

3. Remove carburetor cap (1, **Figure 3**), then disconnect throttle cable (3) from the throttle valve (2).

4. Remove the headlight, then disconnect all wiring from the handlebar.

5a. Remove 4 mounting bolts, then lift the handlebar assembly from the motorcycle.

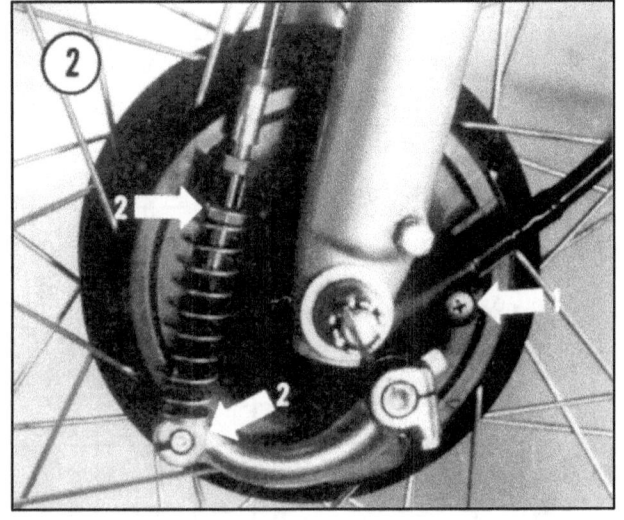

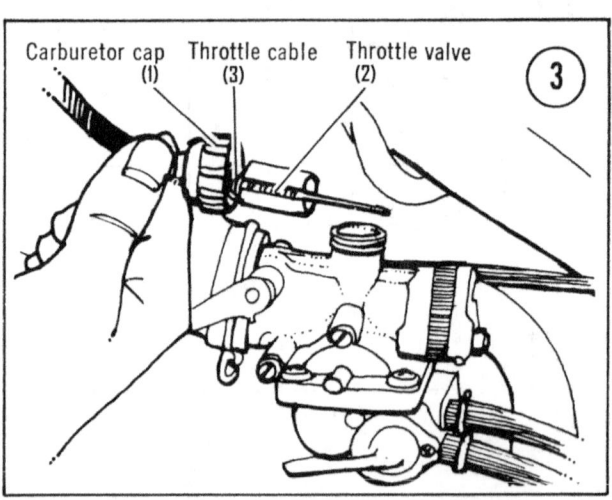

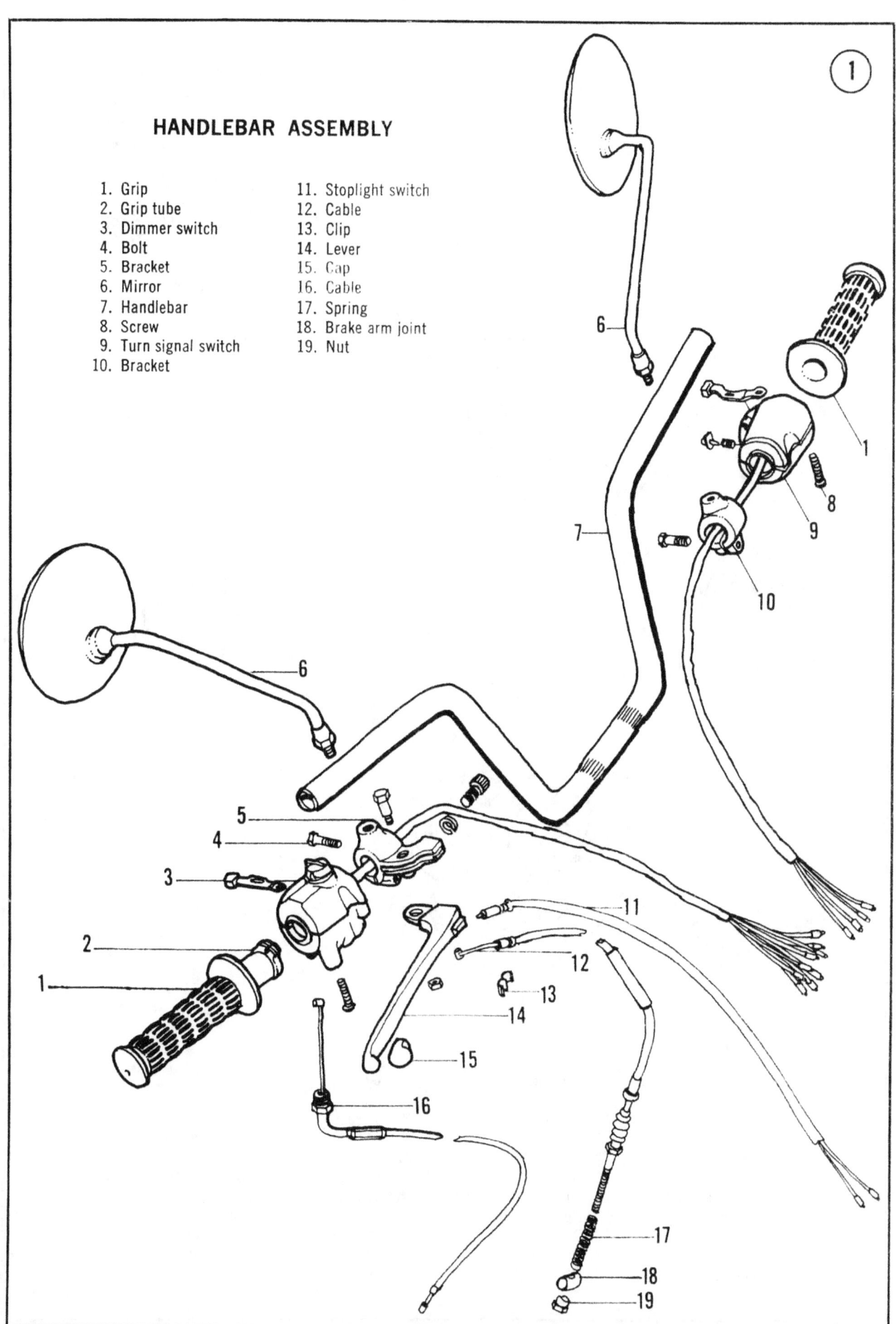

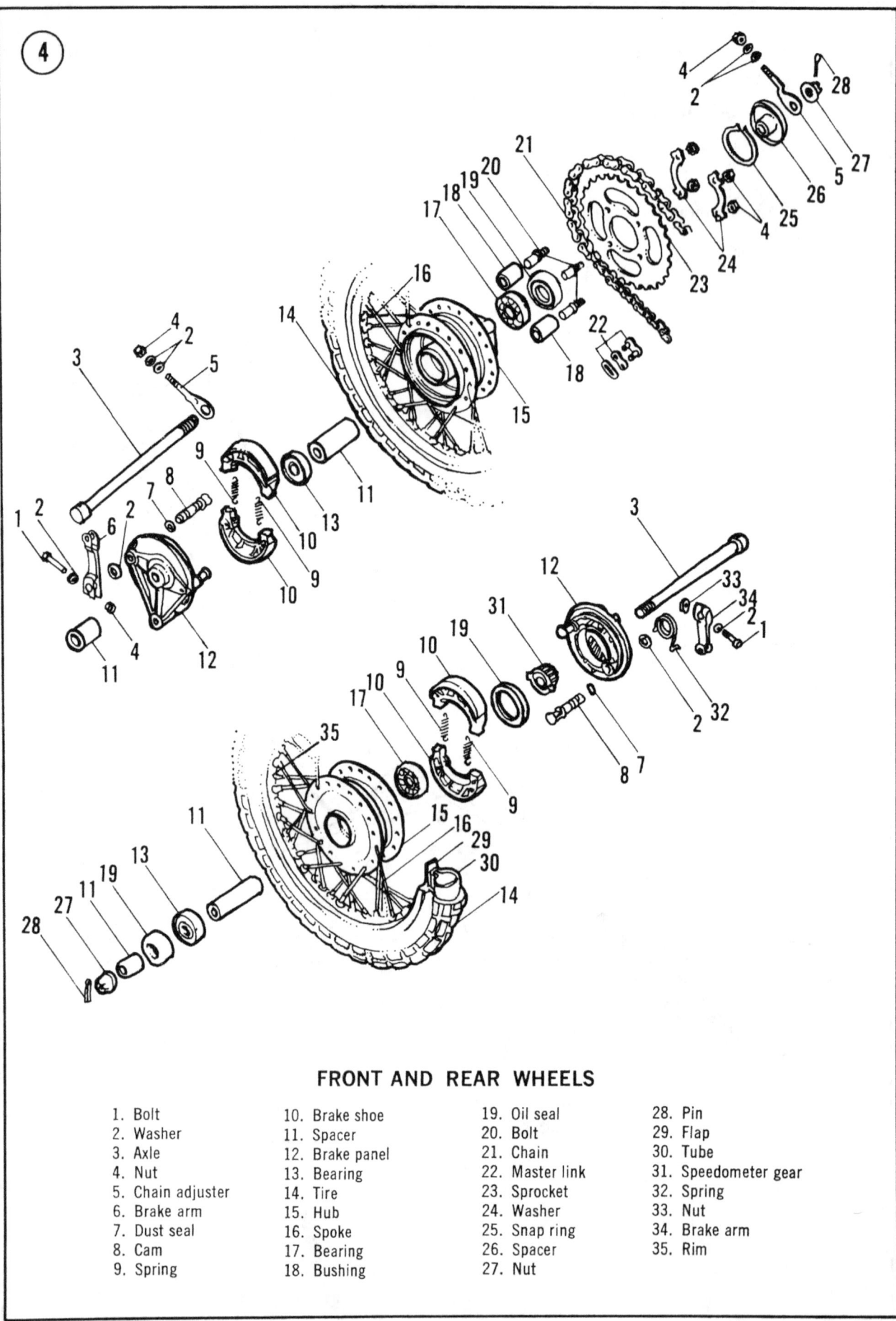

FRONT AND REAR WHEELS

1. Bolt
2. Washer
3. Axle
4. Nut
5. Chain adjuster
6. Brake arm
7. Dust seal
8. Cam
9. Spring
10. Brake shoe
11. Spacer
12. Brake panel
13. Bearing
14. Tire
15. Hub
16. Spoke
17. Bearing
18. Bushing
19. Oil seal
20. Bolt
21. Chain
22. Master link
23. Sprocket
24. Washer
25. Snap ring
26. Spacer
27. Nut
28. Pin
29. Flap
30. Tube
31. Speedometer gear
32. Spring
33. Nut
34. Brake arm
35. Rim

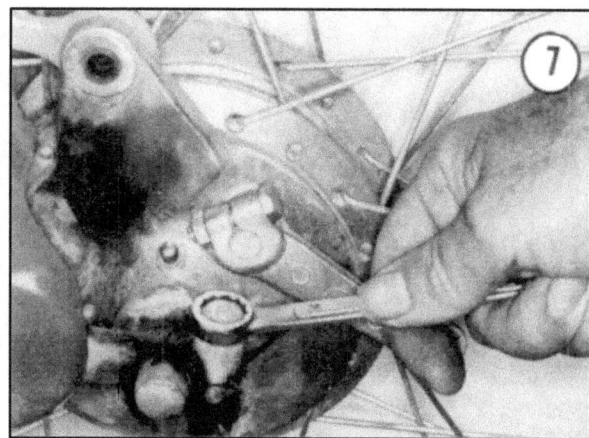
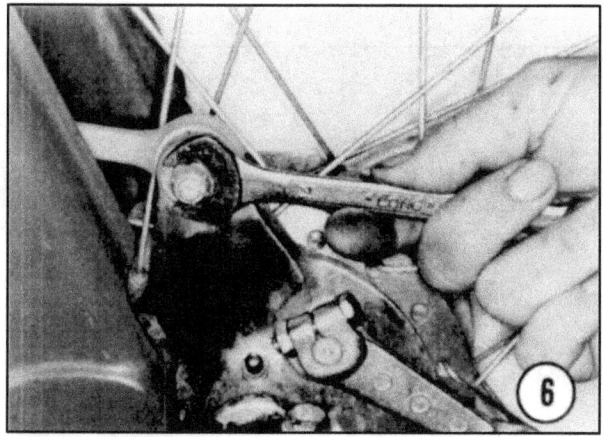
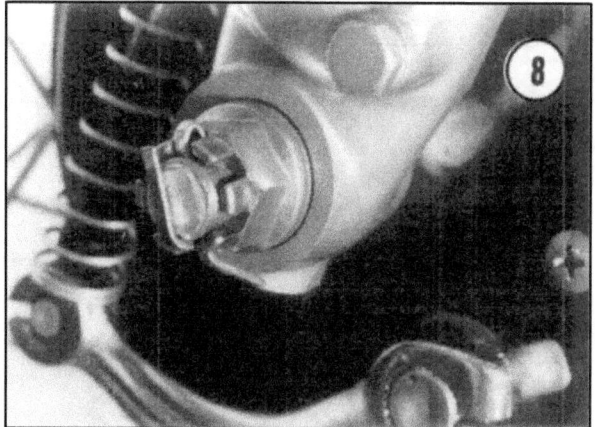

5b. On split bars, remove the 2 mounts and locking knobs.

Inspection

1. Check throttle, clutch, and brake cables for chafing and smooth operation.
2. Be sure levers operate smoothly.
3. Check for bends or cracks in the handlebar, especially after a collision or hard spill.
4. Check operation of all switches.

Installation

Reverse the removal procedure to install the handlebar. Observe the following notes.

1. Position cables and wires carefully, so that they do not become pinched or chafed.
2. Tighten the 2 forward mounting bolts first, until there is 0.008-0.010 in. (0.2-0.3mm) clearance at the rear of the upper clamp. Then tighten both rear bolts.
3. Torque mounting bolts to 5.8-8.7 ft.-lb. (8.0-12.0 N•m).

4. When reconnecting wiring, be very sure that like colors are connected.
5. Adjust the clutch and front brake.

WHEELS

Figure 4 is an exploded view of typical front and rear wheels. Refer to that illustration during the following procedure.

Disassembly/Assembly (Front)

1. Support the motorcycle so that the front wheel is off the ground.
2. Disconnect front brake cable (A, **Figure 5**).
3. Disconnect speedometer cable (B, **Figure 5**).
4. Disconnect the front brake torque strut at the front brake (**Figure 6**).
5. Loosen, but do not remove, the pinch bolts at both ends of the front axle (**Figure 7**).
6. Remove the axle nut (**Figure 8**), then insert a Phillips screwdriver or similar tool in the end of the axle. Simultaneously, twist and pull on the front axle until the front wheel is free.

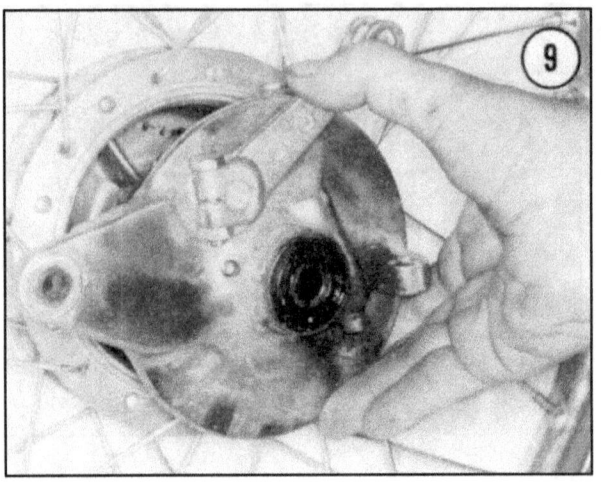

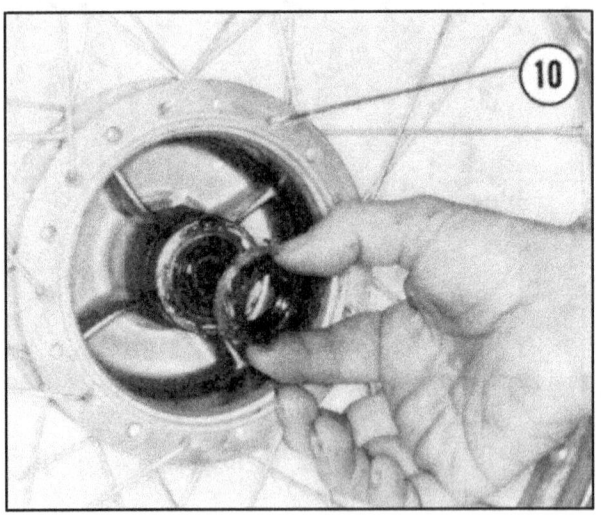

7. Roll the front wheel from the motorcycle. Be sure to catch any spacers or loose parts as they fall.

8. Pull out the brake panel (**Figure 9**).

9. Remove speedometer drive gear (**Figure 10**).

10. Reverse procedure for assembly.

Disassembly/Assembly (Rear)

1. Disconnect the master link.
2. Disconnect the rear brake rod (**Figure 11**).
3. Remove the muffler.
4. Disconnect the rear brake torque link from the rear brake panel (**Figure 12**).
5. Remove the rear axle nut (the smaller of 2 nuts), then simultaneously twist and pull out the rear axle.
6. Remove the rear axle sleeve nut (**Figure 13**), then remove the rear sprocket assembly.
7. Reverse procedure for assembly.

BRAKE

Operation

Figure 14 illustrates a typical brake. When the brake cable or brake rod is pulled, it moves the brake arm as shown by the arrow. The arm turns a cam, which forces both brake shoes outward against the inside of the brake drum, thereby slowing or stopping the wheel.

Inspection

1. Check that friction surfaces of brake shoes are not glazed. Glazing can be removed by light sanding with coarse sandpaper.

2. If there is any grease or oil on brake friction surfaces, replace both shoes of that brake immediately.

3. Check interior surfaces of brake drums for scratches. Any scratch deep enough to catch a fingernail is cause for turning or replacing drum.

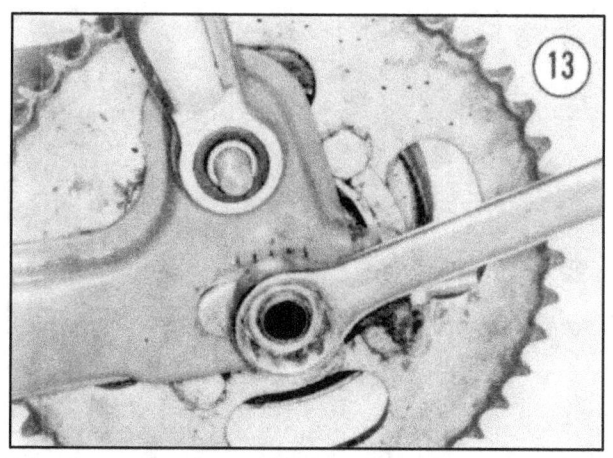

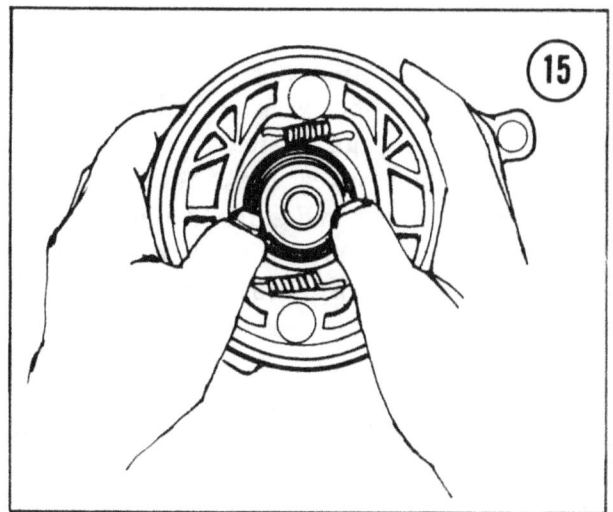

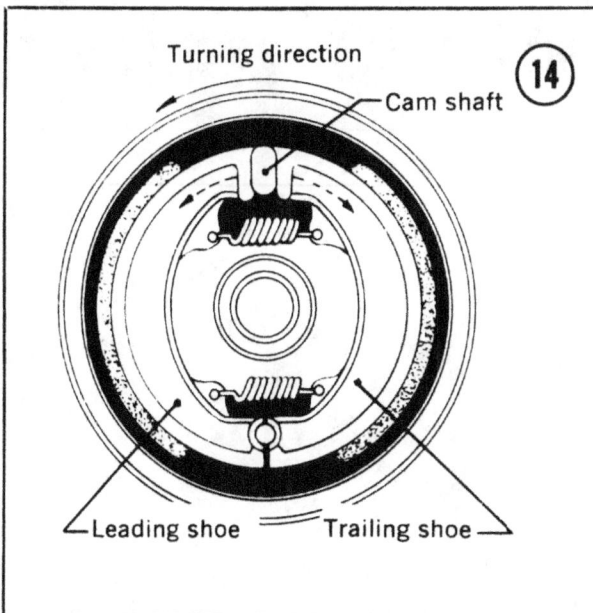

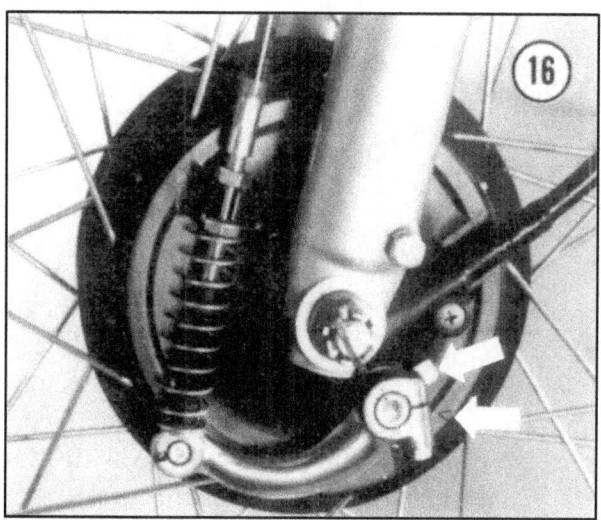

Table 1   BRAKE SHOE WEAR LIMITS

Model	Service Limit Inch	(Millimeters)
50cc-65cc	0.06	(1.5)
70cc	0.10	(2.5)
90cc	0.118	(3.0)

4. Measure brake lining thickness. Replace both brake shoes if the thinnest part of the lining on either brake shoe is worn down to its service limit. See **Table 1**.

Shoe Replacement

Refer to **Figure 15**. Spread both shoes against their retraction springs, then pull them away from brake panel. Reverse the procedure to install new shoes. Always replace both shoes when either needs replacement. Front and rear brakes wear at different rates, so it is not always necessary to replace brake shoes on both brakes at the same time.

Brake Shoe Wear Indicators

Brake shoe wear indicators are fitted to the front and rear brakes on 1978 models. **Figure 16** shows the front brake shoe wear indicator. If the 2 wear indicator marks align when the brake is applied, the shoes on that wheel must be replaced.

The front and rear brake arm can be adjusted as required until the wear indicators show that the brake shoes need replacing.

NOTE: *When replacing the brake shoes, make sure the brake arm is positioned with the punch marks in alignment. See* ***Figure 17***.

Adjustment

Brakes must be adjusted periodically to compensate for brake shoe wear. To adjust brakes, turn the adjusting nut located at the end of the front brake cable or rear brake rod. These adjustments are shown in **Figures 18 and 19**.

As brake shoes wear, it is not always possible to obtain a satisfactory adjustment with the adjuster. When this situation occurs, remove the brake arm and reposition it on its splined shaft a few degrees. This procedure may be repeated as necessary, but take care that brake lining thickness does not wear down beyond the specified service limit.

STEERING STEM AND FORKS

Figure 20 is an exploded view of a typical steering stem and telescoping front fork assembly. Machines with leading link front suspension, such as CD90 and early CT90 models, are discussed separately.

The steering stem is the pivot point for the front wheel. It is supported in the frame headpiece by 2 sets of cone races and steel ball bearings. The steering stem is made of high strength heat-treated steeel to withstand shock loads imposed by rough riding, and also to withstand vibration which tends to fatigue the metal.

Stem Removal/Installation
(Telescopic Forks)

1. Remove the handlebar.
2. Refer to **Figure 21**. Remove fork bridge.
3. Remove the headlight assembly.
4. Refer to **Figure 22**. Remove both fork covers.
5. Remove the front wheel.
6. Remove the front fender.
7. Loosen both fork tube clamp bolts (**Figure 23**), then pull each fork leg downward to remove it. Be sure to mark fork legs so that they are not interchanged upon installation.
8. Refer to **Figure 24**. Using a 36mm spanner wrench, remove the steering stem top nut.
9. Carefully pull the steering stem out from underneath. Do not lose any of the steel balls (**Figure 25**).
10. Reverse procedure for installation.

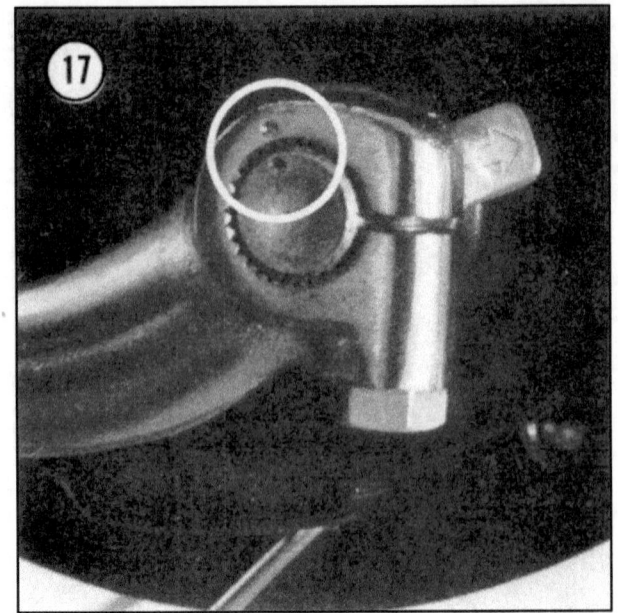

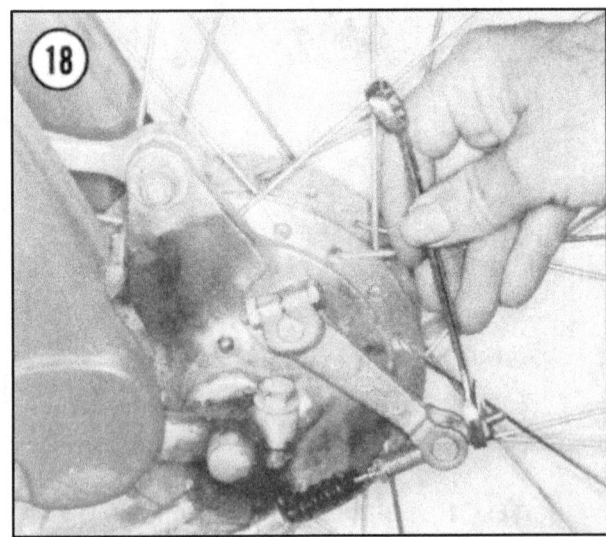

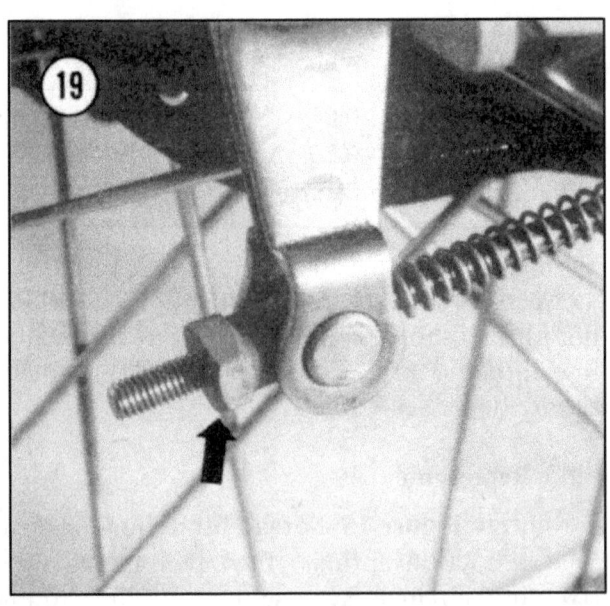

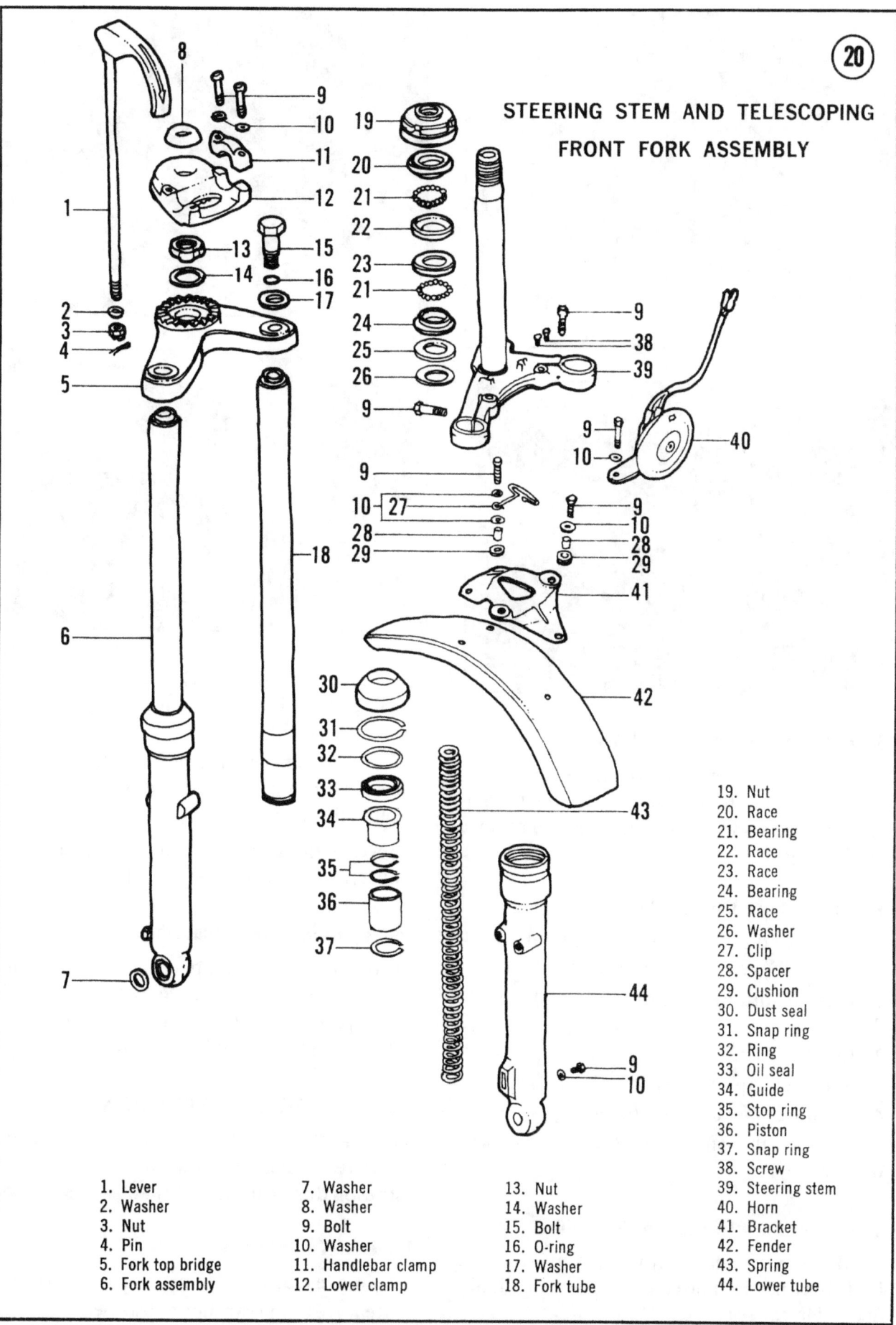

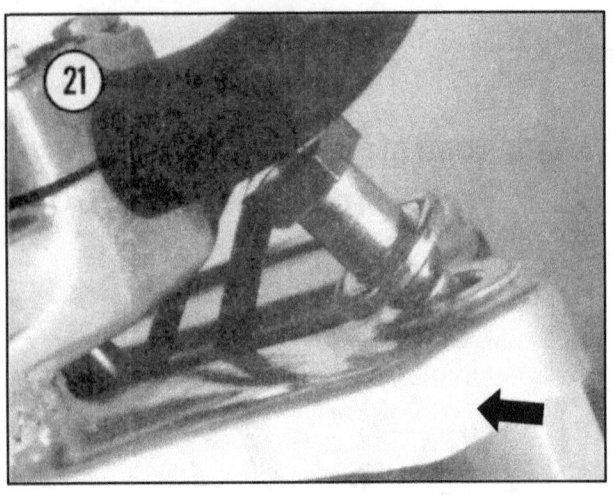

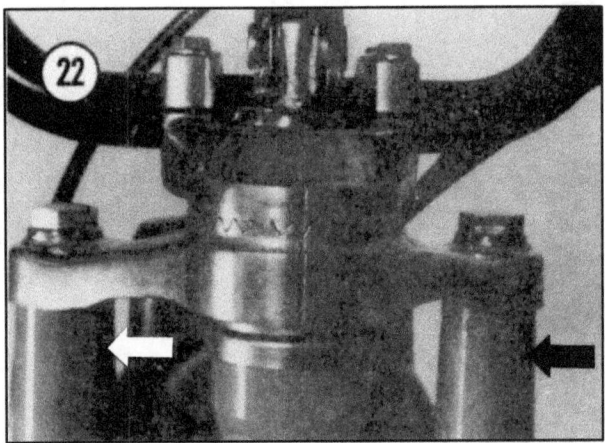

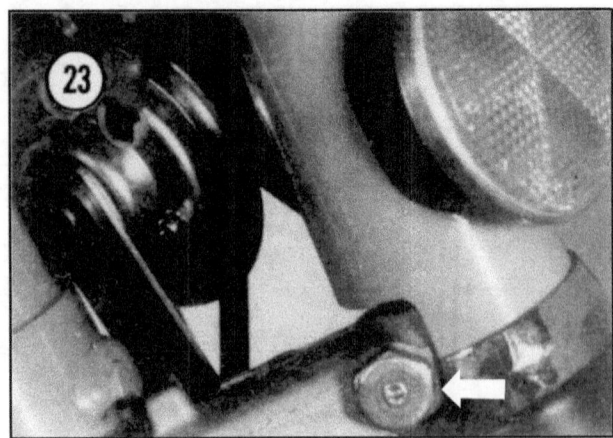

Stem Removal (Leading Link Forks)

Steering stem removal on these models is generally similar to that described in the foregoing paragraph, but it is not necessary to remove the fork legs.

Telescopic Fork Disassembly

If fork leg disassembly is required, refer back to **Figure 20**, then proceed as follows.

1. Remove drain plug and allow the oil to drain.
2. Remove dust seal (30).
3. Remove snap ring (31).
4. Separate inner and fork tubes.
5. Remove the snap ring (37) to complete disassembly.

Telescopic Fork Inspection/Assembly

1. Measure length of fork springs. Replace both if either is shorter than its service limit. See **Table 2**.

2. Check each inner fork tube for bends. If bending is minor, it may be possible to straighten the tube.

3. Be sure that there are no scratches or rough areas on the inner fork tube where it passes through the dust seal.

Reverse the disassembly procedure to reassemble the fork legs. Always replace oil seals.

Leading Link Fork Replacement

Front forks are equipped with leading-link type suspension (**Figure 26,** page 122). The front shock absorbers are not serviceable, and must be replaced if malfunctioning.

REAR SUSPENSION

Figure 27 (page 123) is an exploded view of a typical rear suspension system. Refer to that illustration during disassembly and service.

Removal/Installation

1. Remove rear wheel as previously described.
2. Remove both rear shock absorbers.

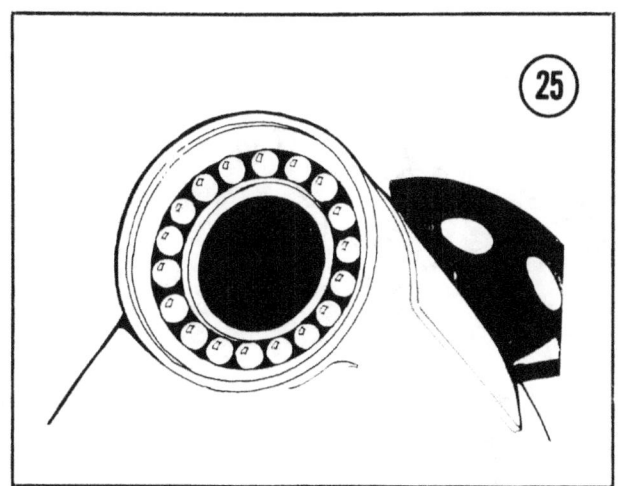

Table 2 FORK SPRING LENGTH

Model	Service Limit Inches	(Millimeters)
C50, C50M, S50	4.72	(120)
C65, C65M, S65	4.72	(120)
C70, C70M, CL70	4.80	(122)
CT70, CT70H	5.43	(138)
SL70	14.20	(360)
S90, CL90, CL90L	7.01	(178)
CD90	5.32	(135)
C90	4.72	(120)
CT90 (from 000001A)	7.28	(185)

3. Remove the pivot shaft.
4. Reverse procedure to install.

Inspection

The pivot section is susceptible to wear, especially in the bushings and shaft. Examine these parts carefully. Replace the pivot shaft if it is bent more than 0.02 in. (0.5mm). Replace both bushings and/or the shaft if clearance between them exceeds 0.014 in. (0.35mm). Shimmy, wander, and rear wheel hop are common symptoms of worn swing arm bushings. If either arm is bent, the rear wheel will be out of alignment. Replace the entire swing arm assembly in the event of any cracked weld.

Shock Absorber Disassembly/Assembly

Rear shock absorbers on Honda motorcycles may be disassembled for service. Refer to **Figure 28**.

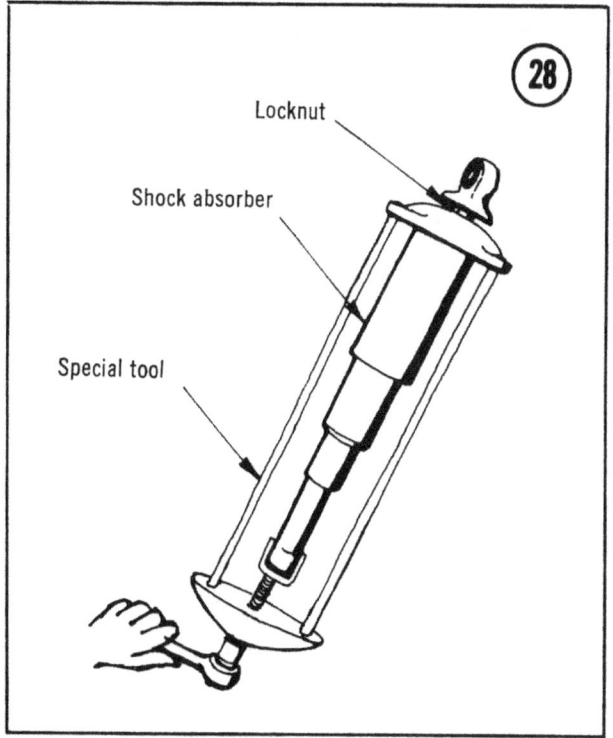

1. Using a compressor, compress shock absorber.
2. Remove locknut.
3. Release pressure and remove tool.
4. Disassemble the shock absorber, using **Figure 29** as a guide to component location.
5. Reverse procedure to assemble.

Shock Absorber Adjustment (1978)

Adjustable rear shock absorbers are fitted as standard equipment to the 1978 CT90 (K9). See **Figure 30**.

1. With the hook wrench, turn the adjusting ring (**Figure 31**).
2. Turning the adjusting ring in a counter-clockwise direction will raise the rear suspension, and clockwise will lower the suspension.

> NOTE: *After adjustment, make sure that the setting is the same on both sides.*

DRIVE CHAIN

The drive chain becomes worn after prolonged use. Wear in pins, bushings, and rollers causes the chain to stretch. Sliding between the roller surface and sprocket teeth also contributes to wear.

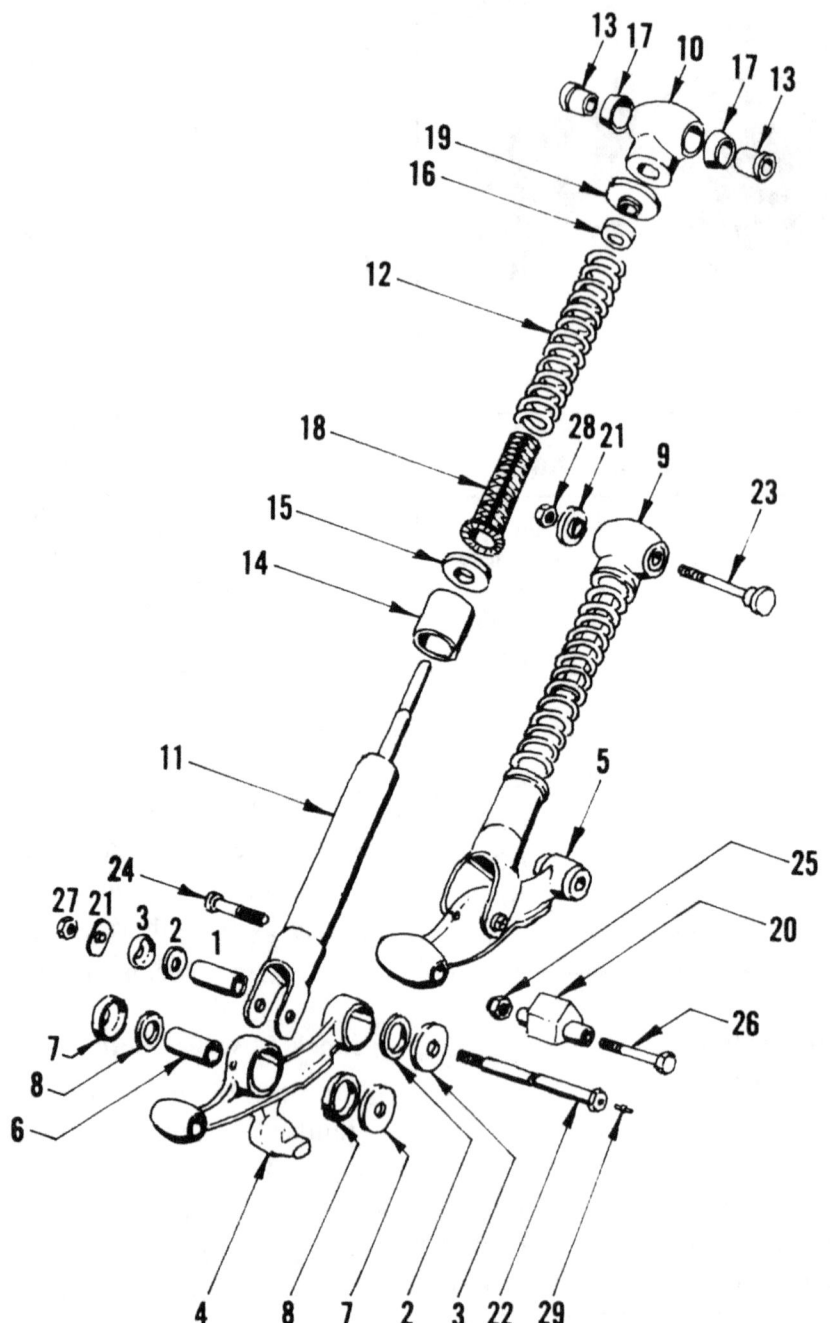

LEADING LINK FRONT FORK

1. Bushing
2. Dust seal
3. Cap
4. Bottom link (right)*
5. Bottom link (left)
6. Bushing
7. Cap
8. Dust seal
9. Suspension unit assembly
10. Upper pivot joint
11. Damper
12. Spring
13. Bushings
14. Collar
15. Spring seat
16. Rubber stop
17. Bushings
18. Spring guide
19. Locking collar
20. Bump stop
21. Collar
22. Pivot bolt
23. Bolt
24. Bolt
25. Self-locking nut
26. Bolt
27. Nut
28. Nut
29. Grease nipple

*Some models may have different right-hand bottom fork link.

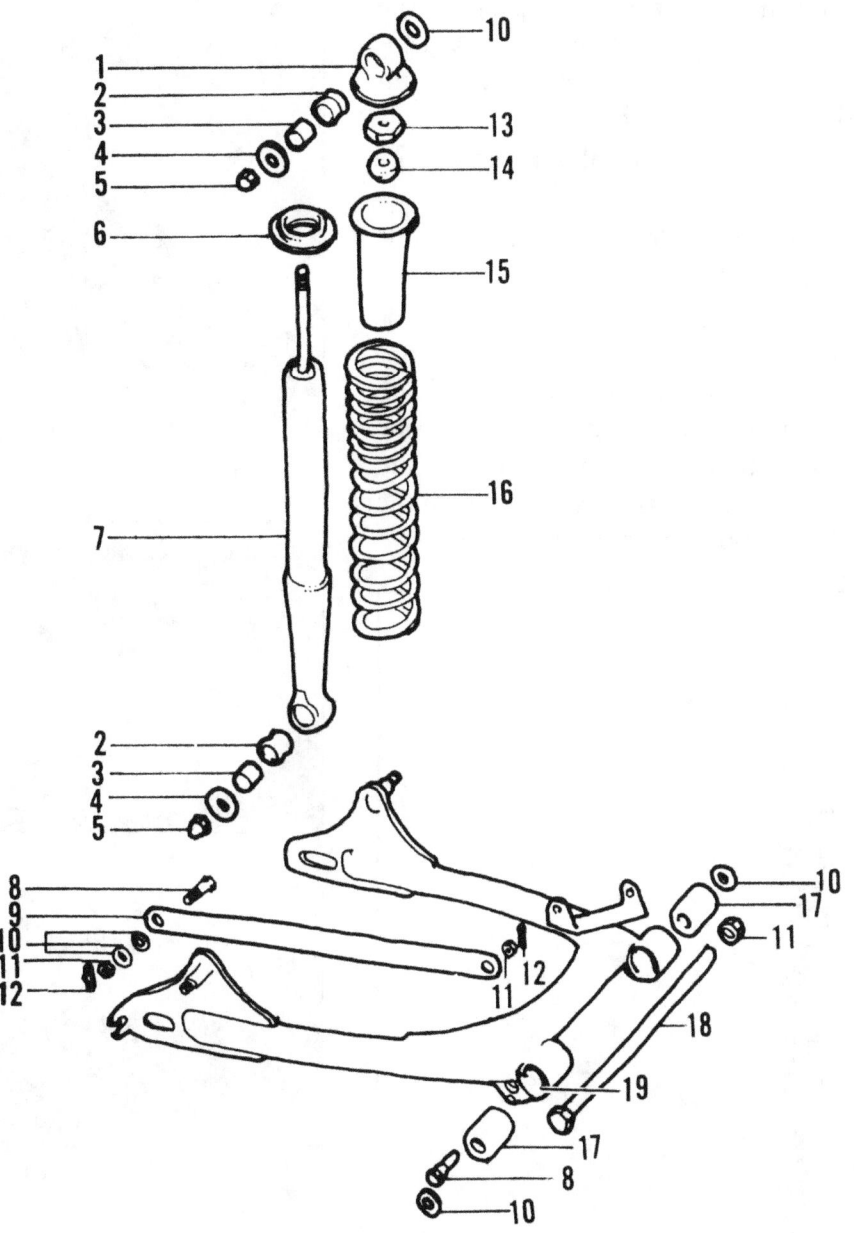

REAR SUSPENSION SYSTEM

1. Upper pivot joint
2. Bushing
3. Collar
4. Washer
5. Nut
6. Spring seat
7. Damper
8. Bolt
9. Torque link
10. Washer
11. Nut
12. Pin
13. Nut
14. Stopper
15. Guide
16. Spring
17. Bushing
18. Bolt
19. Swing arm

Removal/Installation

1. Disconnect the master link. It may be necessary to turn the rear wheel to position the master link for convenient removal. Upon installation, be sure that the master link clip is installed as shown in **Figure 32**.

2. Clean the chain with solvent and a stiff bristle brush.

3. Rinse thoroughly in clean solvent, then blow dry with compressed air.

4. Examine the chain carefully for wear or damage. Replace it if there is any doubt about its condition. If its condition is good, lubricate it by soaking in oil or melted grease, or use one of the special chain lubricants sold by any motorcycle shop. Follow the instructions on the container. Reverse procedure to install.

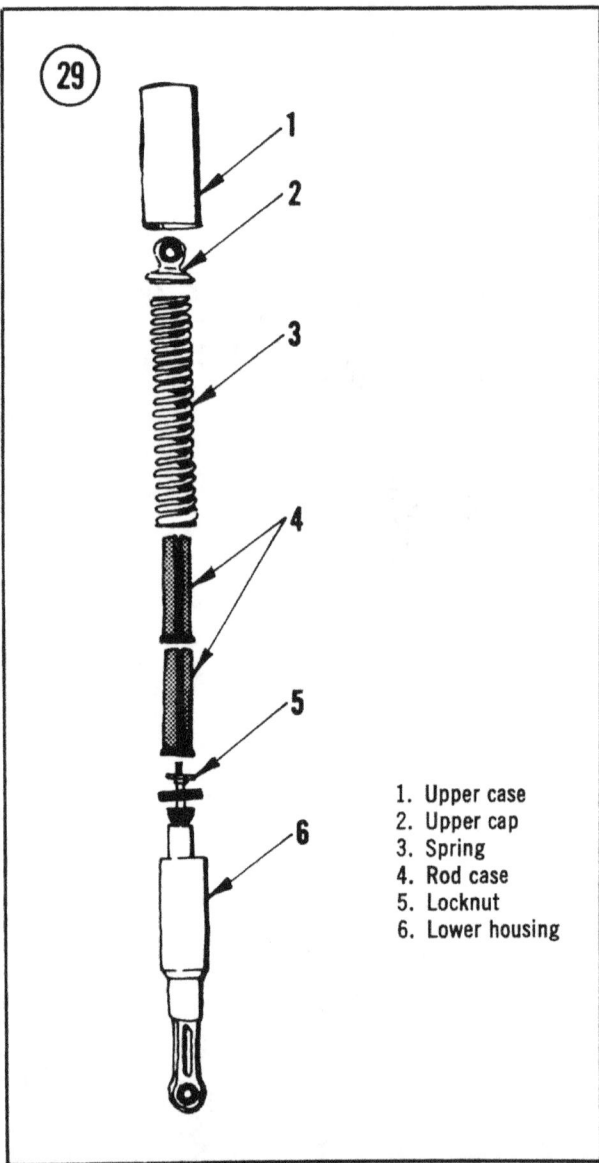

1. Upper case
2. Upper cap
3. Spring
4. Rod case
5. Locknut
6. Lower housing

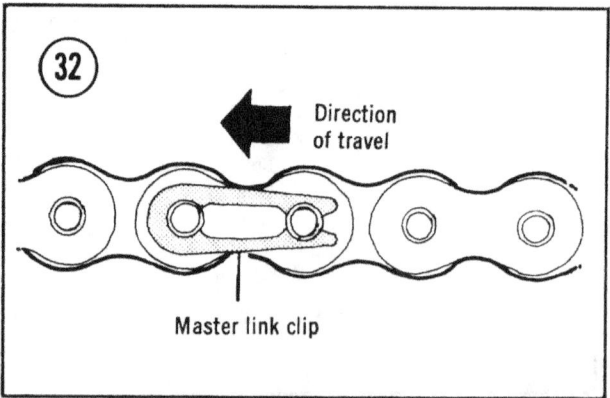

Adjustment

1. Loosen axle nut and axle sleeve nut.

2. There is one adjustment nut (**Figure 33**) on each side of the motorcycle. Turning these nuts clockwise increases chain tension; turning them counterclockwise decreases chain tension.

3. Turn each nut until there is approximately ¾ in. free play in the center of the lower chain run. See **Figure 34**.

> NOTE: *There are alignment marks (A) on the swing arm and an index mark on chain adjuster (B). Be sure that the index mark is in the same relative position on each side.*

4. Tighten the axle sleeve nut and axle nut.

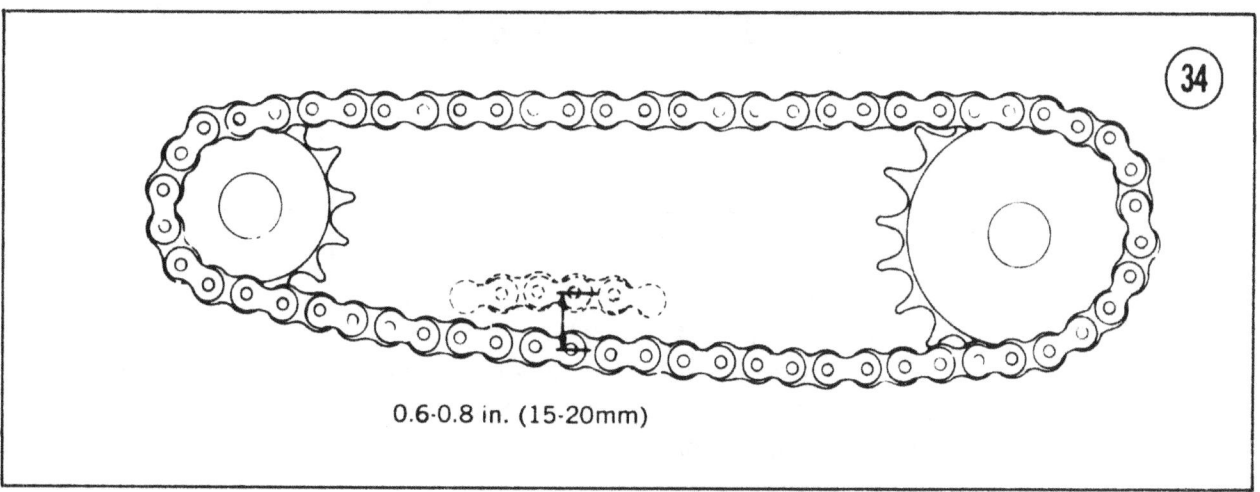

0.6-0.8 in. (15-20mm)

APPENDIX

SPECIFICATIONS

> This chapter contains major specifications for the more popular Honda bikes covered in this manual. Since there are variations between bikes of the same engine size, be sure to consult the proper table. Specification tables are arranged in order of increasing engine size.

MODEL C50 AND C50M

DIMENSIONS	C50	C50M
Overall length	70.7 inches	70.7 inches
Overall width	25.2 inches	25.2 inches
Ground clearance	5.1 inches	5.1 inches
Wheelbase	46.6 inches	46.6 inches
Weight	152 pounds	166 pounds
ENGINE		
Bore and stroke	39 x 41.4 millimeters	39 x 41.4 millimeters
Displacement	49 cubic centimeters	49 cubic centimeters
Horsepower/rpm	4.8/10,000	4.8/10,000
Torque/rpm	2.7 foot-pounds/8,200	2.7 foot-pounds/8,200
TRANSMISSION		
Primary reduction ratio	3.72 to 1	3.72 to 1
1st gear ratio	3.36 to 1	3.36 to 1
2nd gear ratio	1.72 to 1	1.72 to 1
3rd gear ratio	1.19 to 1	1.19 to 1
ELECTRICAL SYSTEM		
Ignition system	Flywheel magneto	Battery and coil
Charging system	Flywheel magneto	Alternator

MODEL S50

DIMENSIONS	
Overall length	69.4 inches
Overall width	24.2 inches
Ground clearance	4.9 inches
Wheelbase	45.3 inches
Weight	168 pounds
ENGINE	
Bore and stroke	39 x 41.4 millimeters
Displacement	49 cubic centimeters
Horsepower/rpm	5.2/10,000
Torque/rpm	4.7 foot-pounds/8,200
TRANSMISSION	
Primary reduction ratio	3.30 to 1
1st gear ratio	3.00 to 1
2nd gear ratio	1.76 to 1
3rd gear ratio	1.30 to 1
4th gear ratio	1.04 to 1
ELECTRICAL SYSTEM	
Ignition system	Flywheel magneto
Charging system	Flywheel magneto

MODEL Z50A

DIMENSIONS
- Overall length — 50.4 inches
- Overall width — 23.2 inches
- Ground clearance — 6.7 inches
- Wheelbase — 34.7 inches
- Weight — 118 pounds

ENGINE
- Bore and stroke — 39 x 41.4 millimeters
- Displacement — 49 cubic centimeters
- Horsepower/rpm — 1.9/5,000
- Torque/rpm — 2.2 foot-pounds/4,200

TRANSMISSION
- Primary reduction ratio — 3.72 to 1
- 1st gear ratio — 3.18 to 1
- 2nd gear ratio — 1.82 to 1
- 3rd gear ratio — 1.19 to 1

ELECTRICAL SYSTEM
- Ignition system — Flywheel magneto
- Charging system — Flywheel magneto

MODEL C65, S65

DIMENSIONS
- Overall length — 70.7 inches
- Overall width — 25.2 inches
- Ground clearance — 5.2 inches
- Wheelbase — 46.6 inches
- Weight — 161 pounds

ENGINE
- Bore and stroke — 44 x 41.4 millimeters
- Displacement — 63 cubic centimeters
- Horsepower/rpm — 5.5/9,000
- Torque/rpm — 3.3 foot-pounds/7,000

TRANSMISSION
- Primary reduction ratio — 3.30 to 1
- 1st gear ratio — 3.36 to 1
- 2nd gear ratio — 1.72 to 1
- 3rd gear ratio — 1.19 to 1

ELECTRICAL SYSTEM
- Ignition system — Flywheel magneto
- Charging system — Flywheel magneto

MODEL C65M

DIMENSIONS
Overall length	70.7 inches
Overall width	38.4 inches
Ground clearance	5.1 inches
Wheelbase	46.6 inches
Weight	174 pounds

ENGINE
Bore and stroke	44 x 41.4 millimeters
Displacement	63 cubic centimeters
Horsepower/rpm	5.5/9,000
Torque/rpm	3.3 foot-pounds/7,000

TRANSMISSION
Primary reduction ratio	3.30 to 1
1st gear ratio	3.15 to 1
2nd gear ratio	1.72 to 1
3rd gear ratio	1.19 to 1

ELECTRICAL SYSTEM
Ignition system	Battery and coil
Charging system	Alternator

MODEL CL70

DIMENSIONS
Overall length	70.1 inches
Overall width	29.7 inches
Ground clearance	5.1 inches
Wheelbase	46.5 inches
Weight	174 pounds

ENGINE
Bore and stroke	47 x 41.4 millimeters
Displacement	72 cubic centimeters
Horsepower/rpm	6.5/9,500
Torque/rpm	3.8 foot-pounds/8,000

TRANSMISSION
Primary reduction ratio	3.72 to 1
1st gear ratio	2.69 to 1
2nd gear ratio	1.82 to 1
3rd gear ratio	1.30 to 1

ELECTRICAL SYSTEM
Ignition system	Flywheel magneto
Charging system	Flywheel magneto

MODEL C70 AND C70M

DIMENSIONS	C70	C70M
Overall length	70.7 inches	70.7 inches
Overall width	25.2 inches	25.2 inches
Ground clearance	5.1 inches	5.1 inches
Wheelbase	46.7 inches	46.7 inches
Weight	165 pounds	174 pounds
ENGINE		
Bore and stroke	47 x 41.4 millimeters	47 x 41.4 millimeters
Displacement	72 cubic centimeters	72 cubic centimeters
Horsepower/rpm	6.2/9,000	6.2/9,000
Torque/rpm	3.8 foot-pounds/7,000	3.8 foot-pounds/7,000
TRANSMISSION		
Primary reduction ratio	3.72 to 1	3.72 to 1
1st gear ratio	3.36 to 1	3.36 to 1
2nd gear ratio	1.72 to 1	1.72 to 1
3rd gear ratio	1.19 to 1	1.19 to 1
ELECTRICAL SYSTEM		
Ignition system	Flywheel magneto	Battery and coil
Charging system	Flywheel magneto	Alternator

MODEL CT70

DIMENSIONS	
Overall length	59.6 inches
Overall width	26.4 inches
Ground clearance	6.5 inches
Wheelbase	41.3 inches
Weight	158 pounds
ENGINE	
Bore and stroke	47 x 41.4 millimeters
Displacement	72 cubic centimeters
Horsepower/rpm	Not specified
Torque/rpm	Not specified
TRANSMISSION	
1st gear ratio	3.27 to 1
2nd gear ratio	1.72 to 1
3rd gear ratio	1.19 to 1
ELECTRICAL SYSTEM	
Ignition system	Flywheel magneto
Charging system	Flywheel magneto

MODEL SL70

DIMENSIONS
- Overall length — 67.5 inches
- Overall width — 28.3 inches
- Ground clearance — 4.9 inches
- Wheelbase — 43.3 inches
- Weight — 198 pounds

ENGINE
- Bore and stroke — 47 x 41.4 millimeters
- Displacement — 72 cubic centimeters
- Horsepower/rpm — 5.0/8,000
- Torque/rpm — 3.6 foot-pounds/5,500

TRANSMISSION
- Primary reduction ratio — 3.72 to 1
- 1st gear ratio — 2.69 to 1
- 2nd gear ratio — 1.82 to 1
- 3rd gear ratio — 1.30 to 1
- 4th gear ratio — 0.96 to 1

ELECTRICAL SYSTEM
- Ignition system — Flywheel magneto
- Charging system — Flywheel magneto

MODEL C90

DIMENSIONS
- Overall length — 72.1 inches
- Overall width — 25.2 inches
- Ground clearance — 5.12 inches
- Wheelbase — 46.9 inches
- Weight — 187 pounds

ENGINE
- Bore and stroke — 50 x 45.6 millimeters
- Displacement — 89.6 cubic centimeters
- Horsepower/rpm — 7.5/9,500
- Torque/rpm — 4.8 foot-pounds/6,000

TRANSMISSION
- Primary reduction ratio — 3.72 to 1
- 1st gear ratio — 2.53 to 1
- 2nd gear ratio — 1.55 to 1
- 3rd gear ratio — 1.00 to 1

ELECTRICAL SYSTEM
- Ignition system — Battery and coil
- Charging system — Alternator

MODEL CL90 AND CL90L

	CL90	CL90L
DIMENSIONS		
Overall length	72.1 inches	72.1 inches
Overall width	31.9 inches	31.9 inches
Ground clearance	6.3 inches	6.3 inches
Wheelbase	47.2 inches	47.2 inches
Weight	203 pounds	203 pounds
ENGINE		
Bore and stroke	50 x 45.6 millimeters	50 x 45.6 millimeters
Displacement	89.6 cubic centimeters	89.6 cubic centimeters
Horsepower/rpm	8.0/9,500	4.9/8,000
Torque/rpm	4.7 foot-pounds/8,000	4.2 foot-pounds/3,500
TRANSMISSION		
Primary reduction ratio	3.72 to 1	3.72 to 1
1st gear ratio	2.54 to 1	2.54 to 1
2nd gear ratio	1.61 to 1	1.61 to 1
3rd gear ratio	1.19 to 1	1.19 to 1
4th gear ratio	0.96 to 1	0.96 to 1
ELECTRICAL SYSTEM		
Ignition system	Battery and coil	Battery and coil
Charging system	Alternator	Alternator

MODEL CD90

DIMENSIONS	
Overall length	70.7 inches
Overall width	25.2 inches
Ground clearance	5.1 inches
Wheelbase	45.4 inches
Weight	191 pounds
ENGINE	
Bore and stroke	50 x 45.6 millimeters
Displacement	89.6 cubic centimeters
Horsepower/rpm	7.5/9,500
Torque/rpm	4.8 foot-pounds/6,000
TRANSMISSION	
Primary reduction ratio	3.72 to 1
1st gear ratio	2.54 to 1
2nd gear ratio	1.61 to 1
3rd gear ratio	1.19 to 1
4th gear ratio	0.96 to 1
ELECTRICAL SYSTEM	
Ignition system	Battery and coil
Charging system	Alternator

MODEL CT90 (Before Frame No. 000001A)

DIMENSIONS
- Overall length — 70.9 inches
- Overall width — 25.6 inches
- Ground clearance — 5.4 inches
- Wheelbase — 46.8 inches
- Weight — 179 pounds

ENGINE
- Bore and stroke — 50 x 45.6 millimeters
- Displacement — 89.6 cubic centimeters
- Horsepower/rpm — 7.0/8,500
- Torque/rpm — 5.0 foot-pounds/6,000

TRANSMISSION
- Primary reduction ratio — 3.72 to 1
- 1st gear ratio — 2.54 to 1
- 2nd gear ratio — 1.61 to 1
- 3rd gear ratio — 1.19 to 1
- 4th gear ratio — 0.96 to 1

ELECTRICAL SYSTEM
- Ignition system — Battery and coil
- Charging system — Alternator

MODEL CT90 (After Frame No. 000001A)

DIMENSIONS
- Overall length — 73.6 inches
- Overall width — 26.8 inches
- Ground clearance — 6.9 inches
- Wheelbase — 47.9 inches
- Weight — 200 pounds

ENGINE
- Bore and stroke — 50 x 45.6 millimeters
- Displacement — 89.6 cubic centimeters
- Horsepower/rpm — 7.0/8,500
- Torque/rpm — 5.0 foot-pounds/6,000

TRANSMISSION
- Primary reduction ratio — 3.72 to 1
- 1st gear ratio — 2.54 to 1
- 2nd gear ratio — 1.61 to 1
- 3rd gear ratio — 1.19 to 1
- 4th gear ratio — 0.96 to 1

ELECTRICAL SYSTEM
- Ignition system — Battery and coil
- Charging system — Alternator

MODEL CT90 (K9)

DIMENSIONS
- Overall length — 73.6 inches
- Overall width — 29.8 inches
- Ground clearance — 6.5 inches
- Wheelbase — 48.0 inches
- Weight — 199 pounds

ENGINE
- Bore and stroke — 50 x 45.6 millimeters
- Displacement — 89.6 cubic centimeters
- Horsepower/rpm — Not specified
- Torque/rpm — Not specified

TRANSMISSION
- Primary reduction ratio — 3.72 to 1
- 1st gear ratio — 2.54 to 1
- 2nd gear ratio — 1.61 to 1
- 3rd gear ratio — 1.19 to 1
- 4th gear ratio — 0.96 to 1

ELECTRICAL SYSTEM
- Ignition system — Battery and coil
- Charging system — Alternator

MODEL S90

DIMENSIONS
- Overall length — 74.5 inches
- Overall width — 26.5 inches
- Ground clearance — 5.7 inches
- Wheelbase — 47.1 inches
- Weight — 191 pounds

ENGINE
- Bore and stroke — 50 x 45.6 millimeters
- Displacement — 89.6 cubic centimeters
- Horsepower/rpm — 8.0/9,500
- Torque/rpm — 4.7 foot-pounds/8,000

TRANSMISSION
- Primary reduction ratio — 3.72 to 1
- 1st gear ratio — 3.21 to 1
- 2nd gear ratio — 2.54 to 1
- 3rd gear ratio — 1.53 to 1
- 4th gear ratio — 0.88 to 1

ELECTRICAL SYSTEM
- Ignition system — Battery and coil
- Charging system — Alternator

MODEL SL90

DIMENSIONS
- Overall length — 73.6 inches
- Overall width — 31.5 inches
- Ground clearance — 9.8 inches
- Wheelbase — 48.8 inches
- Weight — 216 pounds

ENGINE
- Bore and stroke — 50 x 45.6 millimeters
- Displacement — 89.6 cubic centimeters
- Horsepower/rpm — 8.0/9,500
- Torque/rpm — 4.8 foot-pounds/8,000

TRANSMISSION
- Primary reduction ratio — 3.72 to 1
- 1st gear ratio — 2.54 to 1
- 2nd gear ratio — 1.61 to 1
- 3rd gear ratio — 1.19 to 1
- 4th gear ratio — 0.96 to 1

ELECTRICAL SYSTEM
- Ignition system — Battery and coil
- Charging system — Alternator

MODEL ST90

DIMENSIONS
- Overall length — 69.1 inches
- Overall width — 29.9 inches
- Ground clearance — 6.7 inches
- Wheelbase — 46.1 inches
- Weight — 190 pounds

ENGINE
- Bore and stroke — 50 x 45.6 millimeters
- Displacement — 89.6 cubic centimeters
- Horsepower/rpm — 5.5/8,000
- Torque/rpm — 4.3 foot-pounds/3,500

TRANSMISSION
- Primary reduction ratio — 3.72 to 1
- 1st gear ratio — 2.54 to 1
- 2nd gear ratio — 1.65 to 1
- 3rd gear ratio — 1.04 to 1

ELECTRICAL SYSTEM
- Ignition system — Battery and coil
- Charging system — Alternator

ALL MODELS - TECHNICAL DATA

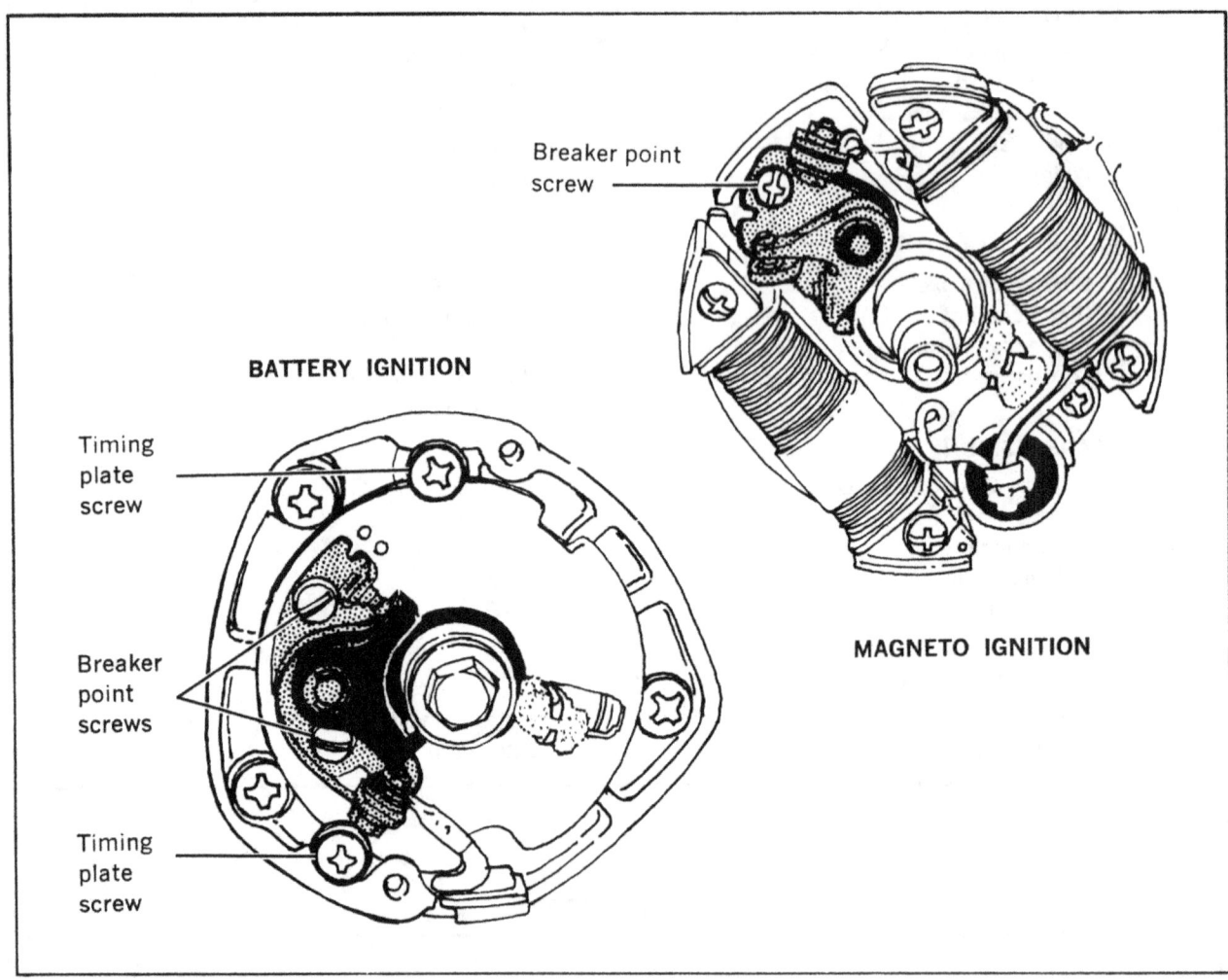

TUNE-UP SPECIFICATIONS

Spark plug type	NGK	ND	Bosch
All 50cc models	C6HB	U20FS	U175T1
All 55, 65, and 70cc models	C7HS	U22FS	U260T1
All 90cc models	D8HS	X24FS	X260T1

Spark plug gap	
Magneto models	0.024-0.028 in. (0.6-0.7mm)
All other models	0.020-0.023 in. (0.5-0.6mm)
Breaker point gap	0.012-0.016 in. (0.3-0.4mm)
Ignition timing	Align "F" marks on stator and rotor
Valve adjustment	0.002 in. (0.05mm) with rotor and stator aligned on the "T" mark
Idle speed	
All 50-70cc models	1,500 rpm
All 90cc models	1,300 rpm
Carburetor air screw	1½ turns from seat

LUBRICANTS AND FUEL

	Capacity	Type
Engine oil		
50cc, OHC automatic clutch	0.85 U.S. qt. (0.7 Imp. qt.; 0.8 liter)	SAE 10W-40
65-70cc, all models	0.74 U.S. qt. (0.6 Imp. qt.; 0.7 liter)	SAE 10W-40
90cc, all models	0.95 U.S. qt. (0.8 Imp. qt.; 0.9 liter)	SAE 10W-40
Drive chain	As needed	SAE 30 or chain lube
Fittings, bearings, and bushings	As needed	Lithium grease
Cables	As needed	WD-40 or LPS-25
Fuel	As needed	86 octane (pump) 91 octane (research)

TIGHTENING TORQUES

Fastener	Ft.-lb.	(N•m)
Cylinder head nuts		
50-70cc models	7.3	(9.3 N•m)
90cc models	14.5-18.1	(19.6-24.5 N•m)
Flywheel nut, rear sprocket nuts	18.22	(24.4-29.8 N•m)
Spark plug	29.32	(39.3-42.7 N•m)
Engine sprocket and clutch retainer	29.32	(39.3-42.7 N•m)
Front and rear axle nuts	29.32	(39.3-42.7 N•m)
Swing arm pivot nut	29.32	(39.2-42.7 N•m)
Fork cap and stem bolts	25.29	(33.8-39.3 N•m)

ADJUSTMENTS

Clutch lever free play	0.08-0.12 in. (2-3mm)
Clutch adjustment	Turn adjuster out ¼ turn from fully seated
Rear brake pedal free play	1.0 in. (25mm)
Front brake lever free play	0.20-0.32 in. (5-8mm)
Throttle grip	10° of grip rotation
Drive chain free play	0.75-1.0 in. (20-25mm) total up-and-down movement

TIRE PRESSURE

	Front	Rear
Street use*	24 psi	28 psi
Off-road use	14 psi	14 psi

*Add 2 psi per tire for sustained high speed riding and 2 psi to the rear tire if a passenger is carried.

NOTES

INDEX

A

Air cleaner 17
Alternator 25

B

Backfiring 21
Battery 90-93
Battery, ignition system
   Breaker points 7-8
   Condenser 84
   Ignition coil 83
   Ignition timing 11-13
   Operation 81
   Troubleshooting 81-83
Bearings, crankcase 61
Brakes 116-118
Breaker points 7-10, 86

C

Cam chain tensioner 18-19, 39-40
Carburetors
   Adjustment, tune-up 17
   Adjustment (1963-1977) 74-77
   Choke valve operation 66
   Disassembly and assembly, Type 1
     (1963-1977) 67-69
   Disassembly and assembly, Type 2
     (1963-1977) 69-72
   Disassembly and assembly, Type 3
     (1963-1977) 72-74
   Float mechanism 62
   Keihin carburetor (1978) 77-79
   Main fuel system 64-66
   Pilot system 62-63
   Troubleshooting 80
Charging system (battery ignition) 87
Charging system (magneto ignition) 87
Clutch
   Adjustment 47-48
   Inspection 44-47
   Installation 47
   Removal 40-44
Compression test 5-7
Condenser, battery ignition 84
Condenser, magneto ignition 86
Crankcase cover, left 23
Crankcase cover, right 40
Crankcase halves, splitting 50-52

Crankshaft 52-53
Cylinder 34-35
Cylinder head
   Description 25-27
   Inspection 30-33
   Installation 33-34
   Removal, 50-70cc 30
   Removal, 90cc 27-29

D

Drive chain 18, 121-125

E

Electrical system
   Alternator 25
   Battery ignition 81-84
   Battery 90-93
   Charging system (battery ignition) 87
   Charging system (magneto ignition) 87
   Horn 94-95
   Lighting problems 21
   Lights and signals 93
   Magneto 24-25
   Magneto ignition 84-87
   Spark plugs 13-17
   Starter, electric 87-90
   Wiring diagrams 96-111
Engine
   Alternator 25
   Bearings 61
   Cam chain tensioner 39-40
   Compression test 5-7
   Crankcase cover, left 23
   Crankcase cover, right 40
   Crankcase halves, splitting 50-52
   Crankshaft 52-53
   Cylinder 34-35
   Cylinder head 25-34
   Disassembly, preparation for 22
   Magneto 24-25
   Oil pump 50
   Piston 35-39
   Posi-torque mechanism (8-speed) ...23-24
   Removal 22-23

F

Flat spots 21
Forks, front (see Steering stem and forks)

Frame
    Brakes 116-118
    Drive chain 121-125
    Handlebar 112-115
    Steering stem and forks 118-120
    Suspension, rear 120-121
    Wheels 115-116
Fuel strainer 17
Fuel system 62-80

G

General information 1-4

H

Handlebars 112-115
Headlight 93
Horn 94-95

I

Idling, poor 21
Ignition system (see Battery ignition system or Magneto ignition system)

K

Kickstarter 53

L

Lighting problems 21
Lights and signals 93

M

Magneto, removal and installation 24-25
Magneto ignition system
    Breaker points 7-10
    Ignition coil 86-87
    Ignition timing 10-11
    Operation 84-85
Maintenance schedule 6
Misfiring 21

O

Oil and filter change 17-18

Oil pump 50
Overheating 21

P

Piston 35-39
Posi-torque mechanism 23-24
Power loss 21
Primary driven gear 49

S

Safety hints 4
Service hints 1
Shifter linkage 49-50
Shock absorbers 120-121
Spark plugs 13-17
Specifications
    C50 127
    C50M 127
    C65 128
    C65M 129
    C70 130
    C70M 130
    C90 131
    CD90 132
    CL70 129
    CL90 132
    CL90L 132
    CT70 130
    CT90 (before frame No. 000001A) 133
    CT90 (after frame No. 000001A) 133
    CT90 (K9) 134
    S50 127
    S65 128
    S90 134
    SL70 131
    SL90 135
    ST90 135
    Z50A 128
Starter, electric 87-90
Starting difficulties 20-21
Steering stem and forks 118-120
Supplies, expendable 4
Suspension, rear 120-121

T

Telescoping fork assembly (see Steering stem and forks)
Timing 10-13
Tools 2-4
Transmission
    Operation 53-55
    Removal, inspection, and installation 55-61
Troubleshooting
    Operating difficulties 21

   Operating requirements 19-20
   Starting difficulties 20-21
Tune-up
   Air cleaner 17
   Battery service 17
   Breaker points 7-10
   Cam chain tensioner 18-19
   Carburetor 17
   Compression test 5-7
   Drive chain 18
   Electrical equipment 18
   Fuel strainer 17
   Ignition timing 10-13
   Oil and filter change 17-18
   Spark plug 13-17
   Valve adjustment 13

V

Valves 13

W

Wheels 115-116
Wiring diagrams
   C50, C65, C70 96
   C50M, C65M, C70M 97
   C90 106
   CD90 105
   CL70 100
   CL90, CL90L 104
   CT70 101
   CT70H 102
   CT90 (before frame No. 000001A) 107
   CT90 (after frame No. 000001A) 108
   CT90 (K9) 109
   S50, S65 98
   S90 103
   SL70, SL90 110
   ST70, ST90 111
   Z50A 99

VELOCEPRESS MANUALS – MOTORCYCLE BY MAKE

AJS 1932-1948 SINGLES & TWINS 250cc THRU 1000cc (BOOK OF)
AJS 1945-1960 SINGLES 350cc & 500cc MODELS 16 & 18 (BOOK OF)
AJS 1955-1965 SINGLES 350cc & 500cc (BOOK OF)
AJS 1957-1966 FACTORY WSM - ALL SINGLES & TWINS
ARIEL UP TO 1932 (BOOK OF)
ARIEL 1932-1939 PREWAR MODELS (BOOK OF)
ARIEL 1933-1951 (WORKSHOP MANUAL)
ARIEL 1939-1960 4 STROKE SINGLES (BOOK OF)
ARIEL 1958-1964 LEADER & ARROW (BOOK OF)
BMW R26 R27 (1956-1967) FACTORY WORKSHOP MANUAL
BMW R50 R50S R60 R69S (1955-1969) FACTORY WORKSHOP MANUAL
BRIDGESTONE 90 SERIES FACTORY WSM & PARTS CATALOGUE
BRIDGESTONE 175 SERIES FACTORY WSM & PARTS CATALOGUE
BRIDGESTONE 350 SERIES FACTORY WSM & PARTS CATALOGUES
BSA SERVICE SHEETS MASTER CATALOGUE ALL MODELS 1945-1967
BSA BANTAM D1 TO D7 1948-1966 FACTORY SERVICE SHEETS MANUAL
BSA BANTAM ALL MODELS FROM 1948 ONWARDS (BOOK OF)
BSA SINGLES & V-TWINS UP TO 1927 (BOOK OF)
BSA SINGLES & V-TWINS UP TO 1930 (BOOK OF)
BSA SINGLES & V-TWINS UP TO 1935 (BOOK OF)
BSA SINGLES & V-TWINS 1936-1939 (BOOK OF)
BSA C10, C11 & C12 1945-1958 FACTORY SERVICE SHEETS MANUAL
BSA OHV & SV SINGLES 250-600cc 1945-1959 (BOOK OF)
BSA C15 & B40 1958-1967 FACTORY SERVICE SHEETS MANUAL
BSA OHV & SV SINGLES 250cc (ONLY) 1954-1970 (BOOK OF)
BSA B31, B32, B33 & B34 1945-60 FACTORY SERVICE SHEETS MANUAL
BSA OHV SINGLES 350 & 500cc 1955-1967 (BOOK OF)
BSA M20, M21 & M33 1945-1963 FACTORY SERVICE SHEETS MANUAL
BSA TWINS A7 & A10 1948-1962 FACTORY SERVICE SHEETS MANUAL
BSA TWINS A7 & A10 1948-1962 (BOOK OF)
BSA TWINS A50 & A65 1962-1965 FACTORY WORKSHOP MANUAL
BSA TWINS A50 & A65 1962-1969 (SECOND BOOK OF)
DOUGLAS 1929-1939 PREWAR ALL MODELS (BOOK OF)
DOUGLAS 1948-1957 POSTWAR ALL MODELS FACTORY SHOP MANUAL
DUCATI 160cc, 250cc & 350cc OHC MODELS FACTORY SHOP MANUAL
HONDA 50 ALL MODELS UP TO 1970 INC MONKEY & TRAIL (BOOK OF)
HONDA 90 ALL MODELS UP TO 1966 (BOOK OF)
HONDA 50-65-70-90Ccc OHC SINGLES 1959-1983 FACTORY WSM
HONDA 125-150cc TWINS C/CS/CB/CA FACTORY WORKSHOP MANUAL
HONDA 250-305 TWINS C/CS/CB 1959-1967 FACTORY WSM
HOHDA 250-305 TWINS CB/CL/SL 1968-1973 FACTORY WSM
HONDA 450 CB/CL 1965-1974 K0 TO K7 WORKSHOP MANUAL
HONDA C100 SUPER CUB FACTORY WORKSHOP MANUAL
HONDA C110 SPORT CUB 1962-1969 FACTORY WORKSHOP MANUAL
HONDA TWINS & SINGLES 50cc THRU 305cc 1960-1966 (BOOK OF)
HONDA TWINS ALL MODELS 125cc THRU 450cc UP TO 1968 (BOOK OF)
INDIAN PONYBIKE, BOY RACER & PAPOOSE ILL PARTS LIST & SALES LIT
J.A.P. ENGINES 1927-1952 & MOTORCYCLES 1934-1952 (BOOK OF)
MATCHLESS 1931-1939 ALL MODELS 250cc THRU 990cc (BOOK OF)
MATCHLESS 1945-1956 350 & 500cc SINGLES (BOOK OF)
MATCHLESS 1955-1966 350 & 500cc SINGLES (BOOK OF)
MATCHLESS 1957-1966 FACTORY WSM - ALL SINGLES & TWINS
NEW IMPERIAL ALL SV & OHV FROM 1935 ONWARDS (BOOK OF)
NORTON 1932-1939 PREWAR MODELS (BOOK OF)
NORTON 1932-1947 (BOOK OF)
NORTON 1938-1956 (BOOK OF)
NORTON 1955-1963 MODELS 19, 50 & ES2 (BOOK OF)
NORTON 1955-1965 DOMINATOR TWINS (BOOK OF)
NORTON 1960-1970 TWIN CYLINDER FACTORY WORKSHOP MANUAL
NORTON 1970-1975 COMMANDO FACTORY WORKSHOP MANUAL
NORTON 1975-1978 MK 3 COMMANDO FACTORY WORKSHOP MANUAL
PANTHER 1932-1958 LIGHTWEIGHT MODELS 250 & 350cc (BOOK OF)
PANTHER 1938-1966 HEAVYWEIGHT MODELS 600 & 650cc (BOOK OF)
RALEIGH MOTORCYCLES 1919-1933 (BOOK OF)
ROYAL ENFIELD 1934-1946 SINGLES & V TWINS (BOOK OF)
ROYAL ENFIELD 1937-1953 SINGLES & V TWINS (BOOK OF)
ROYAL ENFIELD 1946-1962 SINGLES (BOOK OF)
ROYAL ENFIELD 1958-1966 250cc & 350cc SINGLES (SECOND BOOK OF)
ROYAL ENFIELD 736cc INTERCEPTOR FACTORY WORKSHOP MANUAL
RUDGE 1933-1939 (BOOK OF)
SUNBEAM 1928-1939 (BOOK OF)
SUNBEAM 1946-1957 S7 & S8 (BOOK OF)
SUZUKI 50cc & 80cc UP TO 1966 (BOOK OF)
SUZUKI T10 1963-1967 FACTORY WORKSHOP MANUAL
SUZUKI T20 & T200 1965-1969 FACTORY WORKSHOP MANUAL
SUZUKI TWINS 1962 ONWARDS 125-500cc WORKSHOP MANUAL
TRIUMPH 1935-1939 PREWAR MODELS (BOOK OF)
TRIUMPH 1935-1949 (BOOK OF)
TRIUMPH 1937-1951 (WORKSHOP MANUAL)
TRIUMPH 1945-1955 FACTORY WORKSHOP MANUAL
TRIUMPH 1945-1958 TWINS (BOOK OF)
TRIUMPH 1956-1969 TWINS (BOOK OF)
VELOCETTE 1925-1970 ALL SINGLES & TWINS (BOOK OF)
VILLIERS ENGINE UP TO 1959 INC. 3 WHEELERS (BOOK OF)
VILLIERS ENGINE UP TO 1969 (BOOK OF)
VINCENT 1935-1955 (WORKSHOP MANUAL)
YAMAHA 1961-1967 YA5 & YA6 (WORKSHOP MANUAL & ILL PARTS LIST)
YAMAHA 1971-1972 JT1& JT2 (WORKSHOP MANUAL & ILL PARTS LIST)

VELOCEPRESS TECHNICAL BOOKS – MOTORCYCLE

1930'S BRITISH MOTORCYCLE CARBS & ELEC COMPONENTS (BOOK OF)
1930'S BRITISH MOTORCYCLE ENGINES (OVERHAUL & MAINTENANCE)
1930'S BRITISH MOTORCYCLE GEARBOXES & CLUTCHES (BOOK OF)
CATALOG OF BRITISH MOTORCYCLES (1951 MODELS)
LUCAS ELECTRONICS BRITISH M/CYCLES REPAIR & PARTS (1950-1977)
MOTORCYCLE ENGINEERING (P.E. Irving)
MOTORCYCLE ROAD TESTS 1949-1953 (Motor Cycle Magazine UK)
SPEED AND HOW TO OBTAIN IT (Motor Cycle Magazine UK)
TUNING FOR SPEED (P.E. Irving)
WIPAC SERVICE MANUAL NUMBER 3

VELOCEPRESS MANUALS – SCOOTERS BY MAKE

BSA SUNBEAM SCOOTER WORKSHOP MANUAL 1959-1965
BSA SUNBEAM SCOOTER 1959-1965 (BOOK OF)
LAMBRETTA 1947-1957 ALL 125 & 150cc MODELS (BOOK OF)
LAMBRETTA 1957-1970 LI & TV MODELS (SECOND BOOK OF)
NSU PRIMA 1956-1964 ALL MODELS (BOOK OF)
TRIUMPH TIGRESS SCOOTER WORKSHOP MANUAL 1959-1965
TRIUMPH TIGRESS SCOOTER (BOOK OF)
VESPA 1951-1961 (BOOK OF)
VESPA 1955-1963 125 & 150cc & GS MODELS (SECOND BOOK OF)
VESPA 1955-1968 GS & SS (BOOK OF)
VESPA 1963-1972 90, 125 & 150cc (THIRD BOOK OF)

VELOCEPRESS MANUALS – MOPEDS & MOTORIZED BICYCLES

CYCLEMOTOR (BOOK OF)
NSU QUICKLY 1953-1963 ALL MODELS (BOOK OF)
PUCH MAXI N & S MAINTENANCE & REPAIR (3 MANUAL COMPILATION)
RALEIGH MOPEDS 1960-1969 (BOOK OF)

VELOCEPRESS MANUALS - THREE WHEELER'S

BOND MINICAR THREE WHEELER 1948-1967 (BOOK OF)
BMW ISETTA FACTORY WORKSHOP MANUAL
BSA THREE WHEELER (BOOK OF)
RELIANT REGAL THREE WHEELER 1952-1973 (BOOK OF)
VINTAGE MORGAN THREE WHEELER (BOOK OF)

VELOCEPRESS MANUALS – AUTOMOBILE BY MAKE

ALFA ROMEO GIULIA WORKSHOP MANUAL 1300 TO 2000cc 1962-1975
ALFA ROMEO GIULIA TECH MANUAL CARBURETED CARS FROM 1962
ALFA ROMEO GIULIA TECH MANUAL FUEL INJECTED CARS FROM 1969
ALFA ROMEO GIULIETTA & GIULIA 750 & 101 SERIES 1955-1965 WSM
AUSTIN-HEALEY SPRITE & MG MIDGET WORKSHOP MANUAL 1958-1971
BMW 600 LIMOUSINE FACTORY WORKSHOP MANUAL
BMW 600 LIMOUSINE OWNERS HAND BOOK & SERVICE MANUAL
BMW 2000 & 2002 1966-1976 WORKSHOP MANUAL
CORVAIR 1960-1969 WORKSHOP MANUAL
CORVETTE V8 1955-1962 WORKSHOP MANUAL
FIAT 500 FACTORY WORKSHOP MANUAL 1957-1973
FIAT 600, 600D & MULTIPLA FACTORY WORKSHOP MANUAL 1955-1969
JAGUAR E-TYPE 3.8 & 4.2 SERIES 1 & 2 WORKSHOP MANUAL
JAGUAR MK 7, 8, 9 & XK120, 140, 150 WORKSHOP MANUAL 1948-1961
METROPOLITAN FACTORY WORKSHOP MANUAL
MGA & MGB OWNERS HANDBOOK & WORKSHOP MANUAL
MG MIDGET TC, TD, TF & TF1500 WORKSHOP MANUAL
PORSCHE 356 1948-1965 WORKSHOP MANUAL
PORSCHE 911 2.0, 2.2, 2.4 LITRE 1964-1973 WORKSHOP MANUAL
PORSCHE 911 2.7, 3.0, 3.2 LITRE 1973-1989 WORKSHOP MANUAL
PORSCHE 912 WORKSHOP MANUAL
TRIUMPH TR2, TR3, TR4 1953-1965 WORKSHOP MANUAL
VOLKSWAGEN TRANSPORTER, TRUCKS & WAGONS 1950-1979 WSM
VOLVO 1944-1968 ALL MODELS WORKSHOP MANUAL

VELOCEPRESS TECHNICAL BOOKS - AUTOMOBILE

FERRARI 250/GT SERVICE AND MAINTENANCE
FERRARI GUIDE TO PERFORMANCE
FERRARI OWNER'S HANDBOOK
FERRARI TUNING TIPS & MAINTENANCE TECHNIQUES
HOW TO BUILD A FIBERGLASS CAR
HOW TO BUILD A RACING CAR
HOW TO RESTORE THE MODEL 'A' FORD
MASERATI OWNER'S HANDBOOK
PERFORMANCE TUNING THE SUNBEAM TIGER
SOUPING THE VOLKSWAGEN
SOLEX CARBURETORS (EMPHASIS ON UK & EU AUTOMOBILES)
SU CARBURETORS (EMPHASIS ON UK AUTOMOBILES)
WEBER CARBURETORS (EMPHASIS ON ALFA & FIAT)

VELOCEPRESS BOOKS & GUIDES - AUTOMOBILE

ABARTH BUYERS GUIDE
COMPLETE CATALOG OF JAPANESE MOTOR VEHICLES
FERRARI 308 SERIES BUYER'S AND OWNER'S GUIDE
FERRARI BERLINETTA LUSSO
FERRARI BROCHURES AND SALES LITERATURE 1946-1967
FERRARI BROCHURES AND SALES LITERATURE 1968-1989
FERRARI SERIAL NUMBERS PART I - ODD NUMBERS TO 21399
FERRARI SERIAL NUMBERS PART II - EVEN NUMBERS TO 1050
FERRARI SPYDER CALIFORNIA
HENRY'S FABULOUS MODEL "A" FORD
MASERATI BROCHURES AND SALES LITERATURE

VELOCEPRESS BOOKS – RACING

CARRERA PANAMERICANA - MEXICAN ROAD RACE (BOOK OF)
DIALED IN - THE JAN OPPERMAN STORY
IF HEMINGWAY HAD WRITTEN A RACING NOVEL
VEDA ORR'S NEW REVISED HOT ROD PICTORIAL

AUTOBOOKS WORKSHOP MANUALS & BROOKLANDS ROAD TEST PORTFOLIOS

FOR A COMPLETE LISTING OF THE AUTOBOOKS & BROOKLANDS TITLES THAT WE CURRENTLY HAVE AVAILABLE, PLEASE VISIT OUR WEBSITE.

www.VelocePress.com

www.ingramcontent.com/pod-product-compliance
Lightning Source LLC
Chambersburg PA
CBHW082206230426
43672CB00015B/2918